ILLUSTRATIONS

CHAPTER 1

WELL, ROBIN, on what folly do you employ yourself? Do you cut sticks for our fire o' mornings?"

Thus spoke Master Hugh Fitzooth, King's Ranger of the Forest at Locksley, as he entered his house.

Robin flushed a little. "These are arrows, sir," he announced, holding one up for inspection.

Dame Fitzooth smiled upon the boy as she rose to meet her lord. "What fortune do you bring us today, Father?" asked she, cheerily.

Fitzooth's face was a mask of discontent. "I bring myself, Dame," answered he, "neither more nor less."

"Surely that is enough for Robin and me!" laughed his wife. "Come, cast off your shoes, and give me your bow and quiver. I have news for you, Hugh, even if you have none for us. George of Gamewell has sent his messenger today, and bids me bring Robin to him for the Fair." She hesitated to give the whole truth.

"That cannot be," began the Ranger, hastily; then checked himself. "What wind is it that blows our Squire's friendship toward me, I wonder?" he went on. "Do we owe him toll?"

"You are not fair to George Montfichet, Hugh—he is an open, honest man, and he is my brother." The dame spoke with spirit, being vexed that her husband should thus slight her item of news. "That Montfichet is of Norman blood is sufficient to turn your thoughts of him as sour as old milk——"

"I am as good as all the Montfichets and De Veres hereabout, Dame, for all I am but plain Saxon," returned Fitzooth, crossly, "and the day may come when they shall know it. Athelstane the Saxon might make full as good a King, when Henry dies, as Richard of Acquitaine, with his harebrained notions and runagate religion. There would be bobbing of heads and curtseying to us then, if you like. Squire George of Gamewell would be sending messengers for me cap in hand—doubt it not."

"For that matter, there is ready welcome for you now at my brother's house," said Mistress Fitzooth, repenting of her sharpness at once. "Montfichet bade us *all* to Gamewell; but here is his scroll, and you may read it for yourself." She took a scroll from her bosom as she spoke and offered it to her husband.

He returned to the open door that he might read it. His brow puckered itself as he strove to decipher the flourished Norman writing. "I have no leisure now for this screed, Mother; read it to me later, an you will."

His tone was kinder again, for he saw how Robin had been busying himself in these last few moments. "Let us sup, Mother. I dare swear we all are hungry after the heat of the day."

"I have made and tipped a full score of arrows, sir; will you see them?" asked Robin.

"That will I, so soon as I have found the bottom of this pasty. Sit yourselves, Mother and Robin, and we'll chatter afterwards."

Robin helped his mother to kindle the flax whereby the dim and flickering tapers might be lighted. His fingers were more deft at this business, it would seem, than in the making of arrows. Fitzooth, in the intervals of his eating, took up Robin's arrows one by one and had some shrewd gibe ready for most of them. Of the score only five were allowed to pass; the rest were tossed contemptuously into the black hearth onto the little heap of smouldering fire.

"By my heart, Robin, but I shall never make a proper bowman of you! Were ever such shafts fashioned to fit across cord and yew!"

"The arrows are pretty enough, Hugh," interposed the dame.

"There 'tis!" cried Fitzooth, triumphantly. "The true bowman's hand showeth not in the *prettiness* of an arrow, Mother, but in the straightness and hardness of the wand. Our Robin can fly a shaft right well, I grant you, and I have no question for his skill, but he cannot yet make me an arrow such as I love."

"Well, I do think them right handsomely done," said Mistress Fitz-ooth, unconvinced. "It is not given to everyone to make such arrows as you can, Husband; but my Robin has other accomplishments. He can play upon the harp sweetly, and sing you a good song——"

Fitzooth must still grumble, however. "I would rather your fingers should bend the bow than pluck at harpstrings, Robin," growled he. "Still, there is time for all things. Read me now our brother's message."

Robin, eager to atone for the faults of his arrows, stretched out the paper upon the table, and read aloud the following:

"From George à Court Montfichet, of the Hall at Gamewell, near Nottingham, Squire of the Hundreds of Sandwell and Sherwood, giving greetings and praying God's blessing on his sister Eleanor and on her husband, Master Hugh Fitzooth, Ranger of the King's Forest at Locksley. Happiness be with you all. I do make you this screed in the desire that you will both of you ride to me at Gamewell, in the light of tomorrow, the fifth day of June, bringing with you our young kinsman Robin. There is a Fair toward at Nottingham for three days of this week, and we are to expect great and astonishing marvels to be performed at it.

"Wherefore, seeing that it will doubtless give him satisfaction and some knowledge (for who can witness wonders without being the wiser for them?), fail not to present yourselves as I honestly wish. I also ask that Robin shall stay with me for the space of one year at least, having no son now and being a lonely man. Him will I treat as my own child in all ways, and return him to you in the June of next year.

"This I send by the hand of Warrenton, my man-at-arms, who shall bear me your reply.

"Given under our hand at Gamewell, the 4th day of June, in the year of grace one thousand one hundred and eighty-eight.

"(Signed) MONTFICHET."

Robin's clear voice ceased, and silence fell upon them all. Fitzooth guessed that both his son and wife waited anxiously for his decision; yet he had so great a pride that he could not at once agree to the courteous invitation.

For himself he had no doubt. Nothing would move Fitzooth to mix with the fine folk of Nottingham whilst his claims to the acres of Broadweald, in Lancashire, went unrecognized. It was an old story, and although, by virtue of his office as Ranger at Locksley, Hugh Fitzooth might very properly claim an honorable position in the county, he swore not to avail himself of it unless he could have a better one. The bar sinister stayed him from Broadweald, so the judges had said, and haughty Fitzooth had perforce to bear with their finding. The king had been much interested in the suit, the estate being a large one, situated in the County Palatine of England, and the matter had caused some stir in the Court. When Fitzooth had failed, Henry, anxious to find favor with his Saxon subjects, had bestowed on him the keeping of a part of the forest of Sherwood, in Nottingham.

So Fitzooth, plain "master" now for good and aye, had come to Locksley, a little village at the further side of the forest, and had taken up the easy duties allotted to him. Here he had nursed his pride in loneliness for some years; then had met one day Eleanor Montfichet a-hunting in the woods. He had unbent to her, and she gave him her simple, true heart.

Strange pair, thrown together by Fate, in sooth; yet no man could say that this was an unhappy union. Within a year came black-eyed Robin to them, and they worshipped their child. But as time passed, and Hugh's claims were again put aside, his nature began to go sour once more. Now they were lonely, unfriendly folk, with no society other than that of the worthy Clerk of Copmanhurst—a hermit too. He had taught Robin his Latin grace, and had given him a fair knowledge of Norman, Saxon, and the middle tongues.

"Say that we all may go tomorrow, Father," cried Robin, breaking the silence. "I have never seen Nottingham Fair, sir, and you have promised to take me often."

"I cannot leave this place; for there is my work, and robbers are to be found even here. I have to post my foresters each day in their tasks, and see that the deer be not killed and stolen."

He paused, and then, noting the disappointment in his son's face, relented. "Yet, since there is the Fair, and I have promised it, Robin, you shall go with your mother to Gamewell, if so be the Friar of Copmanhurst can go also. So get ready your clothes, for I know that you would wish to be at your best in our brother's hall. I will speed you tomorrow so far as Copmanhurst, and will send two hinds to serve you to Nottingham gates."

"Warrenton, my brother's man, spoke grievously of the outlaw bands near Gamewell, and told how he had to journey warily." So spoke Mistress Fitzooth, trying yet to bring her husband to say that he too would go.

"The Sheriff administers his portion of the forest very abominably then," returned Fitzooth. "We have no fears and whinings here; but I do not doubt that Warrenton chattered with a view to test our courage, or perchance to make more certain of my refusal."

"But we *are* to go, are we not, sir?" Robin was anxious again, for his father's tone had already changed.

"I have said it; and there it ends," said Fitzooth, shortly. "If the clerk will make the journey, you shall make it too. Further, an the Squire will have you, you shall stay at Gamewell and learn the tricks and prettinesses of Court and town. But look to your bow for use in life, and to your own hands and eyes for help. Kiss me, Robin, and get to bed. Learn all you can; and if Warrenton can show you how to fashion arrows within the year I'll ask no more of brother George of Gamewell."

"You shall be proud of me, sir; I swear it. But I will not stay longer than a month; for I am to watch over my mother's garden."

"Never will shafts such as yours find quarry, Robin. I think that they would sooner kill the archer than the birds. There, mind not my jesting. Men shall talk of you; and I may live to hear them. Be just always; and be honest."

★   ★   ★

The day broke clear and sweet. From Locksley to the borders of Sherwood Forest was but a stone's cast.

Robin was in high glee, and had been awake long ere daylight. He had dressed himself in his best doublet, green trunk hose, and pointed shoes, and had strung and unstrung his bow full a score of times. A sumpter mule had been saddled to carry the baggage, for the dame had, at the last moment, discovered a wondrous assortment of fineries and fripperies that must perforce be translated to Gamewell.

Robin was carolling like any bird.

"Are you glad to be leaving Locksley, my son?" asked Hugh Fitzooth.

"Ay, rarely!"

" 'Tis a dull place, no doubt. And glad to be leaving home too?"

"No, sir; only happy at the thought of the Fair. Doubt it not that I shall be returned to you long ere a month is gone."

"A year, Robin, a year! Twelve changing months ere you will see me again. I have given my word now. Keep me a place in your heart, Robin."

"You have it all now, sir, be sure, and I am not really so glad within as I seem without."

"Tut, I am not chiding you. Get you upon your jennet, Dame; and, Robin, do you show the way. Roderick and the other shall lead the baggage mule. Have you pikes with you, men, and full sheaths?"

"I have brought me a dagger, Father," cried Robin, joyfully.

So, bravely they set forth from their quiet house at Locksley, and came within the hour to Copmanhurst. Here only were the ruins of the chapel and the clerk's hermitage, a rude stone building of two small rooms.

Enclosed with high oaken stakes and well guarded by two gaunt hounds was the humble abode of the anchorite.

The clerk came to the verge of his enclosure to greet them, and stood peering above the palisade. "Give you good morrow, Father," cried Robin; "get your steed and tie up the dogs. We go to Nottingham this day and you are to come with us!"

The monk shook his head. "I may not leave this spot, child, for matters of vanity," he answered, in would-be solemn tones.

"Will you not ride with the dame and my son, Father?" asked Fitzooth. "George of Gamewell has sent in for Robin, and I wish that you should journey with him, giving him such sage counsel as may fit him for a year's service in the great and worshipful company that he now may meet."

"Come with us today, Father," urged Mistress Fitzooth also. "I have brought a veal pasty and some bread, so that we may not be hungry on the road. Also, there is a flask of wine."

"Nay, daughter, I have no thought for the carnal things of life. I will go with you, since the Ranger of Locksley orders it. It is my place to obey him whom the King has put in charge of our greenwood. Bide here whilst I make brief preparation."

His eyes had twinkled, though, when the dame had spoken; and one could see that 'twas not on roots and fresh water alone that the clerk had thrived. Full and round were the lines of him under his monkly gown; and his face was red as any harvest moon.

Hugh bade farewell briefly to them, while the clerk was tying up his hounds and chattering with them.

When the clerk was ready Fitzooth kissed his dame and bade her be firm with their son; then, embracing Robin, ordered him to protect his mother from all mischance. Also he was to bear himself honourably and quietly; and, whilst being courteous to all folk, he was not to give way unduly to anyone who should attempt to browbeat or to cozen him.

"Remember always that your father is a proud man; and see, take those arrows of my own making and learn from them how to trim the hazel. You have a steady hand and bold eye; be a craftsman when you return to Locksley, and I will give you control of some part of the forest, under me. Now, farewell—take my greetings to our brother at Game-well."

Then the King's Forester turned on his heel and strode back towards Locksley. Once he paused and faced about to wave his cap to them: then his figure vanished into the green of the trees.

A sadness fell upon Robin—unaccountable and perplexing. But the hermit soberly journeyed toward Nottingham, the two men-at-arms, with the sumpter mule, riding in front.

The road wound in and about the forest, and at noon they came to a part where the trees nigh shut out the sky.

Robin spied out a fine old stag, and his fingers itched to fit one of his new arrows to his bow. "These be all of them King's deer, Father?" he asked the friar, thoughtfully.

"Every beast within Sherwood, royal or mean, belongs to our King, child."

"Do they not say that Henry is away in a foreign land, Father?"

"Ay, but he will return. His deer are not yet to be slain by your arrows, child. When you are Ranger at Locksley, in your father's stead, who shall then say you nay?"

"My father does not shoot the King's deer, except those past their time," answered Robin, quickly. "He tends them, and slays instead any robbers who would maltreat or kill the does. Do you think I could hit yon beast, Father? He makes a pretty mark, and my arrow would but prick him."

The clerk glanced toward Mistress Fitzooth. "Dame," said he, gravely, "do you not think that here, in this cool shadow, we might well stay our travelling? Surely it is near the hour of noon? And," here he sank his voice to a sly whisper, "it would be well perhaps to let this temptation pass away from before our Robin! Else, I doubt not, the King will be one stag the less in Sherwood."

"I like not this dark road, Father," began the dame. "We shall surely come to a brighter place. Robin, do you ride near to me, and let your bow be at rest. Warrenton, your uncle's man, told me but yesterday——"

Her voice was suddenly drowned in the noise of a horn, wound so shrilly and distantly as to cause them all to start. Then, in a moment, half a score of lusty rascals appeared, springing out of the earth almost. The men-at-arms were seized, and the little cavalcade brought to a rude halt.

"Toll, toll!" called out the leader. "Toll must you pay, everyone, ere your journey be continued!"

"Forbear," cried Robin, waving his dagger so soon as the man made attempt to take his mother's jennet by the bridle. "Tell me the toll, and the reason for it; and be more mannerly."

The man just then spied that great stag which Robin had longed to shoot, bounding away to the left of them. Swiftly he slipped an arrow across his longbow and winged it after the flying beast.

"A miss, an easy miss!" called Robin, impatiently. Dropping his dagger, he snatched an arrow from his quiver, fitted it to his bow and sent it speeding towards the stag. "Had I but aimed sooner!" murmured Robin, regretfully, when his arrow failed by a yard to reach its quarry; and the clerk held up his hands in pious horror of his words.

*The road wound in
and about the forest, and
at noon they came to
a part where the trees nigh
shut out the sky.*

"The shot was a long one, young Master," spoke the robber, and he stooped to pick up Robin's little weapon. "Here is your bodkin—'tis no fault of yours that the arrow was not true."

They all laughed right merrily; but Robin was vexed.

"Stand away, fellows," said he, "and let us pass on. Else shall you all be whipped."

Again the leader of the band spoke. "Toll first, lording; tender it prettily to us, and you shall only tender it once."

"I'll tender it not at all," retorted young Fitzooth. "Fie upon you for staying a woman upon the King's highroad! Pretty men, forsooth, to attack in so cowardly a fashion!"

"All must buy freedom of the greenwood, Master," answered the man, quite civilly. "We, who exact the toll, take no heed of sex. Pay us now, and when you return there shall be no questioning."

"A woman should be a safe convoy and free from all toll," argued Robin. "Now here are my two men."

"Slaves, Master; and they have only your mule and the two pikes. It is not enough."

"You will leave us nothing then, it seems," said Dame Fitzooth, in trembling but brave voice.

"There is one thing that we all do value, Mistress, and I purpose sparing you that. We will do no one of you any bodily harm."

"Take my purse, then," sighed Mistress Fitzooth. "There is little enough in it, for we are poor folk."

"Ask toll of the Church," cried Robin, staying his mother. "The Church is rich, and has to spare. And afterwards, she can grant absolution to you all."

Again the robbers laughed, as the clerk began explaining very volubly to them that they were welcome to all that Mother Church could on this occasion offer.

"We know better than to stay a monk for toll," said the robber. "Beside, would Your Excellence have us commit sacrilege?"

"I would have you leave hold of my bridle," answered Robin, very wrathfully.

"Pay the toll cheerfully, youngling," cried one of the others, "and be not so wordy in the business. We have other folk to visit; the day is already half gone from Sherwood."

"I will shoot with you for the freedom of the forest," said Robin, desperately. "An I lose, then shall you take all but my mother's jennet. She shall be allowed to carry my mother into Gamewell, whilst I remain here, as hostage, for her return."

"Let the dam bring back a hundred crowns in each of her hands, then," replied the chief of the robbers.

"It is agreed," answered Robin, after one appealing glance towards the dam. "Now help me down from my horse, and let the clerk see fair play. Set us a mark, good Father, and pray Heaven to speed my arrows cunningly."

The clerk, who had kept himself much in the background, now spoke. "This wager seems to savor of unholiness, friends," said he, solemnly. "Yet, in that it also smacks of manliness, I will even consent to be judge. You, sir, since you are doubtless well acquainted with the part, can speak for distance. Now, I do appoint the trunk of yon birch tree as first mark in this business."

"Speed your arrow, then, lording," laughed the robber, gaily. " 'Tis but forty ells away! I will follow you respectfully, never doubt it."

Robin bent his bow and trained his eyes upon the birch.

Then suddenly came back upon him his father's words: "Remember that I am a proud man, Robin."

"I will," muttered Robin, betwixt set teeth, and he aimed with all his heart and soul in it. There came the twang of the bowstring, and the next moment the gooseshaft was flying towards its mark.

"A pretty shot, Master," said the robber, glancing carelessly towards the arrow, quivering still in the trunk of the birch tree. "But you have scarce taken the centre of our mark. Let me see if I may not mend your aim."

His arrow sang through the summer air, and took root fairly in the middle of the trunk, side by side with Robin's.

"You win first round, friend," said the clerk, with seeming reluctance. "Now, listen, both, whilst I make you a better test." He was about to continue, when an interruption occurred, one that saved him necessity of further speech.

CHAPTER 2

SUDDENLY THROUGH the greenwood came full four score of the King's Foresters, running towards the robbers, ready to seize them.

These were the foresters of Nottingham, roving far afield. The Sheriff of Nottingham had become angered at the impudent robberies of late, and now all of his foresters had spread themselves about Sherwood in the hope of making such a capture of the outlaws as would please their master and bring substantial reward to themselves. On the head of Will o' th' Green, the chief of the band, was set the price of ten golden crowns.

But alas! these crowns were still to seek; for Will o' th' Green, at first hint of the danger, had put his horn to his lips and given a long, low call upon it, and next instant not a robber was to be seen.

Each man had dropped to his hands and knees as soon as he had reached the bushes; and the foresters might beat and belabor Mother Sherwood in vain, for she would never betray her children.

Fitzooth's men-at-arms were glad to be released, and were eager now to give all information against their assailants. One of the fellows swore roundly that the learned clerk had given Will o' th' Green a very plain hint: but this assertion was most properly put aside by all who heard it.

Robin gave his story of the business, and then, having thanked the captain of the foresters, would have continued the journey. The clerk was no longer to be denied, however, from his food: and so it came about that presently the four of them were at a meal together under the trees—the captain of the foresters having agreed to join with Robin, the hermit, and Mistress Fitzooth in an attack upon the good wine and pasty which the latter had provided.

The foresters returned in twos and threes from their fruitless search, and stood about in little knots discussing the chase. All agreed that the outlaws had some stronghold underground, with many entrances and ways into it; easily to be found by those in the secret, but impossible of passage to persons in pursuit.

"Do you go to Gamewell, friends?" asked the captain, after the meal had been finished. When he had been answered yes, he told Mistress Fitzooth that she might have an escort for the rest of the way; since he and his men must travel to Gamewell themselves, to report the encounter to Squire George of Gamewell.

Gladly Mistress Fitzooth heard this, and very cheerfully they all started afresh upon the journey.

Robin alone was sad; the fact that the robber chief's arrow had flown more near a woodman's mark than his own rankled within his breast.

Ah, but a time would come when Master Will o' th' Green should see better archery than he now dreamed of. And Robin should be the master who would teach the lesson.

Building such daydreams, he cantered quietly enough beside his mother's jennet; whilst the clerk and the captain of the foresters chattered amiably together. The dame listened to their gossip, and put in her own word and question; she had an easy mind now and could give herself to talk of Prince John and his impudent rebellion.

"So the barons would really make him King?" asked she, round-eyed: "King of all these lands and forests?"

"Some of our barons have sworn so much," answered the forester, lightly; "but men speak best with their swords, Dame. Have you not heard of young Montfichet's doings? He has undone himself indeed——"

"Waldemar Fitzurse is behind it all, and young De Brocy," the clerk interrupted, loudly, giving him a warning glance.

The friar pointed to Robin. " 'Tis the lad's cousin, and he does not know of Geoffrey Montfichet's outlawry," he whispered.

"Some say that the King will establish an assize of arms on his return from France, whereby every knight, freeholder, and burgess must arm himself for England's defense," continued the clerk, easily. " 'Tis a pretty notion, and like our King."

"There are tales about our Henry, and ballads more than enough," replied the forester, shrugging his shoulders. "Will o' th' Green knows a good one, I am told."

At the mention of the outlaw's name Robin pricked up his ears. He asked many questions concerning Master Will; and learned that he had been outlawed by Henry himself for the accidental slaying of a younger brother in a quarrel years since. Before that he had been a dutiful and loyal subject, and there were some who vowed that Master Will was as loyal now as many of Henry's barons. Will shot the King's deer, truly, but only that he might live: the others conspired against their monarch's honor, in order that their own might be increased.

The cavalcade came into sight of Gamewell Hall while still at this gossip. The night was falling and lights burned behind the embrasured windows of the castle, for such it was in truth, being embattled and surrounded properly by a moat and heavy walls.

The captain wound his horn to such purpose that the bridge was soon lowered, and the whole party began to trot over it into the wide courtyard before the hall. That it was a very magnificent place was apparent, despite the shadows.

Before the door of the hall Robin sprang lightly from his horse and ran to help his mother from her saddle with tender care; then moved to give assistance to the clerk. The latter had bundled himself to firm ground, however, and now stood stolidly expectant.

Master Montfichet—George of Gamewell, as the country folk called him mostly—had come down to greet his guests, and was waiting upon them ere Robin could turn about. The Squire was an old man, with white hair curling from under a little round cap. He wore long black robes, loose and rather monkish in their fashion. He seemed as unlike his sister as Robin could well imagine, besides being so much more advanced in years. His face was hairless and rather pale; but his eyes shone brightly. There was a very pleasant expression in the lines about his mouth, and his manner was perfect. He embraced Robin with kindliness; and real affection for his sister seemed to underlie his few words of welcome. To the Friar of Copmanhurst he was so courteous and respectful that Robin began to wonder whether he himself had ever properly regarded the clerk in the past. If so great a man should bow to him, what ought Robin to do? Robin remembered that he had often ventured to rally and tease this good-natured master who had taught him his letters.

The Squire bade them follow him, so soon as their horses and baggage had been duly given over to the servants and he had heard the forester's complaint against the outlaws. The Squire made little comment, but frowned.

At the conclusion of the captain's report, they came into the hall, lighted by a thousand fat tapers.

"Sister Nell—do you please dismiss us," said the Squire, in his courtly way, after he had signed to some waiting-maids to take charge of Mistress Fitzooth. "I will lead Robin to his chamber myself, and show him the arrangement we have made for his stay at Gamewell. Supper will be served us here in less than an hour. Father, your apartments shall be near my own. Come with me, also."

In the room allotted to him Robin found new and gay clothes laid out upon a fair, white bed, with a little rush mat beside it. A high latticed window looked out upon the court, and there was a bench in the nook, curiously carven and filled with stuffs and naperies the like of which Robin had never seen before.

The walls were hung with tapestries, and very fierce and amazing were the pictures embroidered upon them. The ceiling was low and raftered with polished beams. Behind the door was a sword suspended by a leathern belt.

"For you, kinsman," the Squire had said, smilingly.

Robin lost no time in doffing his green jerkin and hose, and then he washed himself and eagerly essayed his new habiliments. When the sword had been buckled on, our young hero of Locksley felt himself equal to Will o' th' Green or any other gallant in Christendom.

He strode along the corridors and found his way back to the great hall. There the Master of Gamewell and his mother awaited him. Mistress Fitzooth's eyes shone approvingly, and Robin slipped his fingers into hers.

"I'll build a castle as fine as this, Mother mine, one of these days,"

Robin told her: and he began to ask Master Montfichet questions as to the number of claims-at-law that he must have won in order to hold so splendid a domain. The Squire smilingly told him that the King had given Gamewell to him as a reward for valor in battle many years agone.

"Then will I fight for the King," cried Robin, with flashing eyes, "so that I may win my father Broadweald and all the lands of it."

"And I will teach you, Robin: be sure of that," said old George Montfichet. "But your sword must be swung for the right King, harkee. Not for rebellious princes will we cry to arms; but for him whom God hath placed over us—Henry the Angevin."

"Amen," murmured the clerk, fervently. "Let law and order be respected always."

"It may mean much to you, Friar," said Montfichet. "Young John has the Priory of York under his hands."

"He has not fingers upon Sherwood, and we are free of it!" cried the clerk. Then he hastily corrected himself. "We hermits can have no fear, since we have no wealth. Happy then the man with naught to lose, and who has a contented mind."

"I will be free of Sherwood Forest, Father, if that boon shall wait upon my archery. Master Will, the robber, swore that if I beat him, sir"—he had turned his bright face to old Gamewell's—"I should go free of the greenwood. And I will win the right."

" 'Tis scarcely Will's to grant," frowned the Squire; "yet, in a way, he has control of the forest. It is a matter which I will look to, since the Sheriff seems so fearful of him," he added, significantly.

CHAPTER 3

THE NEXT DAY they journeyed quietly into Nottingham, taking only a few retainers with them. The clerk chose to stay at the hall, fearing, as he said, that his eyes would be offended with the vanity of the town.

When they had come to the meadows wherein the Fair was held, Robin was overcome with joy at the sight of the wonderments before him.

That which most pleased him was the tumbling and wrestling of a company of itinerant players, merry fellows, all in a great flutter of tinsel and noise. They were father and three sons, and while the old man blew vigorously upon some instrument, the three sons amused themselves and the crowd by cutting capers.

Again and again did Robin entice Master Montfichet to return to these strollers. It was the wrestling that most moved him, for they put such heart into it as to make the thing seem real. "Give them another penny, sir," requested Robin, with heightened color. "Nay, give them a silver one. Did you ever see the like? The little one has the trick of it, for sure . . . I do believe that he will throw the elder in the next bout."

"Will you try a turn with me, young Master?" asked the little stroller, overhearing these words. "If you can stand twice to me, I'll teach you the trick and more besides."

"Nay, nay," said the Squire, hastily. "We have no leisure for such play, Robin. Your mother is waiting for us at yonder booth. Let us go to her."

Robin turned away reluctantly. "I do think I could stand twice to him. The grass is dry within the ring, sir—do you think I should hurt my clothes?"

Such pleading as this moved the capricious old Master of Gamewell. Although it was scarce a proper thing for one of gentle blood to mix with these commoners, yet the Squire could not forgo his own appetite for sport. He turned about to the strollers: "I will give a purse of silver pennies to the one who wins the next bout," said he. "Let any and all be welcome to the ring, and the bout shall be one of three falls. Challenge anyone in Nottingham; I dare swear some lad will be found who shall show you how to grip and throw."

The father of the players struck a most pompous attitude and blew three piercing blasts. "Come one, come all!" cried he. "Here be the three great wrestlers from Cumberland, where wrestling is practised by every lad and man! Here are the wrestlers who have beaten all in their own county, and who now seek to overcome other champions! Oyez, oyez! There is a price of twenty silver pennies to be handed to the winner of the next bout (did you say twenty or thirty pennies, lording?). Come one, come all—the lads from Cumberland challenge you!"

"Now let me wrestle for the pence, sir," pleaded Robin, catching hold of the Squire's sleeve. "Why should not I try to win them? They might become the foundation of that fortune which I would have for my father's sake."

"Twenty pennies would buy him little of Broadweald, boy," laughed the Squire. "Nor should a Montfichet struggle in the mob for vulgar gain. You are a Montfichet—remember it—on your mother's side. We will see how they fare, these men of Cumberland, against the lads of Nottingham and Sherwood. Here comes one in answer to the challenge."

A thin, pale-faced fellow had claimed the purse whilst the Squire had been speaking. " 'Tis yours if you can take it," answered the old stroller, as he and his lads cleared the ring. A great crowd of folk gathered about, and Montfichet and Robin were in danger of being jostled into the background.

"Stand here beside me, lording," commanded the stroller. "Do you keep back there, impudent dogs! This is the noble who gives the purse. There shall be no purse at all, an you harry us so sorely. Stand back, you and you!" He pushed back the mob with vigorous thrusts. "Now let the best man win."

The two lads had stripped to their waists, and were eyeing each other warily. The Nottingham youth, despite his slimness, showed clean and muscular against the swarthy thickset boy from Cumberland. They suddenly closed in and clutched each other, then swayed uncertainly from side to side. The crowd cheered madly.

The competitors for Montfichet's purse were evenly matched in strength: it remained for one of them to throw the other by means of some trick or feint. The stroller tried a simple ruse, and nigh lost his feet in doing it.

"You must show us a better attempt than that, Cumberland!" called out someone. Robin, quick-eared to recognize a voice, turned his head instantly, and in time to catch a glimpse of Will o' th' Green, the robber of Sherwood!

Seeing Robin's gaze fixed upon him, Master Will deemed it prudent to discreetly withdraw. He nodded boldly to the lad first, however; then moved slowly away. "Hold fast to him, Nottingham, for your credit's sake," he cried, ere disappearing.

Meanwhile the wrestlers tugged and strained every nerve. Great beads of perspiration stood out upon their brows. Neither made any use of the many common tricks of wrestling: each perceived in the other no usual foe.

Suddenly the Nottingham lad slipped, or seemed to slip, and instantly the other gripped him for a throw. Fatal mistake—'twas but a ruse—and so clear a one as to end the first round. The Nottingham lad recovered adroitly, and now that the other had his arm low about the enemy's body, his equipoise was readily disturbed. The stroller felt himself swiftly thrust downward, and as they both fell together it was he who went undermost.

"A Nottingham! A Nottingham!" clamored the crowd, approvingly. Then all prepared themselves for the second round.

This, to Robin's surprise, was ended as soon as begun. The Cumberland lad knew of a clever grip, and practised it upon the other immediately, and the Nottingham hero went down heavily.

The third bout was a stubborn match, but fortune decided it at length in favor of the stroller. Montfichet handed the purse to the winner without regret. "Spend the money worthily as you have won it, Cumberland," spoke the Squire. "Now, Robin, let us join your mother. She will be weary waiting for us."

"And if your stomach sickens for a fight with me, Master, here may I be found until Saturday at noon." So said the little tumbler, roguishly. " 'Tis a pity that we could not tussle for the purse, eh? But I would have given your ribs a basting."

"Now shall I twist his ears for him, Squire?" said Robin.

"Nay, boy, let his ears grow longer, as befitteth; then you will have freer play with them. Come with me to see the miracle play, and be not so ready to answer these rascallions. I begin to think that we should not have gone the round of the shows by ourselves, Master Spitfire. Travelling unattended with you is too dangerous a business."

Montfichet smiled despite his chidings. He had already taken a fancy to this high-spirited youth. He walked affectionately, with his hand upon Robin's shoulder, towards the booth where, with her maids, Mistress Fitzooth was waiting for them. "Are you sorry for Nottingham, Robin?" he asked, as they passed by the pale-faced, rueful wrestler. "Then take him this little purse quietly. Tell him it is for consolation, from a friend."

Robin gladly performed the task; then, as he returned to the Squire's side, thought to ask instruction on a point which had perplexed him not a little. "Yesterday, sir," he began, "when we were in the greenwood, all men seemed eager to catch the robber chief."

"Well, Robin?"

"Today he walks about Nottingham Fair, and no one attempts to tarry him. Why is this, sir? Is the ground sanctuary?"

"Have you spied out Will o' th' Green indeed?" began Montfichet, eagerly. "That were hard to believe, for all he is so audacious."

"Truly, sir, I saw him when we were at the wrestling. He peered at me above the caps of the people."

"Point him out now to me, Robin, if you can." The Squire became humorously doubtful, and his amusement grew upon him as Robin vainly searched with his bright eyes about the throng. "No Will o' th' Green is here, child; he would be a fish out of water, indeed, in

Nottingham town. Dearly would I love to catch him, though."

"Yet I did see him, sir, and he knew me. Now here is my mother, who shall tell you how long we talked together yesterday. It is not likely that I would forget his voice."

"Well, well, perhaps you are right," said the Squire. "At any rate, we'll keep sharp eyes for the rogue. Have you seen the miracle play, Sister Nell?" he added now to Mistress Fitzooth.

"I have been waiting here for you," answered she, briefly. "Robin, what do you think of it all?"

Robin's reply was drowned in the noise of the music made within the tents. It was so dreadful a din that all were fain to move away.

"See, Mother, here is a wizard; let us go in here!" Robin had spied a dim, mysterious booth, outside of which were triangles and cones and fiery serpents coming forth from a golden pot, with cabalistic signs and figures about the sides of it. Standing there was a tall, aged man, clad in a long red robe and leaning upon a star-capped wand.

"Will you have the stars read to you, lording?" he asked, gravely.

"Ay, surely!" clamored Robin. "Come, Mother mine; come, sir, let us ask him questions of Locksley, and hear what my father may be doing."

"Do you think that you will hear truth, child? Well, have your way. Will you join us, Nell—the business is a pleasing one, for these knaves have the tricks of their trade. But harkee, friends, give no real heed to the mummery."

The wizard ushered them into his tent. Then he dropped the edge of the canvas over the opening, shrouding them in complete darkness.

The Squire began an angry protest, thinking that now was a good chance for any confederate to rob them or cut their pockets: but the wizard, unheeding, struck suddenly upon a small gong. A little blue flame sprang up from a brazier at the far end of the tent.

In the strange light one could now see the furniture and appurtenances of this quaint place. They were curious enough, although few in number. A globe, and a small table covered with a black cloth; a bench strewn with papers and parchments; and a skeleton of an ape, terribly deformed, were the chief items of the collection.

A curtain concealed part of the tent. Behind the brazier were hanging shelves covered with little bottles and phials. The wizard stretched his wand out towards the dancing blue flame, and it forthwith leaped up into a golden glory.

"Approach, Robin, son of Fitzooth the Ranger," commanded the wizard. "Place your hand upon the globe and look down upon this table." He pushed away the black cloth, showing that the centre of the table was made of flat green glass. "Look steadily, and tell me what you see."

"I see through it the grass on the ground on which we stand," said Robin. "There is naught else."

"Look again, Robin of Locksley."

Robin strained his eyes in the hope of discovering something of mystery. But the flat glass was clear and disappointing.

"Let me take your place, Robin," said Mistress Fitzooth, impatiently.

But now the green of the glass began to fade; and it seemed to become opaque and misty. Robin dimly saw in it a sudden miniature picture of a glade in the forest of Sherwood, the trees moving under a southwest wind, and the grasses and flowers bowing together and trembling.

It seemed to be summer; the bracken was high and green. A man, clad in doublet and hose of Lincoln green, strode forward into the centre of the picture. He was a slim fellow, not over tall, with a likeable face, bearded and bronzed; and a forester, too, if one might judge by the longbow which he carried. He wore no badge nor mark of servitude, however, and walked as a free man. His face, vaguely familiar, wore an expectant look. He turned his glances right and left. A low call sounded from the bushes on his left. Robin could hear it as a sound afar off.

The man cautiously moved towards the verge of the glade, and as he did so there came a shower of light laughter from the undergrowth. Pushing aside the bracken came forth two arms; a merry face appeared; then, quick as a flash, upstood a page, gaily clad, with black curly hair and strange eyes.

The man opened his arms to the lad, and then Robin saw that 'twas no boy at all. It was a maid, joyous with life, playing such a prank as this that she might bring herself to her true love's side.

Robin watched them delightedly. In some way he knew that in this mirrored picture *he* was concerned to a curious degree; and when a cold cloud passing above the glade took the sun and the light from it Robin felt an intense anxiety.

"Can you see aught now, Robin of the Woods?" murmured the soft voice of the wizard, and Robin would have asked him who was the man, if his tongue had been at command.

His eyes took all the strength of his brain. They waited furiously for the cloud to pass.

When all had become clear again the man was alone. His face was sorrowful, ill, and old. He was fitting an arrow to his bow, and his hand trembled as his fingers drew the string. He drew it slowly, almost wearily, yet with a practised gesture. Robin, watching him, saw the arrow leap forth from the picture.

"He is dying and shoots his last arrow—is it not so?" he uttered thickly, striving to understand.

While he spoke the vision faded and was gone.

CHAPTER 4

ROBIN STARTED BACK angrily and faced the Squire. He began a confused complaint against the wizard, who had vanished behind the curtain on the left. Master Montfichet shrugged his shoulders indulgently.

"Give not so earnest a mind to these mummeries, child. 'Twas all a trick! What did you see? A golden fortune and a happy life?"

"I did see a man, sir, dressed all in Lincoln green. He was like unto my father, in a way, and yet was not my father. Also there was a stripling page, who turned into a maid. Very beautiful she was, and I would know her again in any guise."

"Ah, Master Robin, have you eyes for the maids already?"

"This was so sweet a lady, sir, and in some manner I do think she died. And the man shot an arrow, meaning me to see where it fell, since there would be her grave. That is what I think he meant. But then the picture was gone as quickly as it came."

"Sister Nell, do you hear these marvels? Take your place and let us see what the crystal can show to you. Most worthy conjurer of dreams, take up your wand again: we all are waiting impatiently to know what is in store for us!"

"These things are true that the glass mirror shows, lording," answered the wizard, reappearing. "The crystal cannot lie."

He spoke unwittingly in a natural key. Robin turned round upon him very shrewdly.

"Friend wizard," said the youth, half at random, "have you ever played at archery in that greenwood which your glass showed us so prettily?"

"Like as not, young Master, though I am an old man."

"Fie on you, friend!" cried Robin, exulting in a sudden discovery. "Remember that the crystal cannot lie. It tells me now that you and I will meet in rivalry, to shoot together for a strange prize—the freedom of Sherwood!"

The wizard hastily drew near and pretended to peer into the glass. "What would you do?" he whispered, fiercely.

"I can be generous, Will o' th' Green," spoke back Robin, quite sure now. "Keep your secret, for I will not betray you."

At this moment there uprose without the booth a most deafening tumult. Forthwith all ran to the opening of the tent to see what might be amiss; but Master Will, who peeped out first, needed no more than one glance. He gave way to the others very readily and retreated unperceived by the Squire and Mistress Fitzooth to the rear of the tent.

Cries of "A Nottingham! A Nottingham!" rent the air, and added to the clangor of bells and trumpetings. As the Squire and Robin looked forth they beheld a flying crowd of men and women, all running and shouting.

Before them fled the stroller and his three sons, capless and terrified. The old man's triangle had been torn from him and was being jangled now by Nottingham fingers.

"There is trouble before us. Come, Robin," said Montfichet, as he stepped out, with the lad close at his heels.

"What is the tumult and rioting?" cried out the Squire, authoritatively, and he blew twice on a silver whistle which hung at his belt.

The strollers rushed at once toward the old man, and faced their enemies resolutely when they had gained his side. They were out of breath, and their story was a confused one.

The little tumbler recovered first. After the Squire had left them, he said, the Nottingham lad had returned with full a score of riotous apprentices, all armed with cudgels. They had demanded a fresh trial of skill for the Squire's purse of pennies.

"Which was denied us in most vile words, lording," cried out one from the crowd, which had come to a halt and was now formed in an angry, sheepish ring about the front of the wizard's tent.

"Nay, we refused their request most politely, Most Noble," said the little stroller. "And then they became vexed, and would have snatched your purse from us. So my brother did stow the pennies quickly into his wallet, and, giving me the purse——"

"You flung it full in my face!" roared the Nottingham wrestler, pushing his way to the front, "you little viper, so I snatched at him to give him the whipping he deserved, when——"

"I could not see my boy injured, Excellence, for but doing his duty as one of Cumberland's sons. So I did push this fellow."

"It is enough," said George Gamewell, sharply, and he turned upon the crowd. "Shame on you, citizens," cried he; "I blush for my fellows of Nottingham. Is this how you play an English game: to force your rivals to lose to you any way? Cumberland has won my purse: the test was fairly set, and fairly were we conquered. Surely we can submit with good grace."

" 'Tis fine for you to talk, old man," answered the lean, sullen apprentice. "But *I* wrestled with this fellow and do know that he played unfairly in the second bout. Else had I not gone down at the clutch, as all did see."

"Insolent!" spoke the Squire, losing all patience; "and it was to *you* that I gave another purse in consolation! Go your ways ere I cause you to be more soundly whipped than your deserts, which should bring heavy enough punishment, for sure. Come to me, men, here, here!" He raised his voice still louder. "A Montfichet! A Montfichet!" he called; and the Gamewell men who had answered to his first whistling now lustily threw themselves upon the back of the mob.

Instantly all was uproar and confusion, worse than when they first had been startled from the wizard's tent. The Nottingham apprentices struck out savagely with their sticks, hitting friend and foe alike. The burgesses and citizens were not slow to return these blows, and a fierce battle was commenced.

The strollers took their part in it with hearty zest now that they had some chance of beating off their foes. Robin and the little tumbler between them tried to force the Squire to stand back, and very valiantly did these two comport themselves.

The head and chief of the riot, the Nottingham apprentice, with clenched fists, threatened Montfichet. Robin and the little stroller sprang upon the wretch and bore him to the ground. The three rolled over and over each other, punching and pummelling when and where they might. Robin at last got fairly upon the back of their enemy and clung desperately to him; whilst the stroller essayed to tie the man's hands with his own garters.

The riot increased, for all were fighting now in two great parties; townsfolk against apprentices. The din and shouting were appalling. Robin and the little tumbler between them rolled their captive into the wizard's tent.

The Squire helped to thrust them all in and entered swiftly himself. Then he pulled down the flap of canvas, hoping that thus they might not be espied. "Now, be silent, on your lives," he began; but the captured apprentice set up an instant shout.

"Silence, you knave!" cried Montfichet. "Stifle him, Robin, if need be; take his cloth." He felt for and found the wizard's black cloth.

The Squire was quite out of breath. "Where is our wizard friend?" he went on, peering about in the semi-darkness. "Most gentle conjurer, we wish your aid."

But Master Will had beaten a prudent retreat through the back of the tent. The canvas was ripped open, letting in a streak of light. They left their prisoner upon the ground, and cautiously drew near the rift.

The noise without showed no abatement. The fighting was nearer to the tent, and the bodies of the combatants bumped ever and anon heavily against the yielding canvas.

"They will pull down the place about our heads," muttered the Squire. "Hurry, friends."

Just then Robin stumbled over the skeleton of the ape, and an idea seized suddenly on his brain, and, picking himself up, he clutched the horrid thing tightly, and turned back with it. Thrusting open the proper entrance of the tent, Robin suddenly rushed forth with his burden, with a great shout.

"A Montfichet! A Montfichet! Gamewell to the rescue!"

He held the ape aloft and thrust with it at the press. The battle melted away like wax under a hot sun at the touch of those musty bones. Terror and affright seized upon the mob, and everywhere they fell back.

Taking advantage of this, the Squire's few men redoubled their efforts, and, encouraged by Robin's and the little stroller's cries, fought their way to him. The tumbler had come bounding to Robin's side and made up in defiant noise that which he lacked in strength of arm. The tide was turned, the other strollers and the Gamewell men came victoriously through the press and formed a ring about the entrance to the wizard's tent.

Robin, still brandishing his hideous skeleton, wished to pursue the beaten and flying rabble; but the Squire counselled prudence.

"You have done right well, Robin of Locksley, and dearly do I love you for your courage and resource. George Montfichet will never forget this day. Here let us wait until the Sheriff's men come to us. I hear them now, come at last, when all the fighting's done."

"What is your name, lording?" asked the little stroller, presently.

"Robin Fitzooth."

"And mine is Will Stuteley. Shall we be comrades?"

"Right willingly, for between us we have won the battle," answered Robin. He had taken a liking to this merry rogue; and gave him his name without fear or doubt. "I like you, Will; you are the second Will that I have met and liked within two days; is there a sign in that?"

"A sign that we will be proper friends," replied the stroller.

Montfichet called out for Robin to give him an arm. The Squire, now that the danger was over, felt the reaction; and he had strange pains about his breast.

"Friends," said Montfichet, faintly, to the wrestlers, "bear us escort so far as the Sheriff's house. It will not be safe for you to stay here now. I would speak with you later, since notice must be taken of this affair. Pray follow us, with mine and my lord Sheriff's men."

He spoke with difficulty, and both Robin and Mistress Fitzooth were much perplexed over him. The party moved slowly across the scattered Fair; nor heeded the mutterings and sour looks of the few who, from a distance, eyed them.

Nottingham Castle was reached, and admittance was demanded.

When the Sheriff heard who was without his gates he came down himself to greet them. He was a small, pompous man, very magnificent in his robes of office, which he was wearing this day in honor of the Fair. In the early morning he had declared it open; and on the last day would bring his daughter to deliver the prizes which would be won at the tourney.

Master Monceux, the Sheriff of Nottingham, was mightily put about when told of the rioting. He protested that the rogues who had conspired to bring about this scandal should all be thrust into the stocks for two whole days, and should afterwards be scourged out of the city. He was profuse in his offers of hospitality to his guests; knowing Montfichet to have a powerful influence with the King. And Henry might return to England at any moment.

The strollers and the Squire's retainers had been told to find refreshment with the Sheriff's men-at-arms in the buttery. Robin pleaded, however, with the Squire for little Will to be left with them.

"I like this impudent fellow," he said, "and he was very willing to help us but a little while since. Let him stay with me and be my squire in the coming tourney."

"Have your will, child, if the boy also wills it," Montfichet answered, feeling too ill to oppose anything very strongly just then. He made an effort to hide his condition from them all, and Robin felt his fingers tighten upon his arm.

"What is it, dear patron?" Robin asked, anxiously.

"Beg me a room of the Sheriff, child, quickly. I do think that my heart is touched with some distemper."

Robin ran to the Sheriff.

"Sir," said he, "my patron is overcome of the heat and commotion. He prays that you will quietly grant him some private chamber wherein he may rest."

"Surely, surely!" said the Sheriff. "Ay, and I will send him a leech— my own man, and a right skilful fellow. Bid your master use this poor house as he would his own." The Sheriff spoke with great affectation. "In the meantime I will see that a proper banquet is served to us within an hour. But who is this fellow plucking at your sleeve? He should be in the kitchen with the rest."

"He is my esquire, Excellency," returned Robin, with dignity.

Mistress Fitzooth had been carried off by the Sheriff's daughter and her maids as soon as they had entered the house, so that Robin alone had the care of Montfichet. With Will Stuteley's assistance they brought the old man safely to the chamber allotted them by the fussy Sheriff. Robin was glad when, at length, they were left to their own devices.

" 'Tis a goblet of good wine that the lording requires to mend him," said the little stroller. "I'll go and get it, Robin Fitzooth."

The wine did certainly bring back the color to the Squire's cheeks. Robin chafed his cold hands and warmed them betwixt his own. Slowly the fit passed away, and George Montfichet felt the life returning to him.

" 'Twas an ugly touch, young Robin. These escapades are not for old Gamewell, lad; his day has come to twilight. Soon 'twill be night for him and time for sleep."

The Squire's voice was sad. He held Robin's hand affectionately, as the latter continued his efforts to bring back warmth to him.

"But I will do some proper service for you, child. You shall not find me one to lightly forget. Will you forgive me now? I will return to Gamewell soon as I may and there rest for a few days."

"I'll take you, sir. It will be no disappointment to me. I have seen all that I wish of Nottingham Fair."

"You shall return for the tourney; and if your father will give you leave, young Cumberland, you shall become my Robin's esquire. No thanks; I am glad to give you such easy happiness. Arm me to the hall, Robin; I am myself again, and surely there is a smell of roasted meats!"

"You are a worthy leech, Will," presently whispered Robin. "The wine has worked a marvel. Come, follow us, and forget not that I still will wrestle with you! Ay, and show you some pretty tricks."

"Unless I have already learned them!" retorted young Stuteley, laughing. Then, becoming serious, the little stroller suddenly bent his knee. "I'll follow you across the earth and sea, Master," he murmured, touching Robin's hand with his lips.

He lightly sprang to his feet again, seeing that Montfichet now impatiently awaited them. Together they made their way to the banquet spread in the Sheriff of Nottingham's wide hall.

CHAPTER 5

SQUIRE GEORGE of Gamewell rested at his ease in the comfort of his own domain during the next day; and, though he would have Robin go into Nottingham, with his new esquire and Warrenton—Montfichet's own man—young Fitzooth was more than content to stay near to his patron's side.

There had been no difficulty in the matter of Master Stuteley's detachment from the other strollers. The old tumbler was shrewd enough to see that his son would considerably better his fortunes by joining them with those of Robin of Locksley. Will was delighted, and wished to commence his duty in Robin's service by instructing his young master at once in the arts of wrestling, singlestick, and quarterstaff.

The Squire laughed at their enthusiasm.

"Do you leave me, Robin, to the care of your mother: I warrant me I'll come to no harm!" he said. "There are matters on which I would talk with her, and we must be at peace."

Montfichet dismissed them. He was quite restored by this time, and settled himself to a serious conversation with his sister.

There were subjects which he touched upon only to her—being a secret man in some things, and very cautious.

"Having now no son, and being a lonely man," he had written in his letter, and Dame Fitzooth had known from this that unhappy relations still existed between George of Gamewell and Geoffrey Montfichet, his only son.

The two men had been for a long time on unfriendly terms, though the Squire latterly had sought honestly to undo that which had been years a-doing. He could not own to himself that the fault was his altogether: but Geoffrey, exiled to London, had been brought back to Gamewell at his father's entreaty. For a time things had gone on in a better direction—then had come Prince John's rebellion.

Geoffrey Montfichet was found to have been implicated in it, and had been condemned to death. Only by the Squire's most strenuous endeavors had this sentence been commuted by the King to life punishment. Geoffrey fled to Scotland whilst the Squire had been exercising himself on his erring son's behalf. It was the last straw, and George Montfichet disinherited his son. The hard-won Manor of Gamewell must pass from the line.

Squire George had suddenly perceived a chance to prevent that catastrophe. He had taken greatly to the lad Robin Fitzooth: and this boy was of the true Montfichet blood—why should he not adopt the Montfichet name and become the Montfichet heir?

This notion had been simmering in the Squire's mind. It had been born at that moment when Robin had so cared for him and fought for him in Nottingham Fair. "Here, at last," said the Squire, "have I found a son, indeed."

Mistress Fitzooth had to listen to her brother's arguments submissively. The dame saw stormy days for her ahead, for well she guessed that Hugh Fitzooth would never agree to what the other in his impetuous way was proposing. She listened and said "yea" and "nay" as the occasion offered: once she mentioned Geoffrey's name, and saw Gamewell's face cloud instantly with anger.

"He is no son of mine," said Montfichet, in a hard voice. "Do not speak of him here, Sister Nell—nor think me an unforgiving man," he hastened to add, "for God knows that I did humble myself to the ground that I might save his head from the axe of the King's executioner! And he disgraced me by running away to Scotland on the very night that I had gained Henry's pardon for him. Nay; I have no kin with cowards!"

"Geoffrey may have some reasonable excuse, Brother mine," began the dame, anxious to make peace.

Gamewell cut her short. "There can be no excuse for him," he said, harshly.

46

His voice softened when he talked of Robin, for he was concerned to gain his point.

"Fitzooth will be difficult in the matter, I do fear me," murmured the dame, perplexed and ill at ease. "He is a Saxon, George, and thinks much of his descent and name. He looks to Robin winning fame for it, as in olden days. I do misdoubt me sorely."

"Well, let the lad be known as Robin Fitzooth Montfichet—'tis but tacking on another name to him," said the Squire. "If he lives here, as I shall devise in my will, right soon will he be known as Gamewell, and that only! That fate has befallen me, and one might believe me now as Saxon as your Hugh, Nell."

"You are none the worse for't, George," answered the dame, proudly. "Either race is a kingly one."

"Saxon or Norman—shall Robin become Montfichet?" asked the Squire, commencing his arguments again.

Fate had in store for young Robin, however, very different plans from those tormenting Fitzooth the Ranger and old Squire George of Gamewell Hall.

★　　★　　★

The two lads strolled arm in arm about the wide court of Gamewell, following Warrenton, in dutiful mood. The old henchman was very proud of the place, and had all the legends of it at his fingers' ends. He told young Robin of hidden treasure and secret passageways, and waxed eloquent concerning the tapestries and carvings.

The hours went pleasantly enough, for, after the building had been duly shown them, Warrenton took Robin about the gardens and orchards. There was a pleasance, and a "Lady's Bower," wherein, Warrenton affirmed, walked a beautiful lady once in every twelve months, at Halloween, on the stroke of midnight. The old man then left them.

Very shocked was the old retainer to find these merry lads engaged together, later, at wrestling and the quarterstaff, as if they had been equals in birth. When Stuteley had thrown Robin thrice at "touch and hold," within sight of the hall—it was indeed upon the soft grass of the pleasance—Warrenton looked to see old Gamewell thundering forth.

When the Squire came not, and Robin nerved himself for yet another tussle, the retainer shrugged his shoulders and even took an interest in the matter.

"Catch him by the middle," he shouted. "Now you have him, lording, fairly. Throw him prettily!" And, sure enough, Stuteley came down.

"Does Master Gamewell play at archery here, Warrenton?" Robin asked, presently, when he and Will were tired of wrestling. "Are they not targets that I see yonder?"

The old man's eye lit up with pride. "Squire's as pretty a marksman as any in Nottingham, lording, for all his years!" cried he. "And old Warrenton it was who taught him. Yon target is a fair mark for any shaft from where we stand. Yet I dare swear that Gamewell's lord would never miss the bull in fifty shots at it!"

"Have you bow and quiver here?" inquired Robin, eagerly. "Mine I have left in my room."

"Crossbow, longbow, or what you will, Most Noble. All that Gamewell has I am to give you. Such were my master's commands. An your esquire will run to the little hut nearby, within the trees, he will find all that we need."

"Go, Will. Haste you, and bring me a proper bow," cried Robin, with sparkling eyes. "Now I'll bend the yew and see if I cannot do better than in Sherwood."

Master Stuteley, having journeyed to the hut, peeped in and started back with a cry of affright.

"The Yellow Woman, Robin!" called he, scampering back to them. "She is in there, and did snatch at me! Let us run, quickly!"

"Beshrew me, Master, but this is an adventure, for sure! The Yellow One, was it? Then your days are numbered, and we had better be seeking a new esquire," said Warrenton.

"Are you afraid, Warrenton?" said Robin, moving involuntarily nearer to him. He glanced from one to the other, undecided whether to believe Will or stand and laugh at his fears.

"I have had the distemper, Master, and cannot again be hurt. But here she comes, by the Lord! Keep near to me, lording, and shut your eyes tight."

Robin was too dazed to heed the old man's advice. He glared in a fascinated way at the figure emerging from the hut.

*C*atch him by the middle,"
he shouted. "*N*ow you have him,
lording, fairly. Throw him
prettily!" *A*nd sure enough
Stutely came down.

"It is a man," cried Robin, at last, "and listen—he is calling you, Warrenton."

The retainer uttered a little sound of astonishment and ran forward. "Sir—sir," he cried, as if in entreaty, to the man approaching: and he made a gesture as though to warn him.

The "Yellow Lady" appeared to be in doubt both of Robin and young Stuteley.

"Who are these, Warrenton?" called out a low, hushed voice.

Warrenton answered not, save with his half-warning, half-commanding sign. But as the stranger drew near, apparently come to a decision, the Squire's man spoke.

"It is your cousin, Master Geoffrey, and his esquire. They are here from Locksley."

"So, 'tis my kinsman, Robin, who has tried to startle me?" said the stranger, as Robin drew near to him. "Greetings, Cousin; here's my hand to you, for all that you come to supplant me. Nay! I bear no ill will. Gamewell has no charms in my eyes compared with those of a life of freedom."

"Is it Geoffrey, indeed?" asked young Fitzooth, gazing with both eyes wide. He had looked to see his cousin young as himself, and here was a man before him, bearded and bronzed, of nigh thirty summers. He was clad in sombre clothes, and wore upon his shoulders a great scarlet cape, cut extravagantly in the Norman fashion. Suddenly Robin laughed, heartily and frankly.

"Yellow, Will, *yellow*, forsooth? Are you color-blind, friend? Cousin Geoffrey, we had believed you none other than the yellow-clad damsel who walks here at Halloween. Forgive us the discourtesy, I pray you. Here is my hand and good fellowship in it. I am to relinquish all right to Gamewell ground at the end of a year an I like—such were your father's terms. I do doubt whether I may stay so long as that."

He spoke fearlessly. The two cousins embraced each other, and for an instant Geoffrey gave play to his better self; then, next moment, suspicion returned upon him.

"I am but come to see you, Warrenton, on a small matter. I must have a horse and armor and a lance, that I may ride at Nottingham in the joustings. I shall be disguised, and will wear my visor down:

a hungry wolf prowling unrecognized about his lord's domain."

His speech was bitter and his voice harsh. "Kinsman," added he, to Robin, "do you keep still tongue in the business, and tell your squire to be as discreet. I am outlawed in England and have no right in it——"

"That is not so, Geoffrey; surely your father will forgive——"

"It is in the King's hands, Cousin. My father has no voice in it, nor would desire to speak again for me, I trow. I have heard all that he hath already done in my behoof, Warrenton—the item was brought to me circuitously. Now I will keep you no longer: this hut has been and will be my shelter until the horse and arms are brought here to me."

"I'll saddle him myself for you, Coz: and choose you as stout a lance as Gamewell can provide. Let me help you in this, and be to you always a true friend."

"You speak soothly, young Robin, and it may be with sincerity. I'll trust you then." Geoffrey drew him on one side. "See that the trappings and armor be of good steel and furbished with red leather: let the note of them be steel and scarlet. No device upon the shield, if you should think to bring me one; and stay, I would like the sword hilt and the lance to be bound in red. Thus may you know me, if so be you are at the jousts; but be secret, and trust no other man than Warrenton. I'll wait you here at midnight—have no fear of the yellow ghost, kinsman!"

"You'll be as red as she is yellow, Cousin," whispered back Robin, with smiling face. "I'll do your behest, and attend you in this pleasance tonight at twelve o' th' clock. My squire can be trusted, I well believe."

"Believe in no man until you have tried him, Coz," answered Geoffrey. He paused. "Does Master Montfichet keep well in health, kinsman?" he asked.

"He is well, now, but has been indisposed. . . . Yesterday at Nottingham——"

"Ay, I heard of the doings there—no matter how," muttered the other, hastily. "Tell me that he is restored again; and that you will keep him from harm always as valiantly as you did then. Does your father still guard the forest at Locksley? 'Tis many years since I have seen Master Fitzooth, but thy mother hath always been kindly disposed to me. Farewell."

He nodded to Warrenton, and slipped back to the little hut, and they heard him push the bolts after him. Robin turned to Stuteley.

"Will, speak not of this meeting with anyone save Warrenton. I have promised for you."

"Right, Master; the matter has already passed from my mind. Shall we try our skill at archery? Warrenton can find me a bow, and I'll fetch yours from the hall. Here comes a priest; surely he were good mark for us had we our arrows here! And with him behold a forester of the King—green-clad and carrying a royal longbow. Do you beg it of him, Master mine, whilst I seek yours. I go."

Young Stuteley hurried across the green, whilst Robin advanced to meet the Clerk of Copmanhurst and the captain of the King's Foresters. They were in earnest converse, and clearly had not spied the gay cloak of Geoffrey Montfichet.

Warrenton, with significant gesture to Robin, began a lecture on the making and choosing of arrows, as he walked beside his master's guest.

"Are you talking of arrow-making, friend?" asked the forester, over-hearing them. "Now I will tell you the true shape and make of such shafts as our Will o' th' Green uses," he struck in. "One bare yard are they in length, and are sealed with red silk, and winged with the feathers of an eagle."

"Peacock," corrected the clerk, interposing. "You're wrong, Master Ford, as I will prove. Here is the head of one of Will's bolts, dropped in the greenwood on the day you rescued us from him. I have kept it in my pouch, for 'tis a pretty thing." He laughed all over his jolly face. "Here, Robin, keep it, and learn therefrom how *not* to make arrows, for vanity is a sin to be avoided and put on one side. The plainer the barb the straighter does it fly, as all true bowmen must admit."

He took Robin's hand, soon as the lad had fastened the trophy in his belt. "I have been bidden to you by the Master of Gamewell. He would speak with you, Robin; and I do counsel you to give all heed and weight to his words, and be both prudent and obedient in your answerings to him."

They moved together towards the hall, whilst Warrenton and the forester argued still on the matter of winging arrows.

CHAPTER 6

I T WAS WARRENTON who brought
Master Geoffrey his red-armored steed and lance, after all; for, although
Robin had had a voice in the choosing of the horse, and had helped the
retainer to bind the shaft and interlace the cuirass and gyres with riband
such as the knight had ordered, events stayed Robin from going out
with these appurtenances of war to the Lady's Bower.

Young Fitzooth had been commanded to his mother's chamber so
soon as he had come out from his converse with the Squire. There befell
an anxious interview, Mistress Fitzooth arguing for and against the
Squire's project in a breath. Robin was perplexed indeed: his ambition
was fired by the Squire's rosy pictures of what he, as a true Montfichet,
must adhere to without fail upon assuming the name and mantle of
Gamewell.

Most of all Robin thought of his father. What would he counsel?
"Remain Fitzooth, and fight your own way in the world, boy." That is
what he *might* say. In the end Robin decided to sleep upon the matter.
In any case he would not consent to rob Geoffrey of his inheritance; and
he told old Gamewell this to his face. "When I am gone you can do what
you will with the place, boy," the old man had answered. "I have no
son; but, of course, the fees and revenues will be yours. If, for a whim,
you beggar yourself, I cannot stay you. But take it whilst I live; and
wear Montfichet's shield in the days when my eyes can be rejoiced by so
brave a sight, for you will ne'er disgrace our 'scutcheon, I warrant me.
Perchance 'tis Geoffrey's sole chance that *you* should wear the badge of
Gamewell. I might choose to bequeath it elsewhere."

The lad had checked him then. "Never that, sir," he had said. "Let Gamewell land be ruled, forever, by Gamewell's proper lord. I pray you to let me take counsel with my mother ere I answer you."

"It is what I would suggest myself. Go to her."

Then had come the argument with his mother, which had unsettled him more than before.

He went down to discuss with Warrenton and Stuteley the means by which they best could bring the horse and arms to Geoffrey, and it soon became evident that no one other than Warrenton dare attempt it, for fear of betraying the son to his still angry father.

"Are you sure, Warrenton, that you will perform this business right carefully?" Robin asked, over and over again, until the old servant became vexed.

"I am part of the house of Montfichet, lording," snapped Warrenton, at last, "and it is not reasonable to think that I will turn against myself, as it were. Be sure that the horse and his trappings will be safely carried to my second master, Geoffrey, at the hour given. Do you keep the Squire employed in talk; and find excuse to lie in the little room next to his own that you may hear him if he moves."

So Robin and Will went back to the hall, and presently the Squire's voice was heard through the arras which covered the north entrance to the apartment. He was in deep converse with the clerk, and entered the hall holding him by the arm. For a moment Robin and Will were unperceived; then the Squire's bright, keen eyes discovered them.

"Now to bed, boy!" cried he, dropping his detaining hold of the priest. " 'Tis late; and I go myself within a short space. Dismiss your squire, Robin, and bid me good e'en. An early sleeper maketh a sound man."

"Did I see you with Warrenton, Robin Fitzooth?" put in the clerk, curiously. "I would fain have some talk with him on the matter of archery. I am told that this old man can draw as pretty a bow as any in Nottingham."

"As any in England, I would say," said Gamewell, proudly. "That is, in his day. Now that age is upon Warrenton and his master, cunning in such matters is to seek. Yet he will teach you a few tricks when morning is come. Now kiss me, boy, and keep clear head and ready hand for the joustings and games tomorrow. Good night; God keep thee, Robin."

He seemed to take it for granted that Robin would, in the end, consent to become of the house of Gamewell. Already Squire George looked upon him as heir to the hall and its acres; even as slowly did Warrenton, the shrewd and faithful man-at-arms. Truth to tell, the old servant did not regard the prospect with too kind an eye.

Young Fitzooth embraced his uncle, and bade him good night with real affection. There was no chance to alter his sleeping-room to one nearer to Gamewell's chamber.

When he had reached his chamber, again came the suspicion of Warrenton. Robin unfastened his tunic slowly and thoughtfully. Presently he crossed the floor of his room with decided step.

"Will," cried he, softly; and Stuteley, who had chosen his couch across the door of his young master's chamber, sprang up at once in answer.

"Do you hold yourself ready, Will, so soon as the house is asleep. We will go out together to the bower; there is a way down to the court from my window. Rest and be still until I warn you."

Stuteley replied in a word to him; and, blowing out his taper, Robin returned to his bed and flung himself upon it in patient expectation.

The hours passed wearily by, and movement could yet be heard about the hall. The open lattice gave entry to all sound from the court below: and from his window Robin could tell when the tapers in the hall were extinguished. Thrice he got up from his bed, and his stock of patience was slipping from him.

At last all was quiet and black in the courtyard of Gamewell.

"Will," whispered Robin, opening his door as he spoke, "are you ready?"

Stuteley nodded as he entered on pointed toes.

"From the window," explained Robin, pushing him towards the lattice. A faint starry radiance illumined the sky, and dim shadows held the angles and nooks of the court below them.

A dense ivy clung to and covered the walls of the house. To one of light and agile body it gave fair footing. Robin had hands and feet in it in a moment; and cautiously, adroitly came to the ground, and signalled to Will Stuteley.

The little ex-tumbler would have liked to have done tricks and shown his cleverness in the business, had there been time for it: as it was, Will dropped beside Robin lightly and easily, and instantly the two began to cross the court.

It was necessary for them to climb over the stables at their left hand. Some dogs, hearing these quiet, stealthy footfalls, began to bay furiously: and both the youths stayed themselves until the beasts went grumbling and suspicious back to the kennels.

They then renewed their journey, and, under the better light, made a safe crossing of the stable roofs.

They managed at length to win the gardens, and then raced across the open ground to gain the shelter of the yew trees bordering the bower. The pleasance, in the soft moonlight, looked ghostly enough: the statues and stone ornaments placed about the place seemed to be instinct with life and to wave signals of horror to Will's starting eyes.

At last they approached the hut, and Robin saw in the bright moonlight that the door gaped black at them. There was no sign to betray either Warrenton or Geoffrey to him. Robin entered the hut, dragging the unwilling esquire after him.

A draught of chill air puffed in their faces as they entered; and a great owl blundered screamingly out into the night, the rush and noise of it startling Will to a cold ecstasy of terror. He would have plunged madly back to the hall had not Robin held firmly to him.

"Be not so foolish, friend," said Fitzooth, crossly. His voice took his father's tone, as always happened when he was angered.

They moved thereafter cautiously about the hut, groping before and about them to find something to show that Warrenton had fulfilled his mission. Presently Will stumbled and fell, pulling down Robin atop of him.

Robin, putting out his hand to save himself, found that his fingers grasped nothing but air. They were upon the verge of an open trap, in the far corner of the hut; and Stuteley had tripped over the edge of the reversed flap mouth of this pit. Fitzooth's hand rested at last upon the top rung of a ladder, and slowly the truth came to him. Quickly he drew himself up and whispered the discovery to the other.

In an instant, then, their fears were dispelled. Will would have gone down first into the pit had not Robin stayed him. Stuteley was anxious that his young master should come to no harm; and where a danger appeared an earthly one, he was quite willing to bear the brunt of it. It was thought of the Yellow Woman which dried up all the courage in his small, wiry body.

Robin carefully descended the ladder and found himself soon upon firm rocky ground. Stuteley was by his side in a flash: and then they both began feeling about them to ascertain the shape and character of this vault. Hardly had they commenced when Robin's quick ears took warning. Sound of a quiet approach was plain.

The darkness of the pit was suddenly illumined, and the lads found themselves suddenly faced by the beams of a lanthorn suspended at about a man's height in the air. From the blackness behind the light they heard a voice—Warrenton's!

"Save me, Masters, but you startled me rarely!" cried he, waving the lanthorn before him to make sure that these were no ghosts in front of him. "I have but this minute left Master Montfichet, having carried his horse to him in safety. He rides into Nottingham tomorrow, unattended. I would that I might be squire to him!"

"Did you indeed bring horse and arms down this ladder, Warrenton?" enquired Robin, with his suspicions still upon him. "Truly such a horse should be worth much in Nottingham Fair! I would dearly have loved to see so brave a business——"

"Nay, nay, lording," answered Warrenton, with a half-laugh. "See"—and again he waved his light, showing them where the underground passage, for such it was, sloped upward to another and larger trap, now closed. "This way is one of the many secret ones about Gamewell, Master: but do you keep the knowledge of it to yourselves, I beg, unless you would wish hurt to our future lord of Gamewell."

Warrenton spoke thus with significance, to show Robin that he was not to think Geoffrey's claims to the estate would be passed by. Robin Fitzooth saw that his doubts of Warrenton had been unfair: and he became ashamed of himself for harboring them.

"Give me your hand, Warrenton, and help me to climb these steps," said he, openly. " 'Tis dark, for all your lamp; and I fain would feel friendly assistance, such as you can give."

His tones rang pleasantly on Warrenton's ears, and forthwith a good-fellowship was heralded between them. This was to mean much to the young hero of Locksley in the time to come; for Warrenton's help and tuition were to make Robin Fitzooth something far better than the clever bowman he was already. This night, in a way, saw the beginning of Robin's fortunes and strange, adventurous afterlife.

The old servant told him quietly as they crept back to Gamewell that this passageway led from the hut in the pleasance to Sherwood; and that Geoffrey for the time was hiding with the outlaws in the forest. "Our master is to be recognized by us as the Scarlet Knight at Nottingham Fair, should one ask of us, lording," Warrenton told him. "He implores us to be discreet as the grave in this matter, for in sooth his life is in the hollow of our hands."

The old servant spoke no more. In silence he led them back into Gamewell by the private door through the stables by which he had himself emerged.

They regained their apartment, apparently without disturbing the household of Gamewell. Only did one pair of eyes and ears look and listen for them, and observe both their exit and return. It was the Clerk of Copmanhurst's door that stood ajar; his busy mind that employed itself in speculation as to the cause and meaning of this midnight adventure.

CHAPTER 7

Geoffrey Montfichet's reason for wishing to be known as the Scarlet Knight was no idle whimsey, as the other had guessed.

To John's rebellion against his father, Henry of England, the younger Montfichet had given himself body and soul. The Prince had shown him kindness, and now that the rebellion had failed, Geoffrey felt it incumbent upon him to remain with the beaten side, and endeavor to recover the advantage lost to them. To this end he now journeyed through the Midlands in many disguises, trying to stir up the outlaws and robbers of the forests to take up arms with John, under a promise that the Prince (if successful) would grant them amnesty and a goodly share of the spoils sure to fall to them.

A spy was to attend at Nottingham Fair to know how matters had progressed with the outlaws of Sherwood; but, since it was too dangerous to attempt an open meeting, Geoffrey had arranged a simple code of signalling by color.

Did he appear as a knight unknown and disinherited, bound on his arms and steed with red trappings, the spy, eyeing him from beside the Sheriff of Nottingham, would know that Will o' th' Green was to be trusted, and would promptly bear the joyful news to his Royal Master. Had sad black been the note, John's man would have guessed that friends were still to seek about Nottingham.

Thus we know that Master Will had more reasons than one for appearing as a wizard at Nottingham Fair. He had gone here chiefly to bear a scroll to the Prince's emissary, and to declare fealty to John; but the affair of the tumblers and Robin's discovery of him had warned Master Will not to stay overlong in the town, so Geoffrey had to depend upon his plan of appearing as the Scarlet Knight.

The morning broke dull and threateningly over Gamewell. Robin and his esquire slept late; but no one offered to disturb their slumbers. The monk knew full well that there was good cause for his pupil's fatigue; and had set himself to discover the true meaning of it. "Boy," said he to Robin, "I pray that you do not think upon Nottingham today. There will be a storm and much rain. The mud in the meadows of Nottingham will surely spoil the bravery of the Fair, and show us too plainly how trumpery and vain a matter it is."

"For that cause alone will we go, dear friend," retorted Robin. "It will be a lesson to us. With you beside us to point the moral, much benefit shall accrue, for sure. Father," Robin added, "come with us now to the pleasance. There Warrenton is to show me how to notch arrows and pick a courtly bow."

"I have no great wisdom in the game, boy; yet readily will I go with you."

The three of them went in search of Warrenton; and found him with the captain of the foresters.

Dame Fitzooth and the Squire followed later to the pleasance, and there one and all tried conclusions. Robin soon found that Warrenton could teach him much; and he was too anxious to excel in the conduct of the bow to neglect this chance of learning the many secrets of it. "Men shall talk of you"—Fitzooth's own words to him—always rang in his heart whenever he drew the cord and fitted ash across yew.

Warrenton took great pleasure in showing Robin some of the tricks in which he was so perfect; and explained them so well that ere an hour had gone the lad had learned and mastered them.

"Lording," said the old servant, watching him as he essayed successfully an exercise shown him but a few minutes before. "Lording, I do not doubt that you will carry away with you today the Sheriff's prize from the older bowmen of Nottingham! You have a keen eye for it, and your fingers seem comfortable upon the yew—which is the sign and mark of a good archer. Now, bear in mind this golden rule: that the feet are to be placed at true angles, with the line of the mark running, as it were, fairly through the heels: thus," and he took the position, fitted an arrow to his bow, and, scarce looking towards the target, flew his shaft so straightly as to pierce the very centre of the bull. "Try now to notch the arrow," said Warrenton, with pardonable pride.

Robin shook his head and laughed.

"Ay, but you shall make far *better* than that, lording, an I have the handling of you!" cried Warrenton. "Now take this bow and these arrows which I have chosen; and we will set forth for Nottingham. We have an hour's journey."

On the way to Nottingham, Robin's mind was so full of all that had lately happened that he lagged behind the others and at last found himself quite alone.

This was where the road curved through the last of the forest about Nottingham. Warrenton and Master Ford of the foresters were at a renewed discussion on longbow against crossbow; and Will Stuteley had become so interested in the matter as to have poked his little horse between the others. Robin trotted his steed to come up with them; then, suddenly spying a brooklet among the trees upon his left hand, found himself mightily athirst. He slipped from off the back of his grey jennet and tethered the beast by the roadside.

The brook was fouled near the highroad from the passing of heavy carts and wagons, so Robin pushed down it into the thicker wood.

Finding that now the stream ran pure and limpid, Robin flung himself flat among the bracken and rushes, and dipped his face in the cool water. He drank heartily, and lay there for a while in lazy content, hid by the undergrowth and bracken.

A whinnying from his jennet warned him at length that he must push on with speed if he intended to rejoin the others ere Nottingham gate was reached. Robin turned himself about, preparatory to rising, then hastily shrank back into the shelter afforded by the forms.

Two men approached noiselessly through the forest. They carried bows and were clad in russet brown. Robin, in that brief glimpse, recognized two of Master Will's freebooting band.

The outlaws walked side by side in earnest conversation. Their mutterings were at first unintelligible to Robin; but, by hazard, they paused close to where he lay hid. Young Fitzooth knew that he would have small chance with these fellows should they espy him.

Said one, an evil-looking man, with a dirty grizzled beard: "Our Will seems to me, friend Roger, to be of open heart towards this youngling. He has given him the key of the forest at first word, as if the place were free to all. Had *you* the knowledge of it so soon, Roger? Tell me, lad."

He spoke sneeringly and with meaning. Robin strained his ears to distinguish the other's reply. "Friend," said Number Two, at last, and speaking in a smooth, milky sort of way, "friend, I would rather counsel you to adopt a persuasive argument with the Scarlet Knight, should we chance on him. I would have no violence done, an it may be avoided, being a man opposed to lawlessness in heart, as you know. It is my eternal misfortune which has brought me to this life."

"Tush! 'tis for murder of an old man at York! I know your story, Roger; seek not to impose upon me."

"He was a Jew, dear friend, and did grievously provoke me. But we have a matter in hand. This man has doubtless been sent in to spy upon us. I have no belief in the faith of these Norman nobles. Further, he has upon his head a goodly sum of money, as I well know. Wherefore, if chance should yield him to our hands, it would seem right and proper that we should bind him."

"Ay, hard and fast, Roger. You have it."

"Bind him with a vow, Micah, but not with ropes and wickedness. Yet should your dagger inadvertently prick him——"

"Be sure that it will, Roger. Some inward voice warns me that it will."

The other made a sign to the last speaker to speak more quietly. Robin cocked his ears in vain, but he had heard enough to show him that the shadow of a great evil was stalking behind his cousin, and without further thought decided that he must save him.

The two villains stood together a plaguey time perfecting their plans, and Robin dared scarcely breathe. Once, when he attempted to wriggle his way through the bracken, at the first sound of movement both men had become utterly silent, showing that they had heard and waited to hear again.

"A squirrel, friend," said the one called Roger at last, and Robin took heart again.

However, knowing that presently they must espy his jennet tethered by the road, Robin became desperate. He writhed his body snake-like through the ferns until he came to the edge of the brook; then, covered by the noise of the falling water, essayed to creep up the course of the stream.

The distance from the road could scarcely have been two hundred ells, but it seemed to Robin more like to a league. He got his feet and legs wet and bemired, and cut his hands over the rocks about the brook. Yet he came nearer and nearer still to the roadway without having given alarm.

Robin saw at length the close turf which bordered the road, and spied his little grey horse. Forthwith he rose to his feet and made a bold dash for it.

The jennet was untethered and Robin upon its back in a flash; then the lad heard the whizz of an arrow past him. He bent his head down close to the neck of his jennet and whispered a word into its ear. The little mare, shaking herself suddenly to a gallop, understood; and now began a race between bow and beast.

These outlaws were no common archers, for sure. Twice did their shafts skim narrow by Robin and his flying steed; the third time a sudden pricking told the youth that he was struck in the back.

He had no time for thought of pain. Everything depended on the beast under him. He pressed his legs softly but firmly against her streaming sides.

She was more swift in the end than the cruel arrows. Robin saw the countryside flashing by him through a cloud of dust; saw that Nottingham gate was reached; that a party with surprised faces watched his furious approach. The little mare swayed and rolled as she went, and Robin came to the ground, with the outlaw's arrow still in him. He was conscious that someone ran to him and lifted him tenderly: he perceived dimly, through circling blackness, the anxious face of Stuteley.

"Are you hurt, dear Master?" he seemed to see, rather than hear, him say.

Then Stuteley, Nottingham, and reason fled swiftly together, and the day became as night.

CHAPTER 8

WHEN HE RECOVERED himself Robin found them binding his shoulder. He smiled up at Warrenton to show that the hurt was little. "Are we too late for the joustings, Will?" he murmured, spying out Stuteley's face of concern.

"We are to bring back the golden arrow with us which the Sheriff has offered as prize to the best marksman," answered Warrenton, before the other could speak. "Now, you are to remember all that I have shown you, and shoot in confidence. Now come: the gates of Nottingham are opened, and your wound is neatly bandaged. Here is the arrow plucked from it: keep it for a trophy."

"Is it a pretty shaft, Warrenton?" asked Robin, carelessly, as the old servant thrust it into his quiver.

"It is one of Will's own, and that suffices."

After Master Ford had briefly bidden them farewell, they left their beasts in charge of a fellow inside the gate, bidding him give the little grey jennet all care and attention.

Here, also, Robin got himself washed and made tidy for the Fair, and had some meat and drink to restore him. He found that it was to the long Norman cape he wore that he owed his life. The outlaw's arrow had been diverted by the flapping garment, and had only pricked him in the fleshy part of his shoulder. The cape was so ripped, however, as to become ridiculous in its rags, so Robin asked for the loan of a pair of shears, and with them trimmed the cape so ruthlessly in his haste as to make it become more like an old woman's hood.

"You have turned Saxon out of Norman very suddenly, Master," laughed young Stuteley.

It was a full three hours past noon ere they came to the Fair. A great ring had been made in the centre of it, and huge wooden stands had been built about this circle. They were covered finely with cloth of red and gold; and many flags and banners were flying above the tops and about the stands.

The blare and discord of trumpets rang out over the noise of the people. A great clamor of voices betokened the arrival of some great man at the front of the chief stand.

"The Sheriff has arrived," cried Stuteley, who knew the ways at these affairs. "Hear how the people do cheer him! For sure he must be a man well liked——"

"These fellows will applaud anyone who has power and office," said Warrenton, scornfully. "Master Monceux is *not* beloved of them, for all that. But hasten, or we shall be shut out. Already they are closing the gates."

The clouds were heavy and grey, and a few large drops of rain began to patter down.

"Look to our bows, Warrenton," cried Robin, in alarm.

"Be easy, lording—your bow shall not be at fault if the prize does not fall to your hand. Follow me."

They were now at the wicket, and Warrenton produced his authority. Gamewell's name was enough. They were ushered into a small box nearby the Sheriff's own, and there awaited events.

First came bouts of singlestick and quarterstaffs, and Master Will was keen to take part in these contests. Warrenton counselled him to remain in the background, however.

"The folk are sure to recognize you, malapert," said he, giving Stuteley his favorite name for him, "and there will be an outcry. Let be, then, and attend to your master."

"It would be better, Will, I do think," said Robin. "I have to find out cousin Geoffrey, and warn him against two villains waiting for him without the town." And Robin gave them briefly the history of his adventure.

Ere he had ended the story, the Sheriff held up his baton as a sign that the jousting would begin. Two knights rode into the ring through the hastily opened gates, heralded by their esquires—amid the noise of a shrill blast of defiance. They were clad in chain mail, bound on and about with white riband, and their armor was burnished in a manner most beautiful to behold. Their esquires threw down their gauntlets before the box of Master Monceux, and challenged the world to a trial of strength in these the lists-magnificent of Nottingham town.

Two black knights had ridden into the lists in answer to the challenge; and now all clamor was hushed. The Sheriff's daughter, a pale, hard-faced girl, with straw-colored hair and mincing ways, announced in inaudible voice the terms of the contest. The heralds repeated them afterwards in stentorian tones; and the rivals wheeled about, the white knights couching their lances from under the Sheriff's box. The others prepared themselves at the wicket gate and waited for the signal.

This was given, and the four rushed together with a shock like a thunder-clap. These four knights gave good account of themselves.

The black knights had been unhorsed, and now they lay helpless in their heavy armor. Once on their feet, they were eager to renew the fray, and were soon again in readiness. At the second tilt they rudely unhorsed the white knights by sheer strength of arm; and all the people shouted themselves hoarse.

So the jousting went on; and, after the white knights had eventually won the first round, yellow and red took their places. Robin eagerly scanned the latter, trying to discover which of the two might be Geoffrey. A small, thin-faced man behind the Sheriff was no less eager to discover Montfichet in this favorable apparel; and evidently had sharper eyes than had Robin in piercing disguise. This wizened-faced fellow leaned back with satisfied smile, after one searching glance; then, drawing out his tablets, he wrote on them, and despatched his man in haste to London town.

Geoffrey was unhorsed in the second tilting; and lay so long upon the ground that Robin's heart stood still. It was then discovered that this knight was unknown and had no esquire. Thus Robin knew him for his cousin.

"Attend him, Will, as you would myself," cried Robin, anxiously, "and see now to his hurt——"

"He is but dazed, Master, with his fall. It seems that these knights are armored so heavily that once down they cannot of themselves rise up again! Protect me from such war gear! I'd sooner have my own skin and be able to be spry in it. What say you, old Warrenton?"

"Go to, malapert. Get down to him, and be as active with your hands as you are with your tongue."

"I go, I go—see how I go!" and Will turned a somersault over him into the ring out of the front of their box. Robin called angrily on him to behave, and the little tumbler ran then to his duties as servant to the unknown Scarlet Knight.

Robin's eager eyes roved hither and thither about the gay scene. Opposite him was a small box near to the ground, wherein sat two people only. One was a grave-faced man of courtly mien and handsome apparel: the other seemed to be his child.

Towards one of these two persons Robin's glances forever wandered. The laughing blue eyes of the girl, the queer little toss of her head which she gave in her unheard answers to her sober father, heartily pleased young Fitzooth, and in some way vaguely disturbed his memory. She was of about fifteen summers; and her hair was black as a winter's night—and curled all waywardly around her merry face. Blue were her eyes when the quick fever induced by the tilting rushed in her blood— blue as meadow violets. Then, when the excitement was passed, they fell to a grey wonderment. Twice she encountered Robin's glances; and the second time her eyes shone blue, as if ashamed, and the tint of her warm cheeks deepened. Demurely she turned away her face from him.

Young Fitzooth turned to Warrenton: "Can you tell me who these may be who sit alone in yon little box?" he asked, and cautiously pointed them out to the old retainer.

Warrenton was stupid, however, and would not see exactly where Robin would have him look. At last, as one making a discovery: "Oh, 'tis Master Fitzwalter you mean, lording? Ay, a right worthy, honest gentleman; and warden of the city gates. Next of importance in Nottingham town is he after Monceux, the Sheriff; and a prettier man in all ways. Now, were he Sheriff, Squire George of Gamewell would oftener be in Nottingham Castle than now, for we like not the Sheriff. The maid with Master Fitzwalter is his only child. She has no mother; and he is both parents to her. Ay, a proper man——"

"She is very beautiful, I think," said Robin, speaking his thoughts almost without knowing it.

"Yes, yes, a passable wench. But I have no faith in them, lording. They are all as the Yellow One of Gamewell. They smile upon you that they may work their will; and evil comes of their favor, if not death. Now see——"

"You are crabbed, indeed, Warrenton; and I'll hear no more. Do you know her name?"

"Fitzwalter, lording. Did I not say this was his child?"

"Has she no other name?" persisted Robin, patiently.

"Oh, ay . . . let me see. 'Tis Judith, or Joan, or some such name. Mayhap, 'tis Catherine. I do misremember it, lording: but 'tis surely of no account. The archery is now to begin; and here I would have you give heed——"

He recommended his cautions, warnings, and hints—being anxious that Robin should shine today for Gamewell's sake.

Robin saw that the jousting was done, and that, after all, the red knights were conquerors. It fell to Geoffrey to ride forward and accept the coveted laurel wreath. Dipping his lance, Geoffrey caused his charger to bend its knees before the regal-looking box: and Master Monceux, after an inflated speech, placed the circlet of bays upon the end of Geoffrey's lance. Then the unknown knight for a brief instant raised his vizor. The lean-faced man near to the Sheriff's right hand exchanged a quick glance of understanding with the knight.

The Sheriff nodded to give the knight to understand that he was satisfied. With closed visor the scarlet one then paced his steed slowly and in quiet dignity around the lists, followed dutifully by Stuteley, until they had returned to the Monceux box. Again saluting gracefully, he extended his lance, with the wreath still depending from it, towards the Sheriff, as it seemed.

"Does he return the wreath, and wherefore?" asked Robin, in puzzled voice.

"To her to whom the wreath is yielded our Sheriff will award the title of Beauty's Queen," explained Warrenton. " 'Tis a foolish custom. Master Geoffrey, in this matter of etiquette, knows that the trifle should go to young Mistress Monceux. Otherwise, the Sheriff would have him beaten, no doubt; or injured in some shameful way upon his departure from the lists."

"So that is the rule of it, eh, Warrenton?" said Robin. "I would like to choose my own Queen——"

"It matters not one jot or tittle to young Master Montfichet. See—the wreath has been duly bestowed and the Sheriff will announce his girl Queen, until the night, of Beauty in all Royal Nottingham. There will be some further mummery when the golden arrow is won. Doubtless, the winner will have to yield it up to Monceux's girl again, on a pretence that all is hers, now she is Queen. So shall my lord the Sheriff keep his prize after all; and be able to offer it again next year——"

Robin checked the garrulous old man with a gesture.

"Now give me my bow, Warrenton," commanded young Fitzooth, somewhat roughly; "and do you tell me how I am to enter myself in the lists."

"Your esquire should announce you," returned the other, respectfully. "See, here he comes——"

"The Red Knight would thank you, Master, for your courtesies," said Stuteley, approaching Robin. "He will wait for us at Nottingham gate; and prays that you will accept the chargers of the unhorsed knights from him. They are his by right of conquest, as you know."

"I will accept them, and thank him for the gift," returned Robin, briefly, guessing that this was the reply that Geoffrey would desire him to make. "Now tell the heralds that Robin of Locksley will enter for the Sheriff's prize. Give no more of my name than that, Will," he added warningly, in a lower voice.

Stuteley vanished, and Robin turned again to the lists. The Sheriff's daughter had already been crowned, and sat now in supercilious state in the Sheriff's own seat. Geoffrey had gone, and Fitzwalter's box was empty.

"I'll not shoot at all," said Robin, suddenly. "Go, Warrenton, bring back Stuteley to me. I have changed my mind in the matter."

"Does your wound fret you, lording?" asked Warrenton, solicitously. "Forgive me that I should have forgot——"

"Nay—'tis not that at all. I have no wish to shoot. Fetch Will to me."

It was too late. Stuteley had already given in Robin's name to the heralds, and signified that he would shoot first of all. He came into the box even as Warrenton went out for him.

Half-angrily, Robin took the bow from the retainer's hands and slung his quiver about him. He strode moodily across the lists to the spot where the other archers had already gathered. When they saw this youngling with his odd little cape preparing himself, they smiled and whispered together. Robin strung his bow and slipped an arrow across it.

The crowd became suddenly silent, and this nerved the lad to be himself once more. He forgot his momentary vexation and aimed carefully. His arrow flew surely to the target and struck it full in the middle. "A bull! A bull!" roared Warrenton and Stuteley, together. Robin stepped back.

"None so bad a shot, Master," said the next archer to him, in a quiet tone. "You have provided yourself now with a truer shaft, I ween?"

It was Will o' th' Green, with stained face and horsehair beard. His eyes challenged Robin's in ironical defiance, as he moved to take his turn. His aim seemed to be made without skill or desire to better Robin's shot; yet his arrow found resting place side by side with the other.

The mob cheered and applauded themselves hoarse; while the markers scored the points evenly to these first two archers.

These two stood apart, silent amidst the din. Once Will seemed to be about to speak: then changed his mind. He glanced sidelong at young Stuteley and Warrenton; then hummed a ballad tune under his breath.

The contest went on and the first round came to an end. Out of twenty and three rivals nineteen had scored bulls at this range. The markers gave the signal to the heralds, and these announced the results with loud flourishings.

The target was taken down and the range increased. The range of the mark from the archers for the second round was fixed at forty ells—the same distance as had chanced before between Robin and Master Will when in the greenwood together. The outlaw offered to shoot first; but the heralds requested them to keep in the same order as in the preceding round.

Robin fitted his arrow quietly and with some confidence to his bow, then sped it unerringly towards the target. "A bull! Another bull to Locksley!" cried out Warrenton, in stentorian tones, and the fickle mob took up the cry: "Locksley! A Locksley!" with gusto.

Will aimed with even more unconcern than before. His arrow took the centre fairly and squarely, however; and was in reality a better shot than Robin's. The shafts were withdrawn; then the other contestants followed. This round brought down the number of competitors to five. The markers carried back the target to a distance of five-and-fifty ells; and truly the painted circles upon it seemed to be now very small.

Robin again took his stand, but with some misgiving. The light was uncertain, and a little fitful wind frolicked across the range in a way very disturbing to a bowman's nerves. His eyes half-anxiously addressed themselves to that box wherein he had spied Mistress Fitzwalter.

His heart leaped—she had returned, and her strange gaze was fixed upon him! Robin drew his bow and flew his shaft. Unconsciously he used the arrow plucked from his own shoulder by Warrenton.

Again did he gain the centre, amid the cries and jubilations of Stuteley and the old retainer.

"Now Master Roughbeard, better that!" shouted Warrenton.

The outlaw smiled scornfully and made ready. He drew his bow with ease and a pretty grace, and made a little gesture of confidence as his agile fingers released the arrow. It leaped forth rushingly towards the target, and all eyes followed it in its flight.

A loud uproar broke forth when the markers gave their score—an inner circle, and not a bull. Master Will made an angry signal of disbelief; and strode forward down the lists to see for himself. It was true: the wind had influenced a pretty shot just to its undoing, and Will had to be content with the hope that the same mischance might come to Robin or any of the other bowmen before the round was ended.

The outlaw wished especially to win—that he might have the satisfaction of vexing the Sheriff of Nottingham. Will had intended to send back this prize—a golden arrow—from his stronghold of Sherwood, snapped into twenty pieces, with a letter of truculent defiance wrapped about the scraps. He wished to make it plain to Master Monceux that the free archers of Sherwood were better men than any *he* might bring against them, and that they despised him very heartily. Now that he saw a likelihood of his being beaten his heart grew hot within him.

"Be not too sure of it, stripling," said he, as he returned to Robin's side. "Fortune may mar your next shot, as she has mine——"

" 'Tis like enough, friend," answered Robin, smiling; "and yet I do hope that the arrow may be won by my hand. This is our second test, Master Will," he added, in a low voice. "Forget it not—the freedom of the greenwood is the reward that I do seek even more than my lord the Sheriff's golden arrow."

The outlaw's anger went suddenly from him.

"Then I do wish you Godspeed, youngling," he said, brightly. "You have in truth beaten me right honestly—for mine was an ill-judged shot."

With Will out of it, the contest came to an easy conclusion; and presently the Sheriff's arrow was duly awarded to Robin of Locksley by the markers.

The lad came forward shyly to receive the prize.

"Master Monceux thinks that you should shoot once more with the second archer," said someone to him, leaning from the Sheriff's box. Looking up, Robin espied the lean-faced man smiling disagreeably down at him.

"Let my lord state the terms of this new contest, then," answered Robin, "and the reason for't."

" 'Tis said that you were overfavored by the wind and by the light."

An angry answer was upon the lad's lips: but he checked himself, and with slow dignity turned and went back to where the archers stood grouped together. Soon as he made known to him the difficulty which the Sheriff had raised, Will o' th' Green became furious.

"Locksley, have none of this trumpery prize," cried he, in loud anger. "I do deny my right to any share in it, or to a fresh contest. Nor will I shoot again. Let Monceux vex his brain as he may with rules and conditions—they are not for Roughbeard, or for you. We have our own notions of right and justice; and since the Sheriff is loth to part with the prize that he has offered—why, yield it back to him, friend—and take the reward from me that you coupled with it."

Other indignant protests were now heard from amongst the onlookers: and the Sheriff saw that he had raised a storm indeed. "Locksley!

Robin Locksley!" was shouted noisily round and about; and Warrenton and Stuteley busily fostered the tumult. Master Monceux at last bade the heralds announce that Robin of Locksley had won the golden arrow—since the archer who had made nearest points to him did not desire nor seek a further trial.

"Were it necessary, lording," muttered old Warrenton, "I would show you how to notch the arrow of the best archer hereabout—a merry trick, and one that I learned in Lancashire, where they have little left to learn of archery, for sure."

"Nay," put in Roughbeard, loudly, "the arrow is his without need of further parleyings. I do admit myself beaten this day—though on another occasion we will, perchance, reverse our present positions. Take or leave the arrow as you will, Locksley. For my part I would love to prick Monceux with it heartily."

"You talk wisely, friend," said Warrenton, approvingly, "and, as for making a match with you, why, that will we today. Do you ride with us to Gamewell and there you shall have archery and to spare."

"Ay, and a welcome, too!" commenced Robin; then paused suddenly, remembering who Roughbeard really was. Montfichet of Gamewell entertaining Will o' th' Green!

The outlaw merely laughed good-humoredly at the lad's confusion.

"Go, take the Sheriff's prize; and vex him in some way, if you can, in the accepting of it!"

Again Robin walked forward towards the Monceux box; this time with flashing eyes and a resolve in his heart.

"Robin of Locksley," said the Sheriff, scarce looking at him, "here is my golden arrow which I have offered as reward to the best bowman in this Fair. You have been accorded the prize; and I do yield it to you with sincere pleasure. Take the bauble now from our daughter's hand, and use the arrow worthily."

The heralds blew a brazen blast, and the demoiselle Monceux, with a thin smile, held out to Robin upon a silk cushion the little shining arrow which now was his. Bowing, and on one knee, Robin took up the glittering trophy.

"Surely 'tis a plaything more suited to a lady's hair than to an archer," murmured the lean-faced man, who stood close by. Catching

Robin's eye, he made a significant sign, as who would say: "Here is the Queen who would adorn it."

Robin had that other notion in his mind, however, and saw that now the moment had arrived in which it should be put into execution. Somehow, he contrived to bring himself before the small low box wherein, half-startled, sat the maid Fitzwalter.

"Lady," stammered the young archer, bowing to her, "do you please accept this little arrow which I have won. It is a pretty thing; but of small use to me. Maybe you could make some ornament with it——"

Then he could go no farther; but dumbly held it out to her.

The girl, having seen that her father was not unwilling, stretched out and took the Sheriff's arrow from Robin's shaking hands.

"Thanks to you, Robin o' th' Hood," she said, with that roguish little toss of her dark curls; "I'll take the dart, and wear it in memory of Locksley and this day!" Her eyes looked frankly into his for a brief instant; then were hid by her silky lashes.

Robin, with bounding heart, walked proudly back to where old Warrenton stood, glowing; and the people thunderingly applauded the archer's choice.

"Right well was it done, Locksley!" roared the outlaw, near forgetting himself. "I love you for it." For he saw only that the Sheriff had been slighted, and cries of: "A Locksley!" were renewed again and again.

Master Monceux looked furiously at this archer who had taken the prize with only the briefest word of thanks to him: and would have spoken, had not his daughter, with chilling gesture, forbidden it. She gave no outward symptom of the anger stirring within her: she wore her worthless but royal crown of bay, whilst the other toyed thoughtfully with the golden arrow, and wondered who the gallant giver of it might be.

Robin, Warrenton, Stuteley, and Roughbeard rode towards the gate of Nottingham on the horses of the defeated knights. They had decided to stay no longer at the Fair: the noisy play and mock joustings that were to follow the archery had no attraction for them.

CHAPTER 9

THIS ESCORT SAVED Geoffrey from the attack planned upon him by the two treacherous robbers. They spied him out, and followed the small cavalcade throughout the journey, but at a respectful distance, uttering deep threats against the lad who had warned the knight of their evil intent. So, whilst making friends, Robin also made enemies: but none so bad as that cold-faced woman of Nottingham Castle. She had recognized in Robin of Locksley the youth who had come with old Montfichet on the first day of the Fair.

Nearby Gamewell, Roughbeard called a halt. He had been strangely silent, being over-doubtful.

"Farewell, friends," said he, doffing his cap to them. "Here our roads do part, for I must go further through the forest."

"I, too, have that direction before me, if so be that you are travelling westward," said Geoffrey to him, with well-assumed diffidence, and speaking through his casque. He had known the outlaw at once; but had forborne to show it, scarce dreaming that Robin also had pierced Will's disguise.

Robin became busy in his thoughts when he saw his cousin and Roughbeard riding off together like this. That secret way from the hut which led into Sherwood; the two villains who had plotted against Geoffrey—why, all was clear! Geoffrey now was with them of the forest; had been seeking to influence Master Will; no doubt the red trappings upon which he had laid such stress were as a signal to someone. To whom? And to what end?

Geoffrey had been cool towards Robin when warned of those scheming against him. "I can protect myself against such rabble, Cousin," was all he would say. "But I would thank you for bidding your lad to me in the joustings; it was a matter I had overlooked that one must have an esquire. I'll not forget the courtesy."

That was all. He had shrunk back into himself again; and with closed visor had ridden silently beside them. Yet he was not ungrateful; and had begun to like Robin very honestly, only Geoffrey Montfichet must be very sure of his man ere he would unbend to him.

It was already nigh on dusk as Robin rode into the court at Gamewell in dreaming abstraction. His thoughts had sprung back again from Geoffrey to the blue-eyed maid: and in cloudlands he saw himself her knight. Wondrous and mighty would be the deeds that he should perform for her dear sake—did she bid him to them.

Then he remembered Broadweald, and how he had sworn within himself to set his life to win that, for his father's happiness.

Ay: but surely in the winning of Broadweald there might chance smaller prizes, which properly he might yield for a smile from this fair maid? Or again, might not he battle for the two together?

"Robin, Robin!" He heard old Montfichet's voice, calling from the shadow of the porch. "Where are you, child? I did not espy you at the bridge. Come here, boy, and let me tell you something of sorrow. There has befallen a sad mischance to your father at Locksley——"

"Sir, sir," cried poor Robin, waking suddenly, "tell me not that he is dead!" He sprang hastily from his grey steed and ran towards the Squire.

"No, not that."

"Ah, but my heart forewarns me. He has been hurt by some beast? It is the season when the deer are wild."

"Master Fitzooth has been attacked by a great stag nearby your home. That is all we know of it, child; and I give it you plainly at once, that you may hear the worst. Your mother has already gone to him, with the clerk and a full two score of men. For the captain of the foresters has kindly joined forces with mine own fellows; so that no further harm may befall."

"I'll follow her, sir. Give me leave to go."

" 'Twere wiser to wait till morning, boy. What could you do now? Mayhap we fret ourselves too much, as 'tis. But you shall go, with Warrenton and your esquire, when morning is here. Ay, and I will come too; and we will bring with us the most skilful leech in Nottingham. I have already sent a messenger to him, an hour since, so soon as the dame had gone."

"I like not my mother having been sent for, sir. That shows me that the hurt is deadly. To think that I was playing so foolishly at the moment when I might have been of use to him!"

So rudely ended Robin's dreaming.

In the morning they set out for Locksley; the Squire with the leech, and six mules bearing such delicacies as old Gamewell's generous mind could think upon. Warrenton headed a full score of men, for fear of the outlaws; and they took a litter with them to bring Master Fitzooth to Gamewell.

The dame met them at the latch gate which Robin knew so well. Her face was deathly pale and her mouth quivered as she tried to frame a welcome to them.

"Mother!" cried Robin, in anguished voice, running to her; and there was no need for further speech. In that one cry and in the expression of her mute, answering face, the truth was told and understood. No use to fight for Broadweald now; were it his a hundred times over, Robin could never do that with it which he in all his boyhood had planned. Hugh Fitzooth, Ranger of the Forest of Locksley, was dead.

★   ★   ★

The good Clerk of Copmanhurst, who had appeared from within the cottage, told the story of Fitzooth's death. Fitzooth had been alone when the huge wild stag had attacked him; was near his death when discovered by two of his men. He had regained consciousness only at the sound of his wife's voice; had kissed her with fainting breath; and, having labored to send Robin a message of love and pride in him, had gradually faded in spirit until the dawn.

It was an unhappy ending to a life soured by disappointment; yet somehow this man had managed to win a way into the hearts of many people. The few villagers of Locksley all had their tender word or humble tribute of affection to offer the dame and her sorrowing son; and thus much of the edge of their grief was blunted. Until the interment the priest stayed with them, and so did old Gamewell, who paid all the fees and expenses inevitable in consequence of Fitzooth's decease.

Afterward, the Squire would have them go back to Gamewell with him; but Robin had determined to ask for his father's post. This bitter time made the lad into a man suddenly. It was the evening of the day when they had laid Fitzooth to rest in the little churchyard of Locksley that Montfichet returned again to talk of his plan of making Robin his heir.

The old man argued reasonably and well; and Robin listened in silence until he was done. Then, "Very generously and indulgently have you talked with us, sir," said Robin, "and sure thing it is that we owe you such debt as I can never hope to pay. Yet I cannot feel that 'twould be a man's part to live an idle life. Surely I should do something, sir, to win the right to wear your name? Moreover, I must not forget that there is another—nay, hear me, sir—thine own son, whose birthright I should be stealing away from him."

"Boy," interrupted old Gamewell, on a sudden resolution, "will you share Gamewell with me as Geoffrey's brother, then? If so be this way out of it will meet your objections, I'll sink my prejudice. Geoffrey shall go halves with you."

"That were the course nearer to my heart, sir; and yet not all that I would desire. I have no right to talk to you so openly; but the matter is, in a manner, forced upon me."

"It is agreed then, Robin?" cried the Squire, eagerly. "And so you will take your mother's olden name and become Montfichet of Gamewell?"

"I would rather serve the King *here* for one year, at least," said Robin, arguing still. "You might think better on't, sir. Let me try my strength or weakness; and find out myself for myself. My father would have wished me to fight my own way in the world."

"The lad speaks soothly, Squire," said the clerk, interposing, "and I would counsel you to agree to his notions. Moreover, he has not yet finished his studyings with myself in the Latin tongue."

"Leave me young Stuteley and Warrenton, sir, and your blessing, and let me win bread for my mother and myself for twelve months from today. Then, if I may, and you wish, I'll come humbly to you." Robin went over to him. "And believe me always as being very grateful, sir. I would that I might not seem obstinate in this."

"Have it so, then, Robin. I'll bear your letter to Monceux myself, and rally him about the arrow which you won!"

"Will the Sheriff appoint me, then?" asked Robin, a trifle disconcerted.

"He will advise the King in the matter. 'Tis but a form. The post of Ranger of Locksley is yours, merely for the asking. Who could gainsay your right to it? Give me the letter; and I will be your messenger. I go tomorrow to Gamewell, and will journey to Nottingham the next day. Now, since I understand that this holy man would wish to see you alone, and I would like to talk with your mother. I'll leave you, boy. Count me always as friend, Robin Fitzooth Montfichet."

He added the last word half-enquiringly, half-lovingly; and twinkled to the clerk to see how Robin might take it. But the lad made no reply beyond kissing the old man's fingers very respectfully and tenderly; and with a sigh, old George of Gamewell offered his arm to the dame, who had silently listened throughout the discussion.

Left alone, the clerk approached Robin. "Now, boy, what I have to say is soon told. Know then that I have learned of your adventures with the Scarlet Knight; and that he is in league with Will o' th' Green. Further, I have had it whispered to me that he is none other than Geoffrey of Montfichet. It matters not how this knowledge came to me; I do but seek to warn you to tread gently and warily in the days now before you. So far, life has been kind to you, and surely there is no reason why you should not prosper very exceedingly. There is for you a good friend in Gamewell's Squire."

"And one also at Copmanhurst, Father."

"Assuredly, boy. But I am a poor anchorite and one unable to help you, save by friendly counsel. Take heed not to touch Montfichet too nearly in the matter of his son," added he, warningly; "he is a strange man, and will brook no meddling."

"I would not see Geoffrey wronged, Father, not even by Robin of Locksley," said Robin, vehemently.

The clerk smiled at him. "You may coax the Squire, an you will, boy," said he, twinkling; "for I do think that one may achieve more that way than by any other. But he careful not to let him see that you would lead him; and, above all, provoke him not. Montfichet is an obstinate man. His heart prompts him to forgive Geoffrey; and doubtless he could get the ban removed from off the young man's head. But the Squire will not readily forgo his oath. So now, rest content that he will share Gamewell with Geoffrey and yourself, and do not let him know that once you did deceive him."

"Deceive him, Father?"

"Did you not go out secretly to meet the Scarlet Knight, boy? And do you not now hide from Gamewell that his son is in hiding with Will o' th' Green? Be prudent and tread no more in this path. Peace be with you, Robin Fitzooth; and discretion also."

He bade Robin good night, and set out towards his lonely cell near St. Dunstan's shrine; leaving the other perplexed and distressed at his words.

The first clouds on Robin's horizon were appearing.

CHAPTER 10

SQUIRE GEORGE left them next morning. He bade Warrenton stay at Locksley, and charged young Stuteley to let him know if the dame or his master should want for aught. Then, having pressed some money upon his sister to meet their necessities, he bade them affectionate farewell.

He took Robin's letter to Monceux, and added his own request to it, never doubting that so ordinary a matter as this would be long a-doing. The Rangership of Locksley Woods was Robin's by every right: for the house and garden had been given to Hugh Fitzooth in perpetuity by the King. So at least they all had understood.

Master Monceux, lord Sheriff of Nottingham, took the letters and read them with a thin smile; then bore them to his daughter's chamber, and laid them before her. "Truly the enemies of our King are not lacking in audacity," sneered Master Monceux, when Mistress Monceux had mastered the scrolls.

"What will you do?" asked she, curiously.

"This is the young archer who won my arrow," remarked the Sheriff. "Robin Fitzooth of Locksley. Observe that his father has been killed by one of the King's deer; like as not whilst he was attempting to snare it. His son asks now for the post: this son who shoots with a peacocked arrow to win my prize."

"Say you so? Then this boy is of the outlaws of Sherwood?" Her thin lips parted over her white teeth in an evil doubt, as she asked her father: "How do you know that the arrow was winged with a peacock's feather? Did you see it yourself?"

"John Ford brought it to me."

"Ford is a very untrustworthy knave. I would that some other of the foresters had told you."

The Sheriff was vexed at this. "I have no hesitation in the matter, child. But give heed, for now I must either agree to this recommendation of my lord Montfichet, or refuse it because I have already appointed some other to the place. Can you not suggest a man to me?"

"Let it be one distasteful both to Montfichet and to this boastful youth," said the demoiselle Monceux, eagerly. "Send Ford, or one of the scullions from our kitchen, that they may know our contempt for them. And bid the young archer to us here; he should be whipped and put in the stocks," she added, vindictively.

"Will you reply to those scrolls then, child?" said the Sheriff, glad to be relieved of a task which he did not relish. "Let it be Ford; he is captain of the foresters hereabouts, and has been staying at Gamewell. I hear that young Locksley is not overfond of him. But be discreet in your scrivening, and say only that which is necessary, child."

"I will bring the letters when they are penned, and will read them to you," said his daughter.

In due course, then, came the Sheriff's reply to Robin's request. It was couched in arrogant terms, and bade the youth report himself within ten days at Nottingham Castle in order that the question of his appointment to a post in the King's Foresters might be weighed and considered. As for the Rangership of Locksley, that had already been given to one Master John Ford, who would take up the duties so soon as Robin and Mistress Fitzooth could arrange to render him the house at Locksley and all it contained. To this end the Sheriff's messenger was empowered to take stock and inventory of all furniture and belongings and to make note of all things broken or in disrepair, since those would have to be counted against them when they left the place.

Robin, not knowing the worse indignities that were to befall did he come to Nottingham, for reply flung the letter into the messenger's face.

"Go, take back this answer to your master," flamed the lad. "Locksley is my mother's and my own and not the Sheriff of Nottingham's. Further, tell him that I will administer Locksley Woods, and the men shall obey me even as they did my father: and this is all that I say in answer to your insolent lord."

"Take this also, fellow," cried Stuteley, heroically: "that my master's squire will very instantly do battle on his behalf with all enemies at quarterstaff, singlestick, or at wrestling with the hands."

"Be sure that you will need practise in all your tricks, friend," snarled the messenger, wrathfully; "Master Monceux will send you enough of pupils and to spare! And I will be glad to have a bout with you."

"Now, if you sicken for't," said Will, valiantly; but Robin bade him be still.

The messenger went back to Nottingham; and Robin continued to go about the duties of a ranger.

On the fifth day after the man's visit, however, one of the Locksley foresters refused to obey young Fitzooth, saying that he had no right to command him.

"I have this right, that you shall obey me!" cried Robin, and he bade Warrenton and Stuteley to seize the man and deprive him of his long-bow and quiver. Nor would he suffer the forester to become repossessed of them until he had humbly asked pardon. Thereafter, seeing that this youth had a man's determination, the men remained loyal to him.

Within ten days came Master Ford himself, at the head of ten fellows, armed with such powers of forcible entry as the Sheriff could grant. Robin received the forester civilly, but told him plainly that Locksley was his and that he would keep it to his death.

Master Ford smiled very superior to these brave words. "Death, Master Robin, is a thing a long way off from us both, I do conceive," said he, "therefore is there small valiance in your prating so lightly of it. This matter is one not between ourselves, howbeit, for the Rangership has come to me through no seeking of mine own. The quarrel, if there be one, is between yourself and Master Monceux; and, in reason, you should let me into possession here, and take your anger to Notting-ham."

"I speak to the Sheriff in that I speak to you, John Ford," retorted the lad: "and you have had your answer. Take back your men and yourself;

be content with the captaincy of the foresters of Sherwood. This part of the forest will be administered, under the King's pleasure, by me."

"What if I could show you the King's dismissal of your father?" snarled the other.

"If you could show it to me, you would," answered Robin, calmly.

"Nevertheless, I will show it to you, insolent," cried Master Ford, losing his temper. "In Nottingham we can play at other games than those you saw at the Fair, Robin o' th' Hood," he went on, furiously, and giving Robin this name out of desire to prick him.

To young Robin the epithet recalled a sudden vision of the maid Fitzwalter and her queer little toss of her curls as she had christened him. Ford must have been near to have overheard it. So was there double insult in his words.

Robin looked him full in the face, and then turned contemptuously from him. "Play all the games you know, friend," said he: and walked into the house.

The forester bit his lip in vexation. He scarce knew how to act. The Sheriff had told him to take forcible possession of the house, but this might only be done now after a sanguinary encounter. For Warrenton, the Squire of Gamewell's man, was there, and had eyed him malevolently, and talk with the Locksley foresters had shown them to be now ranged on Robin's side.

After waiting for three hours, Master Ford set about a return into Nottingham, meaning to ask for permission to bring back the Sherwood foresters with him to Locksley. In his return he was met by Will o' th' Green and his men near Copmanhurst, was beaten and robbed of all he had, and sent back in ignominious fashion into Nottingham town—he and all the ten men that the Sheriff had sent with him!

Master Ford made a fine story of this for the greedy ears of Mistress Monceux. She had always disliked the maid Fitzwalter; and had now seen a chance to injure her through Robin. Since he had given this girl the arrow which he had denied to her, the Sheriff's daughter, there could be no doubt that strong friendship, at the least, existed between them, so that any blow at Robin must recoil upon Mistress Fitzwalter.

Demoiselle Monceux therefore credited largely Master Ford's story.

"Go to the hall, and there await my father, Master Ford," said Mistress Monceux, at last. "I will speak again with him when he has returned from Gamewell. He is there now on your behalf, in a way," she added, meaningly.

Monceux, knowing that Montfichet would require an explanation of the refusal to instal Robin in his father's place, had set himself out to be beforehand with the Squire. At once he had endeavored to satisfy old Gamewell by telling him the story of the peacocked arrow. "Readily can I unfold that mystery to you," said Montfichet. "Our Robin was pursued by two of the outlaws when on the way to your tourney. 'Tis like enough that he picked up one of their arrows."

"When they were in chase of him?" asked the Sheriff, with ready reply.

"Well, that is true; and yet, stay—I do mind me that the Clerk of Copmanhurst did speak of some shooting match in which Robin was forced to employ himself with Will o' th' Green, on the day that they journeyed here from Locksley. Then it was that Robin must have become owner of the peacocked arrow. The thing is quite plain to me."

"The clerk himself has been suspected of colleaguing with these robbers of the forest, friend Gamewell," whispered the Sheriff, leaning forward towards the Squire. "And they do say that Will was at our tourney—was none other, indeed, than the very Roughbeard from whom young Robin so cleverly did snatch my arrow of gold. Nay, nay, I think the evidence points very strongly against Fitzooth; yet since he is your nephew I have forborne to press my charge against him."

"I believe no harm of Robin," said the Squire, decisively.

"Still you will see there is reason in my refusal of his request," smiled Monceux. And old Gamewell had to agree, although unwillingly.

So were the clouds upon Robin's horizon gathering apace.

He gravely continued in his duties at Locksley, filling up his leisure with long and frequent practise in archery with Warrenton. A month went by and he had heard no more of Master Ford nor of the Sheriff, and so engrossed did Robin become in his present life and the necessity of making a living for them all that Master Monceux, his summons, and his "appointment" of Ford were forgotten.

He killed such of the deer as his father had, under the King's charter, for their own sustenance, and gathered the fruits from the garden at Locksley. There were cows to be milked and sheep to be sheared.

The men worked for him without question. There had been no further rebellion since Warrenton and Stuteley had so promptly checked the first sign of it.

The Squire had sent twice to them such presents as he knew they would accept, and he made no mention of Master Monceux.

Only one matter troubled Robin. Soon would come round the time when the emoluments of the Rangership would be due; and *then* Robin would have to face the Sheriff and make him pay the moneys.

Having stifled any objections Montfichet might have had to his refusal to recognize Robin as Ranger, the Sheriff was quite content to bide his time, knowing that once in Nottingham, Robin would be entirely in his power. Unforeseen events, however, upset these schemes and hastened matters, even while Robin was perfecting himself in the use of the longbow under Warrenton and in the art of wrestling with little lithe Stuteley. The lean-faced man whom he saw at the tourney returned suddenly to Nottingham from London, bearing news to the Sheriff that he was to prepare the town at once for a visit from the young Prince John.

Master Simeon Carfax, to give the lean-faced one his full style, bade them arrange for a great tourney to be held in Sherwood itself.

"Certes, Prince John may well be King over us in the end," murmured the Sheriff to himself; and he dismissed all thought of Robin and his defiance.

The Sheriff had some suspicion that Master Carfax had had more to do with this sudden visit of the erstwhile rebellious Prince than that pinch-nosed gentleman would allow. Further, he saw with some misgiving that between Carfax and his own daughter there was an understanding, and he decided to speak firmly with her; but, as she was still vexed with him for not having dealt with young Fitzooth as promptly as she had designed, the Sheriff thought it wise to wait his opportunity.

Meanwhile Robin passed his days equably: and now he could notch Warrenton's shaft at one hundred paces, a feat difficult in the extreme.

The old retainer took huge delight in training the lad. "I do hear of a brave business in archery to be done in Sherwood Forest," he said, "and I would have you enter there in the lists, and bear away the Prince's bag of gold, even as you did the Sheriff's arrow."

"Tell me of this, Warrenton," cried Robin, interested at once. "Where did you learn this item?"

" 'Twas told to me a week agone by the Friar of Copmanhurst, a right worthy, pious gentleman," gabbled Warrenton. "It seems that the young Prince is already tired of London ways and the Court of his father the King, and has agreed to come here to us at Nottingham so that he may be more free. He brings with him many of the fine ladies of the Court, and full a hundred score of followers. And they do tell me that some of the barons are with him, Master Fitzurse to wit. Howbeit, 'tis no matter of ours. We have but to remember that he has offered a purse of a hundred pieces to the best bowman in Nottingham town. That purse should be yours, lording."

Robin smiled at the old man's emphatic speech. "When is this prize to be offered, Warrenton, and what other marvels are there to be?"

The man-at-arms commenced afresh. "There is to be a tourney, held in Sherwood Forest."

"Ay; but the archery?"

"I have told you that the Prince offers a fine prize. Know also that he brings with him Hubert, the most renowned of all archers, so that he deems the prize already won. The Prince puts a hundred gold pieces into the purse, and Hubert pockets it in advance."

"Is he a fair bowman, this Hubert?"

"I know but one archer better than he, lording—yourself; and I have seen the finest archery in the world."

"You talk heedlessly, Warrenton," said Robin, rebuking him. Yet secretly he was flattered by this sincere belief in him.

"I'll go with you to Nottingham—and Stuteley shall stay here, on guard," said Robin.

But Stuteley begged most earnestly that he should be allowed to go also, so that Robin came nigh to giving up the plan all together. For he would not consent to leave the dame unprotected.

In the end Warrenton himself, with fine self-sacrifice, offered to remain at Locksley.

"It will be wisest that you should go unattended, after all, lording," concluded Warrenton. "Enter the lists unknown, unannounced, as though you were some forester. Master Monceux means no good to you, and surely he will be there. So be circumspect; and forget not the things that I have taught you. Beat Hubert if you can, but be not overcome if you should fail. He is a very pretty bowman, and experienced."

CHAPTER 11

PROFITING BY A lesson learned
from Will o' th' Green, Robin stained his face and bade Stuteley do the
same ere starting to the Royal tourney.

The morning was overcast and doubtful when the two lads set forth.
They had put on foresters' clothes of green cloth, with long tunics and
green trunk hose. Their hands and faces were brown as walnut juice
could make them; and whilst Robin carried only his best longbow and
a good quiver of arrows, young Will had loaded himself with quarterstaff, axe, and pike, all very difficult to carry.

Robin bade him leave one or the other of these weapons, and reluctantly the pike was returned to Warrenton. Then merrily they started
away through the forest, and came at noon to that glade where Robin
had first met Will o' th' Green. Even while Robin wondered whether
Will or his men might again demand toll of him, Master Will himself
suddenly appeared, and without a word placed his bow across their
path.

"Greetings to you, Will," said Robin, blithely. "Is it toll of us that
you desire?"

"Are you dumb, friend?" added Stuteley, impudently, as the outlaw
made no immediate reply.

Will smiled then. "So old Warrenton has persuaded you to seek the
Prince's gold, youngling?" said he, at last. Without waiting an answer,
he stepped back and withdrew his bow. "Pass, then, Locksley, and
good fortune attend you," he went on. "We may meet again ere the day
be done; but it is not sure——"

"You will not try for the purse, Will?" cried Robin, as if surprised.

"I have no use for it," answered Will, with some egotism. "Nay, fear not, our third trial is yet to come. I did but stay you to speak of your cousin—" He paused, and glanced towards Stuteley.

"I am deaf and dumb as you were, friend, a minute agone," spoke the little esquire.

"Your cousin, Geoffrey of Montfichet, has gone to France," continued Will, speaking freely so soon as Robin had nodded in confirmation of Stuteley's discretion. "Like as not, Master Geoffrey has not talked with you as to his business with us in this greenwood?"

"I know nothing beyond that we did bind my cousin's armor about with red ribbon," replied Robin, uneasily. He remembered the clerk's warning, and a presentiment of coming evil pricked him. "But I am right glad that Geoffrey has encountered no danger, and has given up his schemes with you."

"I did not say that he had done that, Locksley," spoke Will, in his gruff way. "Nor do I see why you should fear danger for him when he is in my company."

"I meant not that, Will, believe me," said Robin, hastily. "But there are two amongst your band who have little love for my cousin, and are jealous also of you——" And he told him of his adventure in the early part of the day when they last had met.

Will listened with a frown. "So they winged you, youngling, and yet for all that you won the Sheriff's arrow? Give me now some token whereby I may know which of my men are traitors."

"I should only know their voices, Will," said Robin, regretfully.

The outlaw shrugged. "It matters not, after all," he remarked, turning to leave them. "Go your ways, Locksley, and win the purse."

"Is there no toll?" enquired Robin, smiling again. "Am I truly free of Sherwood, Will?"

" 'Twould seem so, Locksley," said the outlaw, briefly. Then, without further ado, he strode away from him.

They watched his lithe form disappear.

" 'Tis sure that our disguise is none too good," sighed Robin, pondering upon the ready way in which the outlaw had recognized him.

Soon afterward rain fell and a heavy storm raged amongst the trees.

The two youths crept into the hollow of one of the larger oaks to shelter themselves. Whilst waiting there they heard the noise of an approaching cavalcade. It was a body of archers coming from Lincoln to compete for the purse of gold.

They cantered past the tree wherein Robin and Stuteley lay hidden, and took no heed of the drenching rain. All were merry with wine and very confident that one amongst them would surely win the prize. The only question was, Which one?

"These Nottingham clods!" cried one, scornfully; "I'll dare swear that many of them have already promised the prize to their maids! Nottingham 'gainst Lincoln——'tis possible that they may stand to us for a round. But after that!"

"We will spend the money in Nottingham town," shouted another of the trotting bowmen. "For sure the Prince himself could do no hand-somer thing. A piece I'll toss to the heralds, and another to you, Staveley, for you are a covetous worm——"

The rest of his speech was lost through the one addressed turning violently upon him and thrusting at him with his pike, thus tumbling him into the mire. Stuteley laughed outright at this, and for a moment startled the rest of this worshipful company.

Robin, rather vexed at his esquire's want of caution, came with him from out of the hollow of the tree. The Lincolnshire men halted, and Robin asked for a lift to the field where already the tourney was being commenced.

"Are you going to the Sherwood tourney, and with a bow?" asked one of the archers, loftily. "What will you shoot there, gipsy boy? There are no targets such as your shafts might reach. But 'tis true that you may learn something of the game, if you should go."

"I'll lay a crown wager with you, friends," said Stuteley, vexed to hear Robin called "gipsy," "that my master's shaft will fly more near the centre of the mark than will any one of yours. So now."

"A crown piece, gipsy! Why, that means twenty crowns for you to find," laughed another of the men, loudly.

"Twenty crowns; why, he has not twenty pence," said another.

"My man has laid the wager and I will stand to it," said Robin, quietly, "though I do not like such boasting, I promise you. Twenty crowns to twenty crowns—who will hold the stakes? Here is my purse in warrant of my words."

"Why, Master, I am surely the very man to hold your purse!" called out the lately fallen champion, readily. "Ask any of them here and (if they have love of truth in them) they will say that Much the Miller is a man of men for honesty, sobriety, and the like! 'Tis known throughout Lincoln that never have I given short measure in all my life. Hand me the purse and be easy."

"Show me your crown, friend," said Robin, eyeing him.

"Now, stirrup me but I have given my last piece to a poor beggar whom we did meet in the wood."

"Then I will hold my purse myself, Master Much," cried Robin, putting it quickly back into his bosom. "But have no fear; if you can beat me, I'll add my crown to the Prince's moneybag. We will meet you here, friends," he continued. "beside this very tree, at noon tomorrow, if I should win. If not, I'll yield this purse to the miller ere I leave the tourney, and he shall share it round. Is it agreed?"

"I do think that you should pay for your travelling, gipsy, since you are so rich," grunted the first archer. "Here's half my saddle: I'll only ask a silver penny for a seat on it."

"I'll take you for ought, gipsy," shouted Much, who really was very tipsy. "You've spoken fair; and I like you! Come, jump up behind me, and hold tight. This horse is one of most wayward character."

"Hurry, then," said the leader. "Whilst we chatter here the tourney will be done; and we shall happen on it just as Hubert takes the prize. Forward, friends; quick march!"

They rattled off at a smart pace. Robin mounted behind the good-natured Much, and Stuteley upon the captain's horse. The miller told Robin confidentially a full score of times that he, Much, was bound to win the archery contest, being admittedly the first bowman in the world.

"Harkee, gipsy," called he at length, over the point of his shoulder to patient Robin behind him, "I'll not take your crown, I swear it! I like you, and I would not rob your sweetheart of a penny piece. Buy ribbons for her, then, with the crown I give you."

Robin expressed his thanks very cordially. This fellow seemed an honest-hearted rogue; and 'twas mainly to his furious urging of his steed that they arrived in time for the great event.

As it was, all the jousting was done, and most of the nobles had already gone away. The Sheriff was fussily preparing himself to escort the Prince to the castle when the horns blew announcing the arrival of the Lincolnshire bowmen.

They had pushed their way clumsily through the array of tents, and now blundered into the lists through the gate. Robin was glad indeed of his stained face and semi-disguise, not being over proud of his companions. He gave Will Stuteley a signal to detach himself from them, and come to his side. The two youths then hastened to the archers' stand.

There had been three deaths already as a result of the joustings; and six others were seriously injured; yet the Prince looked far from being satisfied, and his glance strayed forever to the gate.

When the Lincoln men had come noisily trooping in, his face had lit up and his hand had made a half-movement to find the jewelled hilt of his sword. Master Carfax, too, had started to his feet in evident concern.

When the heralds announced these newcomers, visible disappointment showed on the faces of the Prince and his followers. Clearly they were eagerly expecting the appearance of other folk; but, quickly recovering himself, John refound all the old elegance of his manners. He courteously acknowledged the rough greeting of the archers, and sat back smilingly in his box.

Master Monceux gave the signal for the archery contest to be begun; and Robin soon saw that the archers against him were men very different from those who had been at Nottingham Fair.

When it came to the turn of the Prince's own bowman, Hubert of Normandy—a man slim, conceited, and overdressed, but nevertheless a very splendid archer—the first shaft flew so cleanly and so swift that it pierced the very middle of the target and stuck out on the other side full half its length.

Robin had to shoot immediately after him, and waited a few moments whilst the markers were tugging at the Norman's arrow. A sudden inspiration flashed across the lad's mind; and, advancing a step, he bade them desist. They wonderingly fell back, leaving Hubert's arrow fixed spitefully in the target.

One of the heralds cried out that this archer had not yet given in his name, but even as he spoke, Robin's arrow flew hissing from his bow. A silence fell upon the onlookers, and even the smiling Prince leaned forward in his box. Then a great shout went up of amazement and incredulity. The markers and heralds thronged about the target and hid it from the general view until they were impatiently pulled away by some of the Prince's bodyguard.

A marvel was seen then by all eyes—Robin's arrow standing stiffly out from the centre of the target, with Hubert's wand split down on either side of it flush to the very face of the mark!

Robin himself could scarcely credit his own success. He had done the thing before, with Warrenton, once out of a dozen times: and he had essayed it now more out of bravado than aught else.

" 'Twas a feat worthy of Hubert himself," said the Sheriff, bombastically, to the Prince. He had not recognized Robin.

"I have seen Hubert perform just such a trick on many occasions, sir," said Carfax. "This fellow has done no uncommon thing, believe me," he went on. "And after all, he has not bettered Hubert's shot."

"That is true," said the Prince, as if thoughtfully. His face showed smiling again. "Let the contest go on: and Hubert shall shoot again with this young trickster."

"The heralds say that he has not given in his name, Sire," said one of the courtiers.

"If that is so, his shooting is of no avail, be it never so good," cried Carfax, triumphantly. "Tell them that the archer is disqualified, my lord," he continued, addressing the Sheriff; "and bid them discover who he may be."

Carfax turned again to the Prince, and began a whispered conversation with him. The Prince listened, nodding his head in approval.

"Well, Monceux, what do they say?" he asked the Sheriff, languidly, as the other returned.

"It seems, Sire, that the archer is one who came in with a company of Lincoln bowmen. No one knows him hereabout. I have said that he is disqualified, and now the others will shoot again. But Hubert has now the purse, for sure."

"In sooth I do think so," answered the Prince, laughing rather conceitedly. "But Monceux, bid this lad to me forthwith. I would speak with him."

The Sheriff went about the task; but Robin had disappeared; for suddenly, amidst the throng, his eyes had encountered those strange grey-blue ones of Mistress Fitzwalter.

She was sitting alone in a little box nearby the targets. Robin had walked down the lists to see for himself that his shaft had split the Norman's fairly, and in turning away to find Stuteley he had become aware of her shrewd, piercing gaze. She allowed her eyes to rest fully on young Fitzooth's ardent glance for the briefest moment. Then she looked away unconcernedly.

But Robin, venturing all, drew nigh. He came to the edge of her box, and began to speak. He had gone so far as "Give you good morrow, lady," when his eyes perceived the Sheriff's little golden arrow fastening her cloak. His mouth became dry at that and his words went back in his throat.

The girl, aware of his confusion, brought her gaze back upon him. She smiled.

"Is it indeed my young champion?" asked she, rather doubtfully at first, in her low, soft tones. "Is it you who have beaten the Prince's best archer, Robin o' the' Hood?"

Her eyes were wells of innocent fun. The way in which she lingered over the last syllables brought Robin still deeper into the deep waters.

"It is your servant, madame," was all that he could find to say.

"You see then that I wear your gift, Robin," she said, trying to make him at ease. "I have not forgotten——"

"Nor I—I shall *never* forget," cried he, impulsively. "Your eyes are always in my memory: they are beautiful as stars," said he, fervently.

"Oh, a gallant Locksley! But there, take my colors, since you will be my knight." She untied a ribbon from her hair, and gave it into his outstretched palm. "And now, farewell; take the Prince's prize, and spend the pennies worthily. Buy your sweetheart some ribbons, but keep that which I have given you."

She tossed her curls again as she added the last word. Robin was beginning a vehement protestation that he had no sweetheart when Stuteley's voice broke in upon him.

"Master, they have disqualified you, and given the prize to Hubert. 'Tis a vile injustice, and I have raised my voice furiously. So, alas! has Master Much the Miller; he is a very worthy gentleman."

"What do you say?" asked Mistress Fitzwalter, in amazement.

"It is even so, lady, that my lord the Sheriff has ruled my master out of the court, for the reason that he did not give in his name before drawing his bow!" cried Stuteley. "A wicked conspiracy it is, and monstrous unjust! 'Tis thus that these prizes are given; the game's arranged beforehand. Ah, but I know how these Nottingham folk do plot: thrice now have I found them false and treacherous."

When Stuteley had begun there were many who were ready to side with him, but his unlucky conclusion turned these possible friends into enemies. Even Mistress Fitzwalter drew back for an instant.

"Be silent, Will," said Robin, vexed at once. "It is enough to be juggled out of this prize without your making it worse. I'll go claim it from Monceux and he shall argue it with me."

"The Prince is asking for you, friend," said Carfax, suddenly appearing. He touched Robin on the shoulder.

As he turned to depart, his gimlet eyes saw how the girl shrank away from them into her box. He looked swiftly at her; then at Robin again. "His Highness graciously condescended to enquire your name and rank," said he, pausing.

"Will he give the purse to me, then?" asked Robin, surprised.

"Nay, that has already been won by Master Hubert," answered Carfax, as if amused at the question. "You cannot win a prize every day, Master—Locksley."

He spoke at a shrewd guess, and saw that his shaft had hit the mark. Mistress Fitzwalter's interest in Robin had given him the clue.

"I'll not go to the Prince," said Robin, wrathfully. "Tell him, Master Fetch-and-Take, that I have won this prize in all fairness; and I will shoot with Hubert again, if he needs another beating."

"You'll cool your heels in the stocks, Locksley," said Carfax, viciously: "so much is evident. The Sheriff has a quarrel with you already, and 'tis well that you are here to answer Master Ford's complaint. The Prince will send for you in style, since you will not go kindly to him. Bide but a few minutes. I'll not keep you waiting!"

*Marian allowed her eyes
to rest fully on young Fitzooth's
ardent glance for the
briefest moment. But Robin,
venturing all, drew nigh.*

He strode off, in heat, followed by Stuteley's scornful gibings.

Robin became aware that the people were eyeing them both with none-too-friendly glances. He felt that he and Will Stuteley were in a difficult position. Escape seemed to be out of the question.

"Jump over the ledge of my box, Robin," whispered a sudden small voice, "and so make your way through the door at the back of it. Hasten!"

Gratefully Robin did as she bade him; and Stuteley, without waiting for invitation, followed. Mistress Fitzwalter instantly opened the door for them. "Hurry, I pray you," cried she; "I see them coming for you both. The Prince has sent his pikemen——"

Robin pushed Will out before him; and, turning, caught her little hand in his.

"Thanks, thanks," he muttered, hurriedly, and strove to kiss her fingers.

Laughing and blushing, she snatched them away.

"Go," she cried, in agitated voice, "and stay not until you reach Locksley. We may meet again—to talk of thanks," she added, seeing that he still hesitated.

"Give me at least your name," panted poor Robin, at the door; "not that I shall ever forget you."

"I am called Marian," answered she, closing the door ruthlessly upon him—"Marian Fitzwalter. . . .Go now, I implore you, and may good fortune be with you always."

CHAPTER 12

So, INGLORIOUSLY, they returned through the night to Locksley. None offered to stay them in the forest of Sherwood; indeed, Robin might well have disbelieved in the existence of Will o' th' Green and his outlaw band, had he not had such good reason to know otherwise. It was as if Will had silently yielded him that freedom of the forest which he boasted was his to give. Tired and footsore, yet filled with a strange elation, Robin came back to Locksley before dawn, with faithful Stuteley forlornly following him.

There were questions to be asked and answered when they arrived; and Warrenton was very indignant when he heard of the Prince's gross favoritism of his archer Hubert.

Robin seemed to show too little vexation in the matter, Warrenton thought. The man-at-arms was both perplexed and amazed by the semi-indifference displayed by the youth: here had he, by marvellous skill, won a fine prize, and had seen the same snatched most unfairly from him, and yet was not furiously enraged; but rather amused, as it were.

"Surely, surely, you will go back with me tomorrow and demand the purse from the Sheriff?" said Warrenton, in argumentative attitude. "Squire George o' th' Hall shall give us the best of Gamewell to enforce respect to you."

"Nay, it matters not so much as that, Warrenton. The money I would like to have had, I'll not deny it, for it would have made me more independent of Master Monceux. But it has not fallen to me, and there it ends."

"Well, 'tis well that you are so easy, lording," said Warrenton, scratching his head. "Now tell us whom you saw, and how you contrived to split the Norman's arrow."

He had already heard the story, but was very fain to listen to it again. "It is a trick that I taught him, Dame," he added, offhandedly, to Mistress Fitzooth. "One that did surprise the Norman too, I'll warrant me. You see, they are so concerned with their crossbows and other fal-lals in France that when good English yew——"

"I saw Master Will," said Robin, to check him. Once Warrenton was started on a dissertation on the virtues of the English longbow there was usually no staying him. "He told me that the Scarlet Knight had gone to France."

Warrenton looked wise. "That is not worthy of belief, Excellence," said he, cunningly. "Prince John is near; and one cannot imagine that Geoffrey of Montfichet——"

"Geoffrey of Montfichet?" asked the dame, wonderingly: and then Warrenton saw how he had blundered. "Why, I did not know that you had met your cousin, Robin. When was it, and why do you call him the Scarlet Knight?"

"Geoffrey is outlawed, Mother mine, and may not appear in Sherwood," answered Robin, temporizing with her. "And the story of our meeting is too long a one for the moment. We are rarely fatigued, and I would gladly get me to bed. Come, Will, rouse yourself. Mother, see that we do not sleep too long. I must go to Gamewell by the day after tomorrow at least; and there is much work between my going and now."

He had determined to ask the Squire to move again in the matter of the Rangership for him whilst John was here. Even if the Prince had unduly favored Hubert in the archery contest, it did not necessarily follow that he would be unjust in such a plain business as this. Robin kissed the dame, struggled with a yawn, and got him to rest. He slept uneasily, his dreams being strangely compounded of happiness and grief.

*　　　*　　　*

Within three days Robin started away for Gamewell, taking only Stuteley, as before. He intended to make his return to Locksley ere dusk of the next night.

When they were far advanced on their journey they heard sounds of a large company upon the road; and prudently Robin bade Stuteley hide with him in the undergrowth until they should see who these might be.

"Maybe 'tis the Sheriff, with Master Ford, coming to seize our home. By watching them unseen we may find a way to bring their schemes to naught. Keep near to me, Will; and scarcely breathe."

It was indeed a body of men from Nottingham; and, although the Sheriff was not with them, Master Carfax and a few of the Lincoln bowmen were amongst the company. So also was Ford, the forester.

In all, there were about two score of men, and most of them were Sherwood foresters. Robin espied Much the Miller in the tail of the procession, looking very dejected and ill, and decided to risk exposing himself. Standing up in the bracken, he called out boldly: "Hold there, Master Much. Here am I, ready to take your money."

"What sprite are you?" answered Much, reining in his steed sharply. "Why! 'tis the gipsy lad, as I live; with his face nicely washed . . .!" He had recognized Robin by his clothes. "Money, forsooth! Do you know that I have not so much as a groat in my pouch?"

"Then must one of the others lend it to you," replied Robin. "Pay me, friends, forthwith. A short reckoning is an easy reckoning. My arrow flew nearer the target than did any of yours."

"How do you know that?" said Much. "After you had gone we all did aim again, and very marvellous was my shooting. For sure, I should have had the prize, even as I told you, had not Hubert already made off with it."

"Is this so?" asked Robin, doubtfully, looking from one to the other of the Lincoln men. Those in front had now stopped also; and Master Carfax came ambling back to see what had occasioned the delay. So soon as he espied Robin his face took a joyful look. "Here, Master Ford," he called, clapping his hands. "Hither—come hither! Here is your quarry found for you. Now you can fight it out, fair and square, whilst we watch to see fair play!"

Ford turned about and glanced at Robin; but he did not like the notion of such a battle. So he affected not to recognize him. "Nay, this is but some vagrant fellow," said he, hesitatingly. "Let us push on,

Master Simeon; 'tis near the hour when we are to meet with him whom you know." He added these words in a low voice, and made a gesture indicating the Copmanhurst road.

Carfax's face took a diabolical expression. He had begun to answer Ford when the whole party were suddenly disturbed by the rush of a great herd of Royal deer.

These beasts, driven by someone from out of their pastures, came scattering blindly adown the track; and men and horses moved quickly to one side to avoid a devastating collision.

After they had passed, Carfax began again. "Form a ring, friends," cried he, coaxingly. "Let neither of these fellows escape. They shall yield us some sport, in any event, whether Ford be right or I."

A solitary stag at this instant appeared before them. He stood, as if carved from stone, in the centre of the road, at three hundred paces' distance. He was clearly uncertain whether to dash through these his usual enemies, in an attempt to rejoin the herd, or fly backward to that unknown danger which had first startled them all.

" 'Tis a fine beast," hiccoughed Much. "Now had I a steady hand!"

Simeon Carfax interrupted him. "By the Lord Harry, here is the very thing," he said, in whispered excitement. "Now, fellow, you shall prove me right and this forester wrong. I say you are Robin of Locksley, who did split the Norman's arrow at the tourney. Fly a shaft now at yon mark; surely none but such a bowman as yourself might dare hope to reach it."

Robin fell into the very palpable trap set for him. Without answering Carfax, he fitted an arrow to his bow, and sent speeding death to the trembling stag. It fell, pierced cleanly to the heart. Robin eyed Ford triumphantly.

But Master Carfax now held up his hands in horror. "See what you have done, wicked youth," ejaculated he, as if quite overcome with dismay. "I bade you shoot at yon birch tree shimmering there to the left of the deer. Did I not say: 'Fly at yon mark'? And now you have killed one of the King's deer."

"I do hear that this fellow has slain others about Locksley," said Ford, meanly. "You are right, Master Simeon; he is, in sooth, Robin of Locksley; your eyes are wiser than mine. Seize him, my men."

At once the foresters sprang upon Robin and Stuteley, and a fierce battle was commenced. Despite a valiant resistance, Robin and Will Stuteley were soon overcome and bound hard and fast.

"You villains," panted Stuteley. "And you, most treacherous," he called to Carfax, "I wish you joy of so contemptible a trick."

"All's fair in war, friend," answered Carfax. "Now, Master Ford, fulfil your duty. You know the law; that if one be found killing the King's deer in the Royal Forest of Sherwood, he or she may be summarily hanged when caught upon the nearest tree."

"It must be *in flagrante delicto*, Master Simeon," said Ford, uneasy again.

"Could there be a plainer case?" cried Carfax, rubbing his hands. "We all did see this fellow shoot the deer. 'Tis the clearest case; and I do counsel you to deal lawfully in it, Master Ford. Remember that he also is suspected of being an outlaw, in that you saw him once use a peacocked arrow. Although I am but a layman, as it were, friend," he added, meaningly, "yet I do know the law, and shall be forced to quit my conscience with the Prince when I return to Nottingham. Wherefore, seeing that your appointment to Locksley still lacks his confirmation——"

"I would rather bring the rogue to Master Monceux, as he did command me," argued Ford, who could not quite brace himself to this. "Besides, we have no leisure at this moment to carry out the law," he went on. "You know that your master the Prince did start us on this journey with two errands upon our shoulders."

"One was to deal with Robin of Locksley," said Carfax, snarlingly, and without yielding his point.

"To take him to Nottingham, Master, I say," put in Much. "I do not think that the Prince meant you to harm him."

"Be silent, knave!" snapped the lean-faced man, sharply. "Who gave you the right to question me? Shut your mouth, or I will have you accounted as accomplice with these fellows, and put a noose about your bull neck also!"

"Why, harkee, Master," said Much, very wrathful. "This is a game where two can play or more. I do forthwith range myself with the gipsy; and you, Midge," he added, turning to one of his company, "surely you will follow?"

"Right instantly," answered the one called Midge, a little ferret of a man.

"And I also." "And I, Master Much"—so spoke the remaining Lincoln men.

"So are we six, then," said Much. He tumbled off his horse, and the other three of them did the like; and then strode over to where Robin stood. "Release him," said the miller, determinedly; and he promptly knocked two of the foresters sprawling.

This was the signal for a general encounter, and all threw themselves very heartily into the mêlée.

The miller and his men struggled to release Robin and Stuteley so that these might help in the fray; but the foresters were too many for them. Twice did Much get his hands upon Robin's bonds, only to be plucked violently backward. The men tumbled one upon the other in the fight, pummelling, clutching, and tearing at each other in a wild confusion. They made little noise, all being too desperately in earnest. Ford encouraged his foresters by word and gesture; and Carfax kept himself as far out of it as possible. Presently three of the foresters overpowered the good-natured, still half-tipsy miller, and held him down.

Then Master Carfax sprang from his horse and rushed in upon the prostrate miller. Seizing one of the foresters' pikes the lean-faced man foully swung it down upon Much's pate with a sounding thwack. The miller gave a groan and became limp in the hands of his assailants.

"Now, surely, that is the meanest of all the mean deeds which you have done!" cried Robin. He tore at his bonds fiercely and vainly— biting at the cord about his wrists with his teeth. Carfax ran to his horse. In an instant he had returned with a cord taken from under his saddle. "I had a notion that this might be useful to me when I set out this morn," he said. "Put it about his neck soon as a noose is fashioned. Now fling the end of it over this branch. Now draw it tight. Steadily, I pray you; be not over-quick. The prisoner has the right to speak a prayer ere he be hanged. Say it then, Robin of Locksley."

Robin caught sight at this instant of poor Stuteley's face. He had been knocked down in the fight, and, being bound, had lain where he had fallen. His eyes met Robin's in an anguished glance, and his lips trembled in attempt at speech.

Robin strove to smile at him; but his own soul was sick within his body. He felt the cord tighten again about his throat, but even as the world reeled black, Robin heard dully the sound of a horn. In familiar tones it came in upon his fainting brain. Next instant came a jerk at the rope, futile, if infuriated; then, suddenly, contact with a body falling heavily against his own.

As he fell he knew that something warm and horrid trickled upon his hands. Then followed a vast confusion of noise: and, in the midst of it, sweet peace.

CHAPTER 13

WHEN ROBIN CAME TO his senses he found himself surrounded by the outlaw band. On this occasion they appeared as friends, however—and welcome ones to boot; for it had been a near matter that Robin's history had been ended by Master Carfax on this day.

Now were the tables turned, and very completely. The foresters had been overcome by Will and his outlaws, thanks to the diversion brought about by the Lincoln men. Much was sitting up with a more rueful countenance than he had when Robin had first spied him on this morning; and little sharp-nosed Midge was busy bathing and binding his cracked poll.

Some half-score of the foresters, with Master Ford, had escaped along the road towards Locksley: the rest were bound, and their horses confiscated by the outlaws.

Master Simeon, with rage and terror depicted plainly upon his countenance, lay writhing at Robin's feet, bound with the very cord with which he had sought to end young Fitzooth's life. His enemies had trussed him across a quarterstaff, and had tied the knots large and tight about him.

"Well, Locksley, how now?" asked Will o' th' Green, with gruff kindliness. "Are the vapours passed? Can you twiddle your bow again?"

"Not skilfully enough now to take place against you, Will," smiled Robin, recovering himself more and more. "I am atrembling yet. I had thought to see the blue sky no more——"

"Ay, my man's arrow was not too soon, Locksley," said Will, gravely. "This fellow's hand was upon the rope, and another moment might have seen you gallows fruit upon this tree." He paused to bend over a forester lying prone near them, with his face buried in the grass. Robin saw that the man's body was transfixed by an arrow.

"He is no more," Will told them, looking up presently; "your aim was a shrew one, Hal," he went on, addressing himself to one of his band.

"Is he indeed *dead*?" asked Robin, in an awestruck voice.

" 'Twas his life or yours," answered Will o' th' Green, grimly. He turned to his men. "Now, comrades," cried he, "have you searched our prisoners and prepared them? 'Tis well. Are they bound together, then, by the arms, twos and threes, as is appointed in our rules; and is the right leg and left leg of each villain shackled together? . . . Stand them up, then, with their faces toward Nottingham, and bid them march."

"There is yet this one, captain," said one of the men, indicating Carfax. "What shall we do with him?"

"Has he been searched closely?" enquired Will. Without waiting a reply, he roughly ran his fingers through Master Carfax's pockets, and unfastened his tunic at the bosom. A parchment dropped out and Will snapped it up.

"I come from the Prince," whined Carfax, speaking at last; "and if so be you are Master Will Cloudesley, or Will o' th' Green—as these folks do call you—why, I have a very gracious message for you."

The outlaw gave a signal to his men. "Set him upon his feet," he ordered, "and loosen these cords. Now, Excellence, speak at your ease."

"Believe him not, Master Will," interposed Stuteley, afraid that Carfax was going to turn the tables on them in some treacherous way. "He is a very proper rogue."

"Be easy, friend," said Will o' th' Green. "Everyone is judged here in fairness. These men," pointing to the shamefaced, miserable foresters, "were caught in the doing of an evil deed, and so were dealt with summarily. But this one did not seem to have a hand in it."

"It was he who commanded them, sir," suddenly shrilled the little Lincoln named Midge. "He is, in sooth, a diabolical villain, and did very foully strike our companion here whilst men were holding him."

"All testify against you, Excellence," said the outlaw, speaking again to Carfax. "What is your story of it? Speak without fear."

"This rascal did imprudently waylay us on the road with a demand for money," began Carfax, "and I, riding back at his noise, did recognize him for one Robin Locksley, a notorious fellow who has defied my lord the Sheriff's authority; and has also been suspect of being of your company—which is a thing, saving your presence, Master Cloudesley, that has been poor recommendation in the past. Further, with our own eyes have we seen him shoot and kill one of his Majesty's stags, a most valued beast with sixteen pointed antlers, as you can see. We were but exercising the law upon him, as is appointed . . . . That is to say, *Master Ford* was directing his men to carry out the law," said Carfax, with his thin cheeks pale with fear. "I did but counsel prudence, and plead for the youth."

"Enough," cried Will, with contempt in his tones. "Now tell me the message which the Prince has sent by so worthy a messenger."

"That is for your private ear," said Simeon, cunningly.

"You may speak plainly before my comrades," said Will. "Doubtless they are as interested in the Royal words as I myself."

"I was to bid you come at once to the city gate, so many of you as would," Carfax said, "there to receive the King's pardon from the hands of our beloved Prince. Indeed, his gracious Highness did well expect to see you before him three days agone, at the tourney."

"Dressed about with red ribbons, I trow?" enquired the outlaw, as if helping him.

"Indeed yes, Master Cloudesley. You have said it, indeed. Knowledge of your loyalty to us was brought to the Prince by me. By me, good friend," he repeated, insinuatingly. "And now give back to me my parchment—which, being writ in the Latin tongue, is truly no more than a cartel to my lord the Abbot of York—and let us set forth joyfully. For henceforth ye will be as free men, and what is past will be forgotten."

"I can read you the scroll, Will," said Robin, quietly. "I have some knowledge of the priestly tongue."

The outlaw handed him the scroll, and all waited in silence whilst Robin deciphered it. Carfax snapped his teeth together in vexation at this unexpected turn. "*He* cannot read the parchment. Is it likely?" he cried. "He will but pretend to read it, and make lies with which to confound me. 'Tis writ in most scholarly Latin, that only few may learn."

"There is treachery here for you, Will," spoke Robin, without heeding these outcries. "This is a notification from the Prince to the Abbot of York saying that his emissaries have sounded you and that you are ready with your men to strike for him."

"I have said so much," commented Will, "naming three conditions."

"They are written herein: first, that a general amnesty is to be granted; second, that the ban of excommunication is to be removed from off you by the Holy Church; and third, that the Prince shall find your men, afterward, honorable employment."

"That is so, Locksley. The letter is exact."

"So the Prince writes to the Abbot, asking him to promise the second of your conditions, saying that it need be only a promise, for he has not the least intention of holding to a bargain with one so evil as yourself, and that after he has won the throne from Henry his father, matters such as these will be disposed of by his soldiery, if need be."

"It is not true," screamed Carfax. "He lies to you, Master Cloudesley, seeking to be revenged on me."

"Any clerk can read these lines to you, Will," answered Robin. "The Prince continues praying for the welfare of them all at York, and saying that he has already promised in the Abbot's name that the loan shall be taken off; that the Abbot is to receive and watch narrowly one Geoffrey of Montfichet, who has been exiled for treason, but who now imprudently has returned to work on their behalf in England."

"Now do I know that you are reading truly," cried Will, and his brow grew black. "For how could you know that your cousin was concerned in this? You false-hearted knave," he added, turning to Carfax, "false as your false master—your doom is sealed. Tie him up by his heels, and let him hang head downward from this tree whereon he would have hung gallant Locksley. Be speedy, men."

At this Simeon Carfax became as one quite demented, and Robin interposed.

"Let us not punish the man for his master's fault, Will," cried he.

"Deal with him only on the score of my quarrel with him, when I shall say—let him go. For I should always feel shame were we to be as harsh with an enemy as he would be with us. It would show us no better than he."

"Take him then, since Locksley will have it so, and tie his legs under the belly of his horse—first setting him face to tail upon it," said Will. "And you, Hal, go and cut me the antlers from off yon poor beast."

When this was done he caused his men to attach the horns by means of a cord to Master Carfax's head; then, with his own hand, Will gave the horse a lead towards Nottingham.

Then, with a "view halloo," the steed bearing the unfortunate man was started in real earnest; and the foresters sent staggering by after it along the road to Nottingham.

When they were out of sight, Robin thanked the outlaw again for all that he had done for them. Will merely shrugged his shoulders, as one who would say: " 'Tis a matter not worth breath"; and, giving his men a signal, prepared to return to his own fastnesses. Robin begged them to take the body of the deer, and, with small reluctance, the outlaws accepted the offer.

The Lincoln men bade Robin farewell also, saying that they would now go on towards their own homes with a light heart: for, having met the outlaws and found them most agreeable company, they had no more fear of Sherwood.

So Robin and little Stuteley, waving farewell to all these strange friends, moved on towards Gamewell, although Robin really had little hope now of coming by the Prince's grace into what seemed to be but his rights. The Sheriff and Simeon Carfax would attend to that, no doubt.

A curious dejection settled upon Robin. He had nothing but gloomy thoughts upon him as he trudged towards the Squire's domain. Nor did his spirits rise at his reception by old Gamewell. The Squire appeared almost uneasy with him, and was short in his speech, although once or twice a kindlier light flashed in his bright eyes.

"Already he regrets that he should have pressed me to take up the Montfichet name," thought Robin to himself, imagining that herein was the cause of the Squire's distemper.

He began to tell Montfichet of their doings and adventures: but had no sooner come to that part of the narrative referring to the Prince's purse than the Squire broke out: "Talk not to me of that man," cried he, vehemently. "He is an unworthy son of a much-tried father. Forsooth, this has become an age of disobedience and unfilial behavior; one has but to look round to find most sons alike. The Fifth Commandment is now without meaning to the younger generation."

"I have no father, sir," said poor Robin, half in defense; for Gamewell looked so fiercely at him. "Nor do I seek to keep you to your offer," added he, in his thoughts.

"I was not thinking so much of you, boy," replied the Squire; and again a better expression shone briefly in his face. "Give you good night, Robin Locksley—you know your chamber. Sleep well and we will talk together in the morning."

★   ★   ★

The morning saw no easement of the Squire's attitude towards Robin; and as soon as breakfast was ended he determined to go without wasting breath upon the errand which had brought him.

"For sure, he is repenting of his offer," reasoned Robin. "Perchance already his heart is moved again towards Geoffrey, and who shall be more glad than I to find this so? I'll let the Squire think it comes from me—as in truth it does—this whimsey to prefer the name of Fitzooth to Montfichet!"

So, bravely, as he was about to leave him, Robin spoke to the old man.

"Sir," he said, "I have it in me to speak plain words with you, an I may."

"Have no fear, boy. I am one who loves an open mind." Montfichet spoke with meaning.

"Well, sir, I would say with reference to that which you once did press upon my mother and myself—that I should take your name and half-fortune with my cousin Geoffrey—that I have thought well upon your kind offer."

"There was to be a year go by, Master Fitzooth, ere you should give answer."

"In a year or now, sir," said Robin, firmly, "I cannot see that I should accept. I have no quarrel with my cousin, and I will not come between him and your heart—which pleads against yourself on his behalf."

Montfichet broke forth then, and Robin learned suddenly what had come between him and this strange, capricious man.

"No quarrel with Geoffrey, say you?" he shouted, bringing his fist down with violence upon the oak table. "No, I trow you have not, Robin Fitzooth! But I have a quarrel both with him and you. Know that I have heard the story of your escapade with that mean son of mine, who must come prowling like a thief in the night about the walls of Gamewell. I know the Scarlet Knight's secret, and yours—who did think it brave to deceive and outwit an old man."

"Sir, sir!" began Robin, aghast at this storm.

"Nay, I will hear no more of it. Treachery and deceit—always they hang about my house. You deceived me, Robin Fitzooth, and cozened my servant Warrenton. So I cast you out of my heart forever. For the rest of my days I will be sufficient unto myself: after I am gone, the dogs may quarrel above my grave for the bones of Gamewell."

He almost pushed Robin from him, and turned brusquely away. Dazed and confounded, Robin faltered rather than walked to reach Stuteley, who stood awaiting him in the courtyard. Without a word, Robin took his hand. "Come, Will; let us go," he muttered, thickly: and with wrathful heart Robin Fitzooth shook the dust of Gamewell from off his feet.

Faintly through his mind came memory of the clerk's warning: but it was all of it so unjust! He had never intended to deceive the Squire: all that he had done had been done without thought. After all, what fault had he committed against Montfichet?

" 'Fore Heaven," said Robin, furiously, "I never will speak with that man again—nor cross the threshold of his house!"

So the clouds gathered more and more thickly over the head of Robin Fitzooth.

CHAPTER 14

THE DEMOISELLE MARIE was behind all this. She had known Geoffrey's plans from her lover, Master Carfax; for Master Carfax had had interviews with those two of Will's band, Roger and Micah, the traitors sworn against Geoffrey.

'Twas all wheel within wheel and plot within plot. Carfax had by nature a face made to show differently on either side of it. Thus he was in service with the Prince; and, whilst knowing the younger Montfichet to be his master's ally, affected outwardly to recognize him as one against whom the hands of all righteous men should be raised.

Master Simeon had gone forth with the Prince's message to Will o' th' Green, and with John Ford, in order that he might install that latter worthy at Locksley. Afterward Simeon was to journey to the Priory of York, as we know. Marie Monceux, to complete Robin's undoing, bade her father go to Gamewell and there tell Montfichet how Robin had helped Geoffrey to his scarlet-ribboned horse, giving the Squire the story as it had come through the two false outlaws. Certain proof she sent in a strip of the red cloth which Montfichet well knew to belong only to his house at Gamewell.

So suddenly Montfichet's mind was poisoned against Robin; with the result that we have seen. The Squire began now to believe Ford's tale that young Fitzooth was of the outlaw band, and at once withdrew all support of Robin so far as the Rangership of Locksley was concerned. "No doubt," thought the Squire, bitterly, "he is son of his father in discontent and false pride. Fitzooth never was frank with me, and has trained his son to distrust and deceive all men."

Truly the Sheriff's daughter was exacting full penalty for Robin's disregard of her at the Nottingham Fair.

She had employed her hand also against the maid Fitzwalter, as we shall find later.

Robin, in forbidding silence, strode along the road until they neared the shrine of St. Dunstan, when he looked eagerly toward the stout little hut of the clerk, hoping to find his old friend standing at the door of it, with his barking dogs.

All was silent, however, and deserted. To Robin's surprise, the gate of the palisade stood wide open; and the door of the hut also. He glanced at Will.

"Surely the priest is abroad imprudently, Master?" said young Stuteley. "See how he has left his little house—open to the world! He must be of a very trusting nature for sure."

"I remember now that the gate was unlatched yesterday," spoke Robin, slowly. "I noticed it then and meant to talk with you on the point, Will. I hope that no evil has befallen the clerk."

" 'Tis three weeks or more since we have had tidings of him," said Stuteley. "Shall we go in and make search?"

They entered the rude dwelling and soon exhausted every hole and corner of it in a vain hunt for some token of the clerk. The kennels at the back were empty and forlorn; and some bread which they found in the hermit's tiny larder was mouldy and very stale.

"Let us push on to Locksley, Will; mayhap we shall have better cheer waiting us there!"

They trudged on quietly. His master's depression had reached and overcome merry Stuteley. They began unconsciously to walk quickly and more quickly still as they approached Locksley. The day was overcast and very still.

Presently Robin, throwing back his head, sniffed the air.

"Surely there is a strange smell in these woods, Will? Does it not seem to you that there is a taste of burning grasses in the breeze?"

"Master," answered Stuteley, his face suddenly paling at some inner fear, "I do smell fire such as a blazing house would give forth. Well do I know the scent of it; having seen our own home burned last year."

"Hurry, hurry, Will; my heart misgives me. Some further disaster is upon us. This is my evil day, I know. Hurry, for the love of me!"

They set off at a frenzied scamper through the woods, taking the short footpath which would lead them to the back of the house of Locksley. Robin broke through the trees and undergrowth and hastily scaled the fence that railed off their garden from the wild woods.

A dread sight met his starting eyes. Dull brown smoke curled from under the eaves of his home in dense clouds; the windows were gaping rounds from which ever and anon red flames gushed forth; a torrid heat was added to the sickening odor of the doomed homestead.

Somebody grasped him by the hand.

"Thanks be that you are returned, Excellence," spoke a rough voice, with emotion. "This is a sorry welcome."

"My mother?" gasped Robin, blankly, and his heart stood still for Warrenton's answer.

"Not a hair of her head has been touched. Old Warrenton would not stand here to tell you the sorry tale were it otherwise. But the house must go; 'tis too old and dry a place for mortal hand to save."

Stuteley had joined them by this, and the three gazed for a minute in stupefied silence on the flaming destruction of that home so dear to Robin Fitzooth. Warrenton, grimed and righteously angry, began his tale.

Yesterday, at dusk, the sound of a winding horn had brought them all anxiously to the garden. "We thought that you had returned with young Stuteley," said the old man-at-arms; "but we found ourselves facing none other than Master Ford the forester, with about six or more of the most insolent of his men. Peremptorily he bade us deliver up this house to him, pulling out a warrant from his bosom and waving it before your mother's face."

"Ford, was it?" questioned Robin. Then light broke in upon him. Yesterday, after the battle between Will's band and that of Master Carfax, some of the defeated foresters had fled to the north of Sherwood.

"You must bear up, young Master," said Warrenton; "the Squire will doubtless build you a new home."

"Alas, Warrenton! Master Montfichet has turned against me now," said Robin then, "and against you also. Continue your story, and you shall hear ours when you have done."

So Warrenton continued, telling them how John Ford had made an attempt to seize the place: how Warrenton and the few servants had striven to beat him back: and how, after valiant fighting, they had succeeded in keeping them from taking the house at least. The garden they could not retain; but Warrenton, having established himself at one of the upper windows, had so shrewdly flown his arrows, that Ford himself had been wounded and one of his men killed outright.

Night had fallen upon them in this way, and the dame thought that it would be a good scheme for one of her maids now to endeavor to slip out and arouse the village to their help. One of the women therefore essayed the journey; but was so clumsy as to attract the enemy's attention. She was seized and made to confess how the house was protected and where it was most likely to fall before a sharp assault. Being a witless wench, she told them truly, and Master Ford then bade her help them collect sticks and leaves in order that they might be able to fire the place as a last resource.

Those within had thought that the girl had managed to evade danger, and cheerfully waited for help from the village.

A determined attack was commenced at daybreak; and Ford and his men succeeded in gaining possession of the kitchens without loss. Another of the servants was captured, also a second maidservant was injured by an arrow, so seriously as to die within twenty minutes.

Warrenton kept the stairs and barricaded the inner door from the kitchens by putting tables and chairs against it. At length a parley was called, and Ford shouted his conditions through the keyhole. The besieged then learned that the distant village was still unaware of their peril. Ford offered to let them all go forth free, if now they would yield up the house to him.

Mistress Fitzooth had a mind to accept, but Warrenton counselled no. After a long argument Ford swore that he would burn the house over their heads if they did not surrender it within an hour; and, going back to the garden, he began to bring in the loose dry pieces of wood and sticks he and his men had collected in the night.

At three hours after noon, Ford, having given one more warning to them, had bidden his fellows do the worst. In a few moments the smell of burning filled the house; and Mistress Fitzooth became as one distraught.

"We had two women left to us," Warrenton continued, "and a lad, who was worth as much as man to me. I bade them open the door softly, and rush forth whilst the wretches were employed at their fiendish work in the rear. This we did, and so gained, unperceived, the little shed nearby the gate. From a crack in the boards, I could command bowshot of the whole front; and I had given the lad a bow of yours. The two maids, taking your mother's hands, pulled her along under the hedge until they gained the road. Then all three ran furiously toward the village.

"We who were left behind had not long to wait. Presently, one came round to the front with a piece of flaming wood and boldly thrust it through the nearest lattice. Him I killed at once with an arrow through the back. They were now but five against us. Presently two others came stealthily from the back: but, seeing their companion dead, ran back hastily.

"Master Ford appeared next, and began to look suspiciously about him. His fellow had rolled over in his death struggles, and so might have been slain from my window in the housefront. Curls of smoke were coming up from under the thatch by now; and Ford, making up his mind, ran out with the others, and flung himself upon the door.

"We had left it latched; and so it gave enough of resistance in his blind attack to justify him in believing it was still held from within. It fell inwards, at last, with a crash; and Ford sprang triumphantly across the threshold. His fellows rushed after him, trying now to beat out the fire."

Warrenton paused, and all fell again to watching the leaping flames.

"Meanwhile I guessed that your mother was safe, and had already alarmed the villagers," continued the old retainer. "So, with a shout, I rushed out upon the villains, with the lad, and pulled the broken door back to its place, shutting them in, that they might enjoy their own fell work in all security. Two of them did attempt escape just since by leaping from out of the window. But my bow was ready strung for them."

"Have you killed four men, then, Warrenton?" said Robin, his blood running cold. Then suddenly the full meaning of it flashed upon him. "And Ford?" he cried, with a gesture of horror, "and the two others?"

"Nay," said Warrenton, grimly. "I had come round here to see whether they had preference for fire or for my arrows, having left the boy to guard the front. Then I saw you and young Stuteley, and in my chattering I had nigh come to forget them. But there is Master Ford beckoning to us from your own room."

A frenzied, dreadful figure had indeed appeared for a brief instant amongst the thick curling smoke. It waved two hopeless hands out towards the falling dusk, and then incontinently vanished.

A thin scream sounded in Robin's ears, as a rush of flame mercifully swallowed up this apparition: like as not, 'twas the sound of the fire itself. The end had come, both to the unhappy foresters and Robin's home. With a huge torrent of noise the roof of it crushed in, half-stifling the fire.

Then the flames seized full mastery; and amid a shower of sparks, the red tongues licked and devoured the last of their prey.

* * *

Robin hastened to find his mother, that he might be relieved of his anxiety and be rid for the moment of the sight of the awful catastrophe of the fire. Warrenton and Stuteley rushed in together, at his command, to try to save the two remaining foresters; but it was a very forlorn hope. Warrenton in his just revenge had pushed things to their extreme limits: Master Ford and all his band had paid the utmost penalty of their failure to overcome this relentless old man.

Mistress Fitzooth had secured refuge and was now much calmer. She embraced her son and wept over him in joy at this reunion. Robin could see, however, that she was indeed much overwrought by these troubles. She had not yet recovered from the loss of her husband.

They stayed with these poor people, who found room for them somehow, out of sheer charity, for neither Robin nor the dame had any money. It was a bitter business, in sooth: and next day Robin, finding his mother far from well, humbled himself to beg assistance from the Squire. He despatched the letter by Warrenton, and then patiently set himself to wait a reply.

Also, he determined to seek an audience with the Prince. His home had been burned, his small patrimony gone: he had now no means of keeping himself and the dame from starvation save by living on another man's bread.

The clerk, his one tried friend, was gone—no one knew where.

The Prince would surely yield him the right to be Ranger at Locksley in his father's place! The house had been given to dead Hugh Fitzooth by Henry, the King.

An uneasy feeling took possession of Robin, for Warrenton had defied and overcome the Sheriff's man when he had been properly empowered to expel mother and son from Locksley, and there were seven dead men, nay, eight, to be accounted for—and they were all of them King's Foresters.

*   *   *

Montfichet answered him by sending a purse of money and a curt letter saying that Mistress Fitzooth was to come to Gamewell, where for the rest of her days she would always find a home. For Robin he could do nothing: already the Sheriff had drawn up a proclamation of outlawry against him, setting the price of a hundred crowns upon him, living or dead.

CHAPTER 15

ISTRESS FITZOOTH never
saw Gamewell or her brother again. Her disorder took a sudden and
fatal turn; and within a week Robin found himself doubly an orphan—
without home, money, or hope. Only two good friends had he—little
Stuteley and staunch Warrenton.

The Squire had refused to see the latter and had sent him the reply to
Robin's note by one of the servants. Montfichet was angered with
Warrenton because he had been deceived by him.

Robin laid his mother to rest beside his father. That was as long as he
might dare stay in Locksley. Every day he feared to be seized by Master
Monceux's myrmidons. Stuteley kept watch on the road through Sherwood by day and Warrenton by night.

The morning of the interment brought news of danger. One of the
few faithful foresters of Locksley was at his post—the rest, having no
master, had disported themselves upon their own various errands—and
he heard from a shepherd that a body of soldiers were journeying to
Locksley. Full two score and ten of them there were; one, the leader,
carrying a warrant for Robin's arrest. The forester hastened to save his
young master.

The time was short. Robin had scarcely pause to perform the last sad
offices above his mother's grave ere he must be flying for his life. His
only chance was to take to the woods and hide in them.

Warrenton urged him to seek shelter in the thicker forest about
Barnesdale, at the northwestern end of Sherwood. Whispers gave a
story that the higher parts were honeycombed with strange caves; and

all the countryside knew that away in Barnesdale were the headquarters and camps of Will o' th' Green. It was the place of all others for shelter; and Stuteley became joyful in the thought of the adventures that must chance to them therein.

Warrenton was sober, however, over it. He had a presentiment that the days would be hard and the food scanty and plain. Still, 'twas a man's life, after all.

They nearly plunged themselves into the hands of the enemy by mistaking their road.

So it chanced that Robin spied his old enemy Simeon Carfax and narrowly missed being seen also by him. The three fugitives hid themselves high up in the branches of a tree; and watched with beating hearts their enemies hurrying onward to Locksley. With the band of soldiers, pikemen, and foresters were two whom Robin observed narrowly. Sounds of their talk reached his ears; and, since these two fellows rode somewhat apart from the rest, Robin was able to distinguish their chattering.

He had unfailing ear for a voice. These were those traitors in Will's band, the two outlaws whom he had encountered on the day of the joustings at Nottingham Fair. "Roger and Micah," murmured Robin to himself, after listening a while. "Yes, those were the names they used *then*. So, friends, I am forearmed against you, for I will step with heavy foot in your concerns by and by—when I do find Master Will o' th' Green! Roger—and Micah—I'll not forget."

Soon as they had passed, the three slid quietly to the ground and thereafter betook themselves very cautiously through the wood. Robin determined to find Will soon as he might and lay his case before him. The outlaw would give him refuge, no doubt.

The noise of the soldiers passed away in a murmuring discordance, and the three fugitives walked now more boldly towards Barnesdale. Ere sundown they were very heartily tired. They lay themselves down in the long grasses and while two slumbered the third watched.

Such foods as dry bread and berries were all that they could command; but there was water in plenty. The evening came, and after it night—and so to break of the next day.

Robin would have recommenced the flight soon as they had bathed themselves in a little shallow stream. Ere an hour of daylight was theirs, sounds of hurried approach warned them to be alert. Someone was crashing recklessly through the wood, following their trail clearly. Robin bade Warrenton and little Stuteley hide on either hand whilst he put himself directly in the path of this pursuer.

It proved to be none other than that one faithful forester of Locksley who had warned him of the soldiery. Robin welcomed him all the more gladly when he heard that this good fellow meant to throw in his own fortunes with those of his unjustly treated young master.

He had news for them, too. It transpired that Master Carfax had several duties in hand—as was his wont. First, he had to seize Robin and bring him, alive or dead, to the Sheriff. Next he was to declare all the Fitzooth property to be confiscated; and, having put seal upon any of it that might be left from the fire, he had to instal as temporary Ranger one of the Sherwood men who he might think fit and trustworthy. Then a messenger was to be dispatched with another parchment to the Abbot of York: writ this time in true Norman tongue.

After these things were executed Master Simeon was to turn his men about, and march them determinedly upon the outlaws' stronghold, which was now known to be at Barnesdale, and exterminate the band.

A task none so easy, after all!

For the satisfactory doing of these small commissions Carfax was to receive one hundred and fifty pieces of gold; and also would be accepted by the Sheriff as a fitting husband for the pale, hard-eyed demoiselle, Marie of Monceux. 'Twas this reward that made Master Simeon desperate and dangerous.

The forester, John Berry by name, told Robin further that Carfax had clothed his body in chain mail, and was carrying a dreadful axe in his belt—with which to avenge the insult put upon him in the matter of the stag's horns.

"Let us seek Barnesdale forthwith," said Robin. "I am all agog to warn Will o' th' Green—for he has been a stout friend to me."

"Hurry then, Master," cried Berry, the forester. "You are not far from the Barnesdale road. In sooth, as I followed your tracks, I wondered how you had come so far within a very short space. You are now within touch of Gamewell."

It was true. In the mazy forest they had nearly described a circle, and were now perilously nigh to Gamewell and the squire.

An idea came to Robin. He turned to Warrenton.

"Could we but find that underground path whereby cousin Geoffrey came and went from the pleasance, old friend," said he, "why—we might play the Yellow Lady to purpose!"

"Excellence," replied Warrenton, "I will undertake to bring you to the forest entrance of Master Will's castle within a score of minutes."

"Lead us, Warrenton—and I prithee be better guide than you have been so far in this adventure."

After taking many bypaths, and through a big tunnel-shaped cave, the path became dry again, and lighter: and soon they saw that the end was near. They emerged presently, tired and dirtied; and found themselves under the bank of a little jumping woodland river—far down in a gorge of rock and brake, studded and overhung with thick trees.

It was a wild spot: and only the notes of the birds and the rush of the falling water disturbed it. But ere they had proceeded a quarter of a mile up the bank of the stream a sudden bend in it brought them the harsh noise of desperate and near fighting.

Loud shouts and battle cries sounded on their left; and, running speedily in this direction, our four adventurers chanced upon a strange sight.

It was strange by the manner of their view of it; for, having clambered up the bank to the top of the gorge, they saw themselves on the highest edge of a spur of ground—with the low-down rocky valley of the river behind, and before them a little narrow plain—as equally below them as was the water they had left. On this plain were a number of men engaged in deadly battle. Round and about were the thick dark woods of Barnesdale.

A moment's glance showed Robin that they had arrived too late to help Will o' th' Green by way of warning. The outlaw's foes were upon him, and seemingly had the robber and his band at a disadvantage.

The ground descended below the four onlookers so abruptly as to cut them off from the plain. They were near to the battle; and yet altogether remote from it.

"Our arrows must do duty for us, then," muttered Robin, grimly, soon as he understood this. "Fit shafts across your bows, friends, and aim with all your hearts in it. Let not those of either side see us. 'Tis thus that our services shall be of most value to Master Will."

They dropped to their knees and aimed their arrows carefully. They had full quivers with them, and Warrenton and Robin felt themselves in a manner to be pitted one against the other. The battle raged so furiously below, however, that for a minute these allies were compelled to remain idle—not daring to loose their shafts for fear of slaying friends as well as foes.

Sounds of a horn, shrill and impatient, suddenly called the soldiers back to their ranks beside Master Carfax. Robin spied this worthy now; and saw that he bestrode a black horse clumsily—as if armored indeed. Simeon evidently had withdrawn his men from a mêlée for fear that in it he might not be properly protected. He was seen to be issuing orders very peremptorily to the men.

Meanwhile the outlaws rallied themselves to their leader's side. They were sadly decreased in numbers; and, whilst the living thus formed about in battle array, there were many poor fellows of both sides left upon the field who stirred not even to the imperative commands of their commanders.

Now was Robin's chance.

"Choose your man, each one of you," said he, in a suppressed eagerness; "and soon as the soldiers issue at the charge shoot down upon your mark."

Carfax gave an order almost as he spoke. Instantly Robin loosed his bow, and singing death flew from it. He overturned the soldier nearest to Master Simeon, even as Warrenton's shaft struck another dead at once.

The forester Berry and little Stuteley added to the confusion—both wounding the same soldier simultaneously. Then Carfax, believing that these arrows came from Will's band, sounded a charge and spurred his horse forward amongst his pikemen.

They rushed forward with swinging axe and clanking sword upon the outlaws, who now delivered a sudden stream of shafts. These Robin's band supplemented by shrewder arrows. Seven of the soldiers rolled over as they ran, killed forthwith; and Robin, having pricked Simeon's horse, shot him again in the ear whilst meaning to find his master.

The beast plunged wildly into the soldiers, trampling and scattering them. But many managed yet to meet the robbers, and the desperate hand-to-hand fighting was recommenced.

Robin bade the others cease. The four of them peered from out of their cover over the crest, and watched breathlessly. Carfax had fallen from his horse and lay floundering on the close grass. Stuteley sped a gooseshaft into his forearm ere Robin could check him.

Warrenton drew his master's attention and anger away from his esquire by a quick whisper.

"See, lording—quick! Look how some of the enemy do creep about Master Will; they will strike him and his fellows from the rear!"

"The two who lead them are not uniformed—like as not they are those treacherous ones whom I have such cause to remember."

So muttered Robin, with parted lips, and gasping his words disjointedly. "Smite them, Warrenton," cried he, suddenly and excitedly. "Speedily, instantly—or they will end this fight against us. *Now!*"

Their arrows flew together, marvellous shots, each finding its prey. The two wretches threw up their arms as they ran; and, uttering dismal cries, fell upon the earth, and in their death struggles tore up vain handfuls of the soil.

"Follow, follow," called Robin, to his three faithful ones. "Locksley! A Locksley! To the rescue!"

They tumbled headlong down the slope, shouting vociferously as they came. The soldiers, alarmed and already disheartened, imagined that these eager enemies were but forerunners of a large reinforcement. Hastily they disengaged themselves from the outlaws and, gathering up Master Carfax, rushed pell-mell with him backward to the woods on the right.

Will o' th' Green's few men hurried them with their arrows; and soon as Robin had come down to level ground he fell to streaming his shafts

"Smite them, Warrenton,"
cried Robin, suddenly and
excitedly. Their arrows
flew together, marvellous shots,
each finding its prey.

into the rout. He was bruised, begrimed, and cut about his face by the thorns and rocks; yet was so furious against Master Simeon and his myrmidons that these things were not even felt by him. Shouting "Locksley! Locksley!" more and more triumphantly, he ran alone in fierce pursuit.

The soldiers disappeared under the trees, and ran even then. Warrenton and the outlaws came on in support of young Robin; and the defeat of Carfax and his men was completed. They were chased through the woods of Barnesdale, which these wild outlaws knew so well. Some were shot with arrows mercifully; others fell under the cruel blows of the outlaws' short axes. A few escaped with Master Carfax back to the Sheriff of Nottingham—not one-third of those who had set out at his command. It was the most desperate of affairs yet betwixt the greenwood men and those representing law and order as conceived by the Sheriff. On either side many were killed—the outlaw band was reduced in numbers, and its leader, Will o' th' Green, was amongst those who were to plot and fight no more in Sherwood.

When Robin and the rest of them returned from their long chase, tired with an immense fatigue, they found sad work still before them. Robin tended Will himself, and bound up his many wounds: and sought to beguile him to live—if but to spite Monceux and his wretches. But Will o' th' Green had been pierced too dreadfully by his enemies' darts: he had only strength to drink a little water and say his last words to his men.

In the dusk of this day he lay in Robin's arms, wizard no more; and asked that someone should give the call he knew so well—the strange, short signal upon the horn which ever had rallied these men. Then as they, with dejected faces, drew nigh to him, he spoke to them all— bidding them hate the laws and defy them so long as they were unjust and harsh. He counselled them to choose amongst themselves a new leader—one who would be impartial and honest; and the one who could bend the best bow.

"Be not robbers to any who are poor and who are good fellows— having only their poverty against them. Be kind to those who help you, but exact toll as heretofore of all who come through the greenwood. The rich to pay in money, and blood—if it be necessary."

He added these words with an effort; and his mind wandered in the shadowy fields of death. Robin saw how his fingers twitched, as if they plucked still the cord of his good yew bow. He smoothed back Will's dark hair from off his brow, and put water to the outlaw's lips. Will o' th' Green glanced up at him, and something of his old expression— half-grim, half-smiling—showed that he struggled still to hold hands with life.

"For you, Locksley," he muttered, puckering his brows, "there are two roads open. One, to yield thyself to Monceux and the rack—for not even your uncle at Gamewell should save you, even did he so wish; the other—to join with these honest fellows and live a free life. What else is left to you? If you would be as dutiful to the laws as the earth to summer sun, it should not avail you. Your lord the Sheriff is in the hands of his girl—and she listens with willing ear to Master Carfax. Ask not how I know these things. Your cousin is outlawed——"

"I shall live in the greenwood, Will," answered Robin, quietly, "with your brave men and you—if so be I may. Have I won now the freedom of the forest?" He showed him the broken peacocked arrow which the Clerk of Copmanhurst had given him.

The outlaw held up his right hand and laid it on Robin's bowed head: "Upon you, Robin of Locksley, do I bestow, with this my last breath, full freedom of the forests of England," he said, very loudly. Then he relaxed from his frown to a rare smile. "Learn this sign——" he said, and showed Robin, with feeble fingers, how the greenwood men knew each other in any disguise. It was a simple signal, very easy to know, yet very sure. No one might suppose it given by accident—yet of design it appeared quite innocent. The smile was fading from Will's face as Robin repeated it carefully after him; and even as he spoke again he died.

"Farewell—friends all—take this brother into your good company, and make him and those with him right welcome. I pray you to remember and abide by those kindly rules which have always— always——"

His speech fell away into meaningless words, and the light left his face. He moved in Robin's arms and sighed. Then, as his body rolled slowly over, and he lay with his back turned to them, they saw that his worst wound was in it—a dastard's blow. So ended the life of Will o' th' Green—or Will of Cloudesley: he of whom many stories have been told in other books.

They took him up reverently and buried him in a secret place—so that none to this day can say where he lies. And the outlaws swore an oath of vengeance against him who had so foully slain their chief.

Robin guessed wisely that the mortal blow had been given by one of those two traitors in Will's own camp. Had they not been riding with Carfax in the early morn—not as prisoners of war—but as informers and spies?

*   *   *

The next day was passed in burying the dead of both sides. The outlaws accepted Robin without question as one full welcome amongst them; and Warrenton, Stuteley, and John Berry were also given the freedom of the woods and taught the signs and freemasonry of them.

The bodies of the soldiers and mercenaries were stripped and heaped together into a pit, and roughly covered with earth and leaves. Then the outlaws betook themselves to their caves to settle who should be chief of the band in Will's place.

Whilst they were employed in this difficult business, the Sheriff sent out another and larger body of armed men—obeying the insolent command of his Prince. Fear sat upon the soul of Monceux then: for he did not doubt that another such disaster as that which had chanced to his other men would mean disgrace and the end of his lord-shrievalty.

This second company who were captained by Hubert the Archer, with bandaged Carfax second in command, had an easy conquest, however, of Sherwood and Barnesdale—for none challenged them, nor questioned their proceedings in any respect. Nor was there sign left in the woods of Robin or the outlaws—they were vanished so utterly that Carfax conceived them all to have either died of their wounds or fled disconsolate from the neighborhood.

In either event this was most excellent news; and, having patrolled the forest and searched it indifferently well, the men-at-arms of Nottingham agreed that peace-loving folk had no more to fear from the wild spirits of Sherwood. They were gone, banished—and the King's forest was now safe of passage to all.

Carfax, poking here and there, found the fresh grave of his own fellows, and disturbed it mightily. He bade Hubert disinter them all; and pretended to recognize each one. Here was the archrebel Will of Cloudesley—this one was the second man of his band. Here was young Robin Fitzooth, as dead as mutton—and here was his fellow Stuteley. So Master Simeon went on, to his own satisfaction and to Hubert's, who foresaw large rewards to be paid for these poor dishonored bodies.

They brought three of them back, with every circumstance of importance. They were shown to the Prince as being the last remains of Will Cloudesley, Robin Fitzooth, and Hall the Outlaw—a well-known marauder in Will's company.

Prince John forthwith praised the pikemen and archers, and bade Monceux give them great rewards—a thing which vexed the mean Sheriff much. Then they all rode about and through the forest in a great hunt of the Royal deer, graciously attended by the Prince himself.

Monceux was forgiven; and Simeon, having quite recovered all his old self-esteem, was duly betrothed to the demoiselle Marie. A new Ranger was appointed at Locksley; and another house was found for him. No one said him nay.

A proclamation against all outlaws and freebooters having been issued and signed with many flourishes by John, he betook his Royal person to York, carrying lean-faced, smiling Carfax with him. Mistress Monceux hid her sorrow and devoted her energies forthwith towards the undoing of the maid Fitzwalter, against whom she yet nursed much spite.

The Prince stayed at Gamewell on his way, and patronized indulgently old George Montfichet, although the latter's dislike of his Royal guest was only too thinly veiled. Then John took farewell of Nottingham and Sherwood, making an easy business of it. Monceux had ridden out on this morning to make dutiful obeisance and escort the Prince through Locksley to the borders.

Outside the gates of Gamewell John delivered himself to the men-at-arms, retainers, burgesses, and citizens of Nottingham, who had inquisitively followed the Sheriff.

"We will not forget your hospitality, friends all," said he, in his slightly swaggering and yet withal effeminate way; "and see, in some measure of return for it, we leave you our Sherwood free from pestilent robbers and evil defiers of the law. When we came to Nottingham there were these and others, but now they are all driven out of our Royal forest—many slain with the arrows of my Hubert, or beaten with the staves of your own fellows. This surely is some sort of gift—see to it that you keep well that which we have secured for you."

Then he rode forth amid the cheerings of the crowd, Hubert and his followers scattering largesses as they rode.

CHAPTER 16

ALL THROUGH that long winter Robin had lain hidden in the Barnesdale caves with the remains of the band of outlaws which had begun with Will of Cloudesley's advent and nigh ended with his death. At first there had been some quarreling and jealousy amongst them as to who should be the new captain.

There were, with Robin and his three recruits, twenty and two men all told. These had decided upon many tests between themselves in order to settle who should lead; and when there were tests of archery Robin had beaten them all.

Yet he had no wish to set himself at their head, having sped his arrows so well more for the reason that a good bowman cannot but aim well when his fingers are upon his weapon. So he had said modestly that they must reckon without him, and that he would gladly obey the man the others should choose.

Then there had been fresh bickerings, and they were once nearly discovered by the Sheriff's foresters, who by some means stumbled upon one of their underground passages.

The winter brought with it many privations; and they decided at length to leave Barnesdale and go into the county of Lincoln. They made their ragged clothes as much like those of the King's Foresters as they could and then set out.

One thing had been agreed on: that they must have some new clothes and induce other bold spirits to join with them, else Sherwood would be lost to them forever.

Robin had quite decided to cast in his lot with these men. He felt that they would be loyal to each other, and he knew that the only traitors which this band had known were now no more. A bitter hatred of the Sheriff, of lying Carfax and of Royalty, as personified by the unjust, indolent Prince, had moulded Robin's character into steel, as it were.

Robin had counselled this journey to Lincoln. In the secret caves about Barnesdale, Will of Cloudesley had amassed and stored away much wealth. It was useless to them here in Nottingham; but in Lincoln one of them might go in to the market and buy sufficient Lincoln cloth and needles and thread to fit them all out.

Swords might also be obtained; and some shirts of chain mail, new bows and new arrows.

The band started away under cover of a crisp February night, and had come into sight of Lincoln within three days. They had just finished their morning meal of the third day when they were overtaken by a stoutish man whose clothing was of the most remarkable description. He wore a cloak which was so clouted and patched that the first part of it hung about him in a dozen folds. He had on his head three hats, one rammed tightly over the other, so that he cared neither for wind nor rain. On his back was a bag held by a thong of strong leather about his neck. In his right hand was a long crooked stick.

The outlaws had naturally hidden themselves at first sound of his footsteps. They watched him go by, and passed jests between themselves concerning him. Stuteley begged that he might be allowed to play a joke upon the fellow.

"Go after him by all means, if you will," said Robin; "but be polite, for I have it in my mind that this is a man known to me. I would that I could hear him speak."

"Follow me, Master, warily, and you shall hear him speak to a purpose!" cried little Stuteley.

When the stranger found that someone walked behind him, he quickened his pace. Stuteley called out to him, but he made no reply.

"Stand, as I bid you, fellow," cried little Stuteley again, "for you shall tarry and speak to me."

"By my troth," said the other, answering him at last, "I have no leisure for talk with you, friend. 'Tis very far to my lodging and the morning grows. Therefore, I will lose my dinner if I do not hasten."

"I have had no meat nor bread betwixt my lips this day," retorted Will Stuteley, coming up with him. "And I do not know where I may get any, for if I go to a tavern they will ask me for money, of which I have not one groat, unless you will lend me some until we do meet again?"

The clouted man replied very peevishly: "I have no money to lend you, friend; for I have lost the little I had in a foolish wager made at Nottingham. But you are a younger man than I, though you seem to be more lazy; so I can promise you a long fast if you wait until you have money from me."

Now, something in the man's tones roused memories in little Stuteley, yet he could not resolve them into shape. The fellow's face was so obscured by the three hats that one could scarcely get a peep at it.

"Since we have met this day," said Stuteley, wrathfully, "I will have money of you, even though it be but one penny. Therefore, lay aside your cloak and the bag about your neck; or I will tear it open. And should you offer to make any noise my arrows shall pierce your fat body like unto a cullender."

The man laughed discordantly; and again Stuteley thought he recognized him.

"Do you think, friend, that I have any fear of your arrows? Stand away or I will beat you into grist."

Stuteley bent his bow and set an arrow upon the cord, but not so quickly as to save himself from a mighty thwack from the man's cudgel. The little esquire sprang back, and in doing so dropped both bow and arrow. Nothing dismayed, he drew his sword, and engaged at once with the stranger.

Their blows fell about each other's bodies like hail, and Stuteley found that not all his Cumberland tricks could help him with so furious an opponent. His enemy had little skill, but plenty of strength and agility; his stick whirled and twirled, beating down Stuteley's guard time after time. He was, besides, a bigger man and much older.

Robin's esquire began to see that he had met a sturdy opponent, and even as this tardy knowledge came into his mind, the stranger gave him a crushing body blow, and he tumbled fairly to the ground. There Stuteley lay, with closed eyes and white face.

" 'Tis a pity to rest so soon, friend," remarked the stranger, with irony. "Would it not be better to snatch my money from me, and take your ease afterwards in that tavern which you wot of?"

Stuteley answered nothing, but lay deadly still. Robin and the rest were too far behind to perceive what had happened. The strange-looking man turned away without bestowing another glance on his little enemy, and soon his quaint figure disappeared over the brow of the next hill.

Within a dozen minutes the outlaws came up and discovered poor Will Stuteley lying on the ground, faintly moaning. They bathed his head, but could find no wounds. Robin was much upset, and began to eagerly question his esquire so soon as he showed signs of returning to his wits.

"Tell me, little Will, what evil mischance has fallen to you?" asked Robin, with emotion.

Stuteley raised his head and looked about him in a dazed manner.

"I have been all through the county of Cumberland, Master," said he, at last, in a weak voice, "and I have wrestled and fenced with many; yet never since I was a child and under my father's hand have I been so put to it." He shut his eyes again; then opened them viciously. "I encountered with our fellow traveller and saw no reason to fear such a clown. Yet he has scratched my back so heartily that I do fear it never will be straight again."

"Nay, nay, Will. I'll nurse you well, be sure on't," murmured Robin, full of pity and despair.

"Dear Master, I speak but as I feel," continued Stuteley, half-shutting his eyes. "But the rascal has not gone far from us; and were some of you to hasten, doubtless he would be brought to book, and I might see him punished ere I die. Go you, old Warrenton, you are a stubborn fighter; and take John Berry and two of the rest."

"I'll e'en fetch him to you myself, malapert," said Warrenton.

"He is more deadly than your Lady in Yellow, I promise you," said Stuteley. "Be wary, and let at least six of you surround him."

"That would be wasting the time of five of us," answered old Warrenton, in an offhand way; "I will go alone."

"Let someone then prepare bandages for our Warrenton, and take my shirt for them. He will need such service."

Warrenton and Berry, with another, ran off at this. Robin saw that Stuteley was not so near his end as he affected to imagine; and made him more comfortable beneath a tree, covered him with a cloak, gave him some drink, and ministered to him considerately.

The old man-at-arms fully intended to capture their quarry alone; feeling to be on his mettle, as it were. So he ran as fast as he could before the other two; but not so fast as to catch up with the man he sought.

Presently he espied him far down the road; and, knowing a shorter path to Lincoln, whither he judged the man was bound, Warrenton called to the others and they struck away from the road.

They made their plans as they walked, and at length cut off the enemy. He did not look so formidable as Stuteley had painted him; and as he drew near they felt this was an easy business. Two of them sprang out upon him, and one, seizing his twisted stick, dragged it violently out of his hands. Warrenton flashed a dagger at his breast, saying sinisterly: "Friend, if you utter any alarm I will be your confessor and hangman. Come back with us forthwith and you may end your fight properly with our companion. He waits greedily for you."

"Give me the chance," answered the fellow, valiantly, "and I will fight with you all."

Berry and the other outlaw instantly gave him the frog's march backward along the road; but the villain struggled so fiercely that they presently began to tire.

"Now grant me my life," said their prisoner, "and I will give you good money to the sum of one hundred pieces. It is all my savings, which I promised to give into the hands of a wicked usurer in Lincoln."

"Well," said Berry, pausing, "this is a fair sum, and might heal our companion's wounds very comfortably. Hold him fast, comrades, whilst I go back for his staff. Without that he cannot do much harm."

Whilst he was gone the fellow began again. "I am a miller, friends," said he, much more at ease already, "and have but lately returned from doing a good bargain in wheat. Also, I am esteemed a fair archer, and, since I perceive that you are foresters all, this matter will tell with you in my favor. I could draw you a pretty bow had I but the use of my arms."

"Nay, Master Miller, but we would sooner hold you tight, and take your skill for granted," answered the outlaw.

Berry came back and stuck the staff into the ground at a little distance.

"Now count out your pieces, Miller," said Warrenton.

There was a keen wind blowing and the miller turned about so as not to face it directly they gave him half-freedom. Warrenton said gruffly to him: "Count, Miller; count truly and honestly."

"Let me open my bag then," said the rogue. He unfastened it from his neck, and, setting it on the ground, took off his patched cloak. He placed his bag carefully upon it, holding the bag as though it were heavy indeed. Then he crouched down over it and fumbled at the leathern thong.

The outlaws had all gathered closely before him as he plunged in his fingers. In the bag were two pecks of fine meal; and as soon as the cunning miller had filled his hands full he suddenly drew them out and dashed the white powder fair into the eager faces of the men about him.

Then he snatched up the bag by the two corners and shook out the rest of the meal. It blew in a blinding cloud about Warrenton and the rest, and filled their eyes so utterly as to leave them all three at the miller's mercy.

He caught up his stick and began to belabor them soundly.

"Since I have dirtied your clothes, friends," cried he, between the blows, " 'tis only right that I should dust them for you! Here are my hundred 'pieces'; how like you them?"

Each word was accompanied by a tremendous thwack. He fell so heartily into the business as to become unwary. Robin and the rest, hearing the shouting and noise, came speeding down the road, with Stuteley recovered already. They chanced on a strange sight.

Berry, old Warrenton, and the outlaw were dancing about in an agony of rage, helpless and blind, and striking vain blows at empty air. The man with the three hats was belaboring them with his staff so thoroughly as to have become a man with no hat at all. They all were tumbled upon the road.

"Why all this haste?" roared he, not noticing Robin or the others. "Why will you not tarry for my money? 'Tis strange that no man will wait upon me this day, whilst I am in so generous a mood!" He sprang up and down, whacking them without ceasing. His feet encountered one of his many hats and ruthlessly kicked it aside.

" 'Tis Much the Miller!" cried Robin, recognizing him by his voice. " 'Tis the miller who helped to save me in Sherwood. Friend, you have never yet paid me my guinea, and I now do claim it of you."

Master Much ceased his occupation. He turned warily about to Robin. So soon as he had looked well at him, he dropped his stick and came over very frankly to him.

"So it's the gipsy?" said he, grinning all over his broad face. "And they have neither flayed you nor hanged you yet? And are these fellows with you?"

"We are the free men of Sherwood," said Robin, "and were coming to Lincoln to get ourselves new clothes and weapons. Also we had hoped to find other good men and true willing to join with us."

Much went up to Stuteley, and craved his pardon very handsomely at this. "Had I but looked at you, friend, I might have known you for the other gipsy, and these fellows for some of those who did save you both from Master Carfax. That is always my way: but never have I been so sorry for't as on this day, for now, through being too hasty, I have lost your good will."

"Nay, Master Miller, but that is not so," said Stuteley.

Warrenton and Berry at first were inclined to play with the miller as he had with them; but Robin pleaded so well for good fellowship that, after a little, peace was proclaimed.

Much, to atone for his misdeeds, undertook to do their business in Lincoln; and set himself busily to work on their behalf. He found them all comfortable and quiet quarters where they might stay unnoticed and unmolested, and Stuteley went with Robin to buy the cloth for their suits.

They stayed in and about the old town for nearly three weeks, until all were well equipped. Much asked that he might join with them and bring his friend Midge and a few other merry souls.

Robin explained to him that they had rules, which, although few and simple, were strict, and that they had, at present, no especial leader, since all had elected to remain equal and free, observing the same laws and pledged to each other in loyalty unto death. A common bond of independence bound them.

"Why, then, Master, we are your men," said Much; "for we are all sick to death of the Normans and their high-handed ways, to tell truth; and right gladly will we take services with you."

"I am not the first or only man of our company," began Robin, smiling; but hasty Much interrupted him with a great oath.

"You shall be my captain, gipsy, I promise you! And captain of us Lincoln men; for you did beat me in archery before the Prince, so I am bound to own you as master. Here's my hand on it; and Midge's too. Come hither, Midge, and swear fealty to Robin of Locksley."

Robin recognized Midge for the ferret-faced man who had been with Much at the tourney. Both insisted on paying over to Stuteley the amount of the wager lost by them on that day.

The outlaws returned to Sherwood well satisfied; and at Barnesdale went on perfecting their plans and adding to their numbers. The day came at length for them to announce themselves.

CHAPTER 17

ONE BRIGHT MORNING in May a slim, straight youth, slightly bearded, dressed in a green suit, with bow unstrung, and a fresh color blowing on his cheeks, came out of the wood upon the highroad by Copmanhurst.

He stood erect, quietly alert, and with his brown eyes watchful of the road. He then moved softly along the road until he came to where but last year the brook had sprawled and scrambled across it. Now a fine stone bridge had been built, at the word of Prince John, who had complained much at having wetted his feet when he had passed by St. Dunstan's shrine eight months agone.

The stranger smiled as he looked at the bridge, half-sadly, half in reverie. He paused to admire the neat work; then slowly walked over the bridge still thinking deeply. Suddenly he plumped himself right into the arms of a tall, ungainly man, who had crossed from the other side.

The youth sprang back; then planted his little body exactly in the center of the bridge.

"Give way, fellow," roared the other, instantly. "Make room for your betters, or I will throw you into the brook!"

The younger man laughed. "I know this little stream right well, friend. Therefore I have no need to make that closer acquaintance of it which you promise."

"You may be acquainted and yet make better acquaintance," returned his big opponent, stirring not an inch. "This bridge is too narrow for us both. One must go back."

"Go back then, friend, by all means. I will not stay you."

"Now will I trounce you right well, stripling," cried the tall man, grasping his cudgel. He made a pass or two with it about the head of the youth.

The latter jumped back and fitted an arrow to his bow.

"Nay, by my body, but this is ungenerous of you, forester," cried the tall man. "I have only a stick and you have a bow! If we are to fight, surely you might fight fairly."

Again the youth laughed brightly. "Nay, by my inches, friend," replied he, "but how can we fight fairly with staves when you are so much the bigger?"

"Cut yourself a longer cudgel, friend," retorted the big fellow.

The youth threw down his bow, and, opening a knife which hung at his waist, went forthwith towards the nearest bush. He cut himself a stout ash staff and fell to trimming it deftly.

When it was complete he came coolly up to his foe.

"Make ready, friend," said he, giving his cudgel a twirl. "Now take tune from me. One, two——"

"Three!" roared the giant, smiting at him instantly.

The fight was a long one, for the youth had such skill and so ready a guard that the other but wasted his anger on him. This "stripling" jumped from one side to the other so lightly and unexpectedly, and parried each thrust so surely, that presently the giant relaxed a little from the fury of his onslaught. Then the youth ran in and gave him such a crack as to make the welkin ring.

"By my life, but you can hit hard!" cried the giant, dropping his stick that he might rub his pate. "For so small a man that was a right hearty blow." He picked up his stick again. "Fall to, spitfire. I am ready!"

They sparred for a minute longer, and then the giant had his chance. He caught the jumping youth so sound a thwack as to send him flying over the low parapet of the bridge far into the bubbling brook. "How now, spitfire? Have you had enough?"

"Marry, that have I," spluttered his antagonist, trying to scramble out of the rushing water. Then he became dizzy again, and fell back with a little cry.

The big man vaulted down to his help, and plucked his foe to the bank. There he laid him down on the grassy sward and fell to bathing his brows with handfuls of fresh water till the youth opened his eyes again.

"Friend," said the stripling, gravely, sitting up, "you dealt me that blow most skilfully. Tell me your name."

"Why," said the giant, a little awkwardly, "as for the blow, 'twas but an undercut that I know well. My name is John Little Nailor."

"You are anything but little, friend," answered the youth, struggling to his feet. "And now I will give you my name also." He put a horn to his lips at this and blew a strange, shrill note.

Forthwith the greenwood was alive with men, all dressed in grass-colored clothes like the youth's. They swarmed about him, full two score and ten of them. One of them, a little man, having eyed the stranger askance, gave a signal to the others to seize him; but the youth forbade this. "The fight was a fair one, friends, and the right of this bridge belongs for the moment to Master John Little Nailor. Take your rights, friend," he went on, turning to the giant, "and go upon your way."

"In a manner, stripling, you have now the better of this adventure, and yet do forbear," returned Master Nailor. "Wherefore I like you well, and would ask again your name."

"Tell him, Will," commanded the youth.

The little man, stepping up to the giant impudently, then announced his master. "Know, fellow, that this is none other than a dead man—a wraith, indeed! At least, so saith Master Monceux, the lord Sheriff of Nottingham. This is Robin Fitzooth."

"Then I am right sorry that I beat you," answered Master Nailor. "And had I known you at the first your head would now be whole and your body unbruised. By my inches, but I would like to join with you and your company."

"Enter our company, then, John Little; and be welcome. The rites are few; but the fee is large: for we shall ask unswerving loyalty of you, and you must give a bond that you will be faithful even unto death."

"I give the bond, with all my soul, and on my very life," cried the tall man.

"Master," said the little man, who was none other than our friend Stuteley, "surely we cannot consent to welcome this fellow amongst us having such a name? Harkee, John Little," he continued, turning to the giant, "take your new name from me, since you are to be of our brotherhood. I christen you Little John!"

At this small jest the merry men laughed long and loud.

"Give him a bow and find a full sheath for our friend Little John, Warrenton," said Robin, joyfully. "And hurry, friends, for surely it is the moment when our first new defiance of Master Monceux is to be made? Fall back into the woods speedily; and bide my signal. Little John, we now will try you. Stand out on the bridge path you have just won from me and parley with those who are coming along the road from York. Speak loudly that I may hear what answers you win."

He gave a signal, and at once all disappeared even as they had come, swiftly and silently. Warrenton and Stuteley placed themselves low down behind bushes of white thorn. Warrenton, who had given his quiver to Little John, now produced a great bag from under a bush; and took out of it a dozen or more long smocks such as shepherds wear. Hastily Robin and Stuteley attired themselves as hinds, and the old retainer gave them each a crook to hold. He explored again his stores under the bushes, and dragged out a fat buck, freshly killed and ready spitted for the fire.

Robin and those of the freemen who were now attired in this simple garb helped to pull the deer to the edge of the road; and, hastily making a fire, they soon had their meat cooking merrily. Little John eyed them askew, but made no offer to question them. He had recognized Robin by a sign which the other had given to him.

Meanwhile the noise of a small company nearing them became more evident; and presently seven horsemen turned a bend of the road. Their leader was a stout and haughty-looking man clothed in episcopal garments, and so soon as he spied these shepherds he spurred his horse until he came level with them.

Then he drew bridle sharply, and addressed himself to Little John.

"Who are these, fellow, that make so free with the King's deer?" he asked, mildly, as one who wishes first to believe the best of every man.

"These are shepherds, Excellence," answered Little John.

"Heaven have mercy! They seem more like to be robbers o' th' greenwood at first glance," said the priest.

"One must not judge on half-hearing or half-seeing, lording," retorted Little John.

"That is true, but I would question you further, good man. Tell me now who has killed this deer, and by what right?" His tones had passed insensibly to an arrogant note.

"Give me first your name, Excellence, so that I may know I speak where 'tis fitting," said Little John, stubbornly.

"This is my lord the Bishop of Hereford, fellow," said one of the guards, fiercely. "Keep a civil tongue in your head, or 'twill surely be bad for you!"

Robin now came forward. "My lord," said he, bowing his curly head before the Bishop, "I did hear your questions, and will answer them in all truth. We are but simple shepherds, and tend our flocks year in and year out about the forest of Sherwood, but, this being our holiday, we thought there would be small harm in holding it upon one of the King's deer, since there are so many."

"You are saucy fellows, in sooth," cried the Bishop, "and the King shall know of your doings. Quit your roast, and come with me, for I will bring you to the Sheriff of Nottingham forthwith! Seize this knave, men, and bind his hands."

"Your pardon, Excellence——"

"No pardon shall you have of me, rascal!" snapped the stout Bishop. "Seize him, my men!"

Robin blew upon his horn a shrill, short note, and at once his freemen sprang out from behind the thornbushes and flung themselves on the bishop's guard. The good Bishop found himself a prisoner, and began to crave indulgence of the men he had been so ready to upbraid.

"Nay, we will grant you no pardon, by my beard!" said Little John, fiercely. "Lend me that sword, friend," he added, turning to Stuteley, who had taken the weapon from one of the Bishop's guards. "Right skilfully will I make this church to be without a head."

"There shall be no shedding of blood," cried Robin, interposing, "where I can stay it. Come, friends, send these fellows unto Nottingham with their legs tied under their horses' bellies. But my lord the Bishop of Hereford shall come with us unto Barnesdale!"

The unwilling prelate was dragged away cheek by jowl with the half-cooked venison on the back of his own horse, and Robin and the band brought their guest to Barnesdale.

As soon as dusk had passed they lighted a great fire in the centre of a little hill-bordered glade, and fell to roasting the deer afresh. Another and fatter beast was set to frizzle upon the other side of the fire; and, as the night was chill, the men gathered close about their savory dinner.

The Bishop sniffed the odorous air from his place of captivity; and was nothing loth when they offered to conduct him to this fine repast. Robin bade him take the best place.

"For you must know, Excellence, that we freemen are all equal in each other's sight in this free land. Therefore we have no one whom we can specially appoint to do the honors such as your station warrants. Take, then, the seat at the head of our feast and give us grace before meat, as the occasion justifies."

The Bishop pronounced grace in the Latin tongue hastily; and then settled himself to make the best of his lot. Red wines and ales were produced and poured out, each man having a horn tankard from which to drink.

Laughter bubbled among the diners; and the Bishop caught himself smiling at more than one jest. Stuteley filled his beaker with good wine each time the Bishop emptied it; and it was not until near midnight that their guest began to show signs that he wished to leave them.

"I wish, mine host," said he, gravely, to Robin, who had soberly drunk but one cup of ale, "that you would now call a reckoning. 'Tis late, and I fear the cost of this entertainment may be more than my poor purse will permit to me."

"Why, there," answered Robin, as if perplexed, "this is a matter in which I am in your lordship's hands, for never have I played tavern-keeper till now."

"I will take the reckoning, friends," said Little John, interposing. He went into the shade and brought out the bishop's steed, then unfastened from the saddle a small bag. Someone gave him a cloak; and, spreading it upon the ground, Little John began to shake the contents of the Bishop's moneybag upon it.

Bright golden pieces tumbled out and glittered in the pale moonlight;

while my lord of Hereford watched with wry face. Stuteley and Warrenton counted the gold aloud.

"Three hundred and two pennies are there, Master," cried Stuteley. "Surely a good sum!"

" 'Tis strange," said Robin, musingly, "but this is the very sum that I was fain to ask of our guest."

"Nay, nay," began the Bishop, hastily, "this is requiting me ill indeed. Did I not deal gently with your venison, which after all is much more the King's venison than yours? Further, I am a poor man."

"You are the Bishop of Hereford," said Robin, "and so can well afford to give in charity this very sum. Who does not know of your hard dealings with the poor and ignorant? Have you not amassed your wealth by less open but more cruel robbery than this? Who speaks a good word for you or loves you, for all you are a Bishop? You have put your heels on men's necks; and have been always an oppressor, greedy and without mercy. For all these things we take your money now, to hold it in trust and will administer it properly and in God's name. There is an end of the matter, then, unless you will lead us in a song to show that a better spirit is come unto your body. Or mayhap you would sooner trip a measure?"

"Neither the one nor the other will I do," snarled the Bishop.

Robin made Stuteley a sign and Will brought his master a harp: whereupon Robin sat himself cross-legged beside the fire and twanged forth a lively tune.

Warrenton and most of the men began forthwith to dance; and Stuteley, seizing the Bishop by one hand, commenced to hop up and down. Little John, laughing immoderately, grasped the luckless Bishop by the other hand, and between the two of them my lord of Hereford was forced to cut some queer capers.

The moon flung their shadows fantastically upon the sward, and the more their guest struggled the more he was compelled to jump about. Robin put heart into his playing, and laughed with the loudest of them.

At last, quite exhausted, the Bishop sank to the ground.

Little John seized him then like a sack of wood, and flung him across the back of his horse. Rapidly they led the beast across the uneven ground until the highroad was reached, the whole of the band accompanying them, shouting and jesting noisily. The Bishop of Hereford, more dead than alive, was then tied to his horse and the animal headed for Nottingham.

" 'Tis the most and the least that we can do for him," said Robin, gleefully. "Give you good night, lording! A fair journey to you! Deliver our respectful homage to Master Monceux and to the rest of law-abiding Nottingham! Come now, Little John, you have borne yourself well this day; and for my part I willingly give the right to be of this worshipful company of free men. What say you, friends all?"

The giant was admitted by acclamation, and then all went back noisily into that hiding place in Barnesdale which had defied both the ferret eyes of lean-faced Simeon Carfax and the Norman archer Hubert.

The Sheriff of Nottingham learned next day that Sherwood had not been purged of its toll collectors, as he had so fondly hoped.

CHAPTER 18

FTER THE ADVENTURE with the good Bishop, Robin and his men waited in some trepidation for a sign from Nottingham.

However, several weeks passed without any untoward incident.

The fourth week after my lord of Hereford's despoilment a quarrel broke out betwixt Stuteley and Little John; and these two hotheaded fellows must needs get from words to blows.

In the bouts of fencing and wrestling Little John could hold his own with all; but at quarterstaff Stuteley could, and did, rap the giant's body very shrewdly. After one bout both lost their temper: and Robin had to stay them by ordering Stuteley to cease the play.

This was in the forenoon. Later on, chance threw Little John and Stuteley into a fresh dispute. It happened just before dusk; the two of them from different parts of the wood had stalked and run to earth the same stag. Little John had already drawn his bow when Stuteley espied him. At once the little esquire called out that no one had the right to shoot such a deer but Robin of Locksley, his master. Little John scoffed at this, and flew his arrow; but between them they had startled the stag and it bounded away. Little John was furious with Stuteley, and the noise of their quarrelling brought Robin again between them. This time young Robin spoke his mind to Little John, saying that he was sorry that Master John Little Nailor had ever come into their free band.

" 'Tis not free at all!" cried Little John, raging. " 'Tis the most galling of service. Here I may not do this nor that. I'll stay no more in Barnesdale, but try my fortunes with your foes."

He flung himself away from them, and when the roll was called that night, the name of Little John evoked no response.

Robin was vexed at this, and saw that they must come to some agreement if they would keep the company alive. He talked with Warrenton and Much and some of the others, and they all pressed him to assume the captaincy by right of his skill with the bow. They decided between them to have a full council on the morrow and come to a decision: for without a captain they were as a ship without a rudder.

The early morning found Robin walking thoughtfully in the greenwood. He hoped that he might discover Little John returning to them, repentant. He had taken a strange liking to this great giant of a man.

As he walked, he drew insensibly toward the highroad; but had not nearly reached it when he came upon a herd of deer feeding peacefully in a glade. Robin got his bow ready. Before he could fit a shaft to it, however, one of the finest beasts fell suddenly, pierced by a clever arrow.

Immediately he thought that Little John had indeed returned; and was about to emerge from his hiding place, when a handsome little page ran gleefully towards the dying buck from the other side of the glade. This was plainly the archer; and Robin, after a swift glance of surprise, moved out upon him. "How dare you shoot the King's beasts, stripling?" asked Robin, very severely.

"I have as much right to shoot them as the King himself," answered the page, haughtily, and by no means afraid. "And who are you who dares to question me?"

His voice stirred Robin strangely; yet he could fit no memory properly to it. The lad was very handsome, slim, dark-haired, and with regular features.

"My name is my own," said Robin to him, "and I do not like your answering of a plain question. Keep a civil tongue in your head, boy, or you will one day be whipped."

"Not by you, forester," cried the page, pulling out a little sword. "Put up your hands, or draw your weapon. You shall have such answering now as you can understand."

He flourished his point valiantly; and Robin saw nothing for it but to draw also. The page thereupon engaged him quite fiercely; but Robin soon perceived that the lad was no great master of the art of fencing.

Still, he played prettily, and to end it Robin allowed himself to be pricked on the hand. "Are you satisfied, fellow?" said the page, seeing the blood rise to the wound.

"Ay, honestly," said Robin, "and now, perhaps, you will grant me the privilege of knowing to whom I owe this scratch?"

"I am Gilbert of Blois," replied the page, with dignity; and again his voice troubled Robin sorely. He was certain that he had met with it before; but this name was strange to his ears.

"What do you in the greenwood at such an hour, good Master Gilbert?"

The lad considered his answer, whilst wiping his sword daintily with a pretty kerchief. The action brought a dim confused memory to Robin—a blurred recollection of that scene discovered in the wizard's crystal troubled his thoughts. Meanwhile the little page had condescended to glance upon him.

"Forester," said he, somewhat awkwardly, "can you tell me—do you know aught of one Robin o' th' Hood? He is believed to have been killed in the fall o' last year, and truly they brought a body into Nottingham. He was a merry youth."

"This is brother to my Marian!" cried Robin, inwardly. "Ay, for sure, 'tis the lad Fitzwalter, and no Gilbert of Blois. Yet Warrenton did not tell me that there was a brother."

He replied to the page. "Did not this fellow, this Robin, have other name? Robin o' th' Hood—why, all of them wear their capes and hoods nowadays—how can such a man as I know him whom you seek, to say whether he be dead or alive?"

"Forester, he was much like to you; but he had no beard, nor was he quite so uncouth as you. I mean no offence. I saw him but twice; but he seemed a lovable fellow. I remember that some called him Robin of Locksley."

"I knew him right well," said Robin, in decided tones. "Come with me, Master Gilbert, and you shall hear of him."

"He lives, then?" The page's blue eyes glistened happily.

"Did your—sister send you, Master Gilbert?" asked Robin, with his heart in his mouth.

The boy gave him a puzzled stare. "My sister—who told you that I had a sister?" Then, changing his policy with swift intuition: "Ay, my sister did send me to find the man. Bring me to him."

"Follow me, Master Gilbert of Blois," cried Robin. So Marian had remembered him. It was a happy morning, indeed!

"This poor stag," began the page, pointing to it. "I wish now that I had not slain it."

" 'Tis one of the King's deer," observed Robin, grave again, "and you may be hanged for the killing of it. What put so desperate a business into your mind, friend?"

"I—to tell truth, had a notion to be made outlaw, like—like unto Master Robin, in short," said the page. "But I did not know that they might hang me for't." He made a grimace.

Robin went up to the beast and drew out the boy's arrow. Then he stuck one of his own peacocked shafts into the wound. "Now you are safe, Gilbert," said he, smiling. "Take the arrow, and keep it in your quiver until we can dispose of it. I leave my mark upon the buck—my fellows will find and deal with it."

They walked together into Barnesdale, and Robin showed the boy their hiding place and presented him to the rest. He asked that he might become one of their company, and all agreed. So he took the vow fervently, and was given Little John's place for the nonce.

Robin asked them not to mention him by name, wishing to know more of Master Gilbert's plans ere disclosing himself. The boy was full of chatter, and had news for them, too. He gave them the sequel to the Bishop's adventure, and told how my lord of Hereford had come into Nottingham in parlous state—more dead than alive: how he had lain prostrate upon a sickbed in the Sheriff's house for the best part of three days: how, having briefly recovered, he had made a full statement of his experiences, and had cursed the greenwood men with bell, book, and candle: how he had sworn that he they thought to be dead—Robin of Locksley—was very much alive and full of wickedness.

"Master Monceux, whom I have no cause to love," continued Gilbert, in quick speech, "has bidden his archers and men to assemble, and has promised a round sum for the head of each greenwood man, such as I perceive you all to be, and since I am now of your company, friends, I suppose my head is worth as much as Master Robin's or any of yours? Which of you is Robin o' th' Hood? I fain would look upon a man who can recover from death so valiantly."

Berry and Much were, both together, preparing to point to Robin, forgetting their promise. Robin gave them a quick glance of warning. "Come, friends, let us to breakfast," he cried, rising. "I am sharp set, and soon we shall be hearing from the Sheriff's men, no doubt. Let us fortify ourselves withal."

All that morning went by, however, without further event. The greenwood men became uneasy. All felt that some terrible plot was being hatched against them, and their unrest grew with the day. Had Little John turned traitor? And was he now preparing their enemies?

Soon after noon Robin called them together into the biggest of their caves. He offered to disguise himself and go into Nottingham—there to learn the best or worst.

Many of them made objection to this, saying that one had no reason to take more risk than another in this free company. Robin persuaded them at last to his own way of thinking, as he had already done before. Unconsciously they were coming to regard him as their head, although any one of them would have fiercely denied this in open council. Robin took a staff, and hurried towards the highroad for the second time that day.

He had another reason for making this adventure: the fond hope of seeing Mistress Marian. Her brother—for so he felt sure this young Gilbert must be—had stirred afresh in Robin's heart all his warm love for her. He wondered what he could say to her.

Why, he could tell her of Gilbert's escapade! Of course she must be trembling at this very moment for the boy and thinking him in a thousand dangers! It was another duty added to that which Robin bore towards the company of freemen. He doubled and trebled his pace.

Suddenly, as he came upon the road, the sound of a lusty singing struck upon his ears. Robin became aware of a shabby cart and a bushy figure leading a bony horse, and the smell of fresh-killed meat. It was an honest butcher on his way to market in Nottingham.

"Give you good day, friend," called Robin to him. "You have a fair load there—what is your price for it?"

"Why, truly, beggar, a bigger price than you will pay, I fear," answered the butcher, in the middle of his song.

"I will give you four pieces of gold for it," said Robin.

The butcher stopped his thin horse at once. "Take the reins then, Master," cried he, joyfully; "the cart and all is yours for the sum! Pay it to me, and I will go back into Locksley forthwith."

"Do you come from that village, friend?" asked Robin, as he paid over the gold, "and are you not afraid to ride through Sherwood alone?"

"You are strange to this country, friend," answered the jolly butcher, "else you would know that now our Sherwood is free as air to all men. The outlaws and wicked ones have all been driven out of it."

"Is this indeed so? Truly I am rejoiced at the news. And Locksley—is not the Ranger there now dead, and his house burned? I do misremember his name."

"Master Fitzooth is dead and lieth in Locksley ground. Also his son, wild Robin, is no more. He gave himself early to the outlaw band, and was slain. We have a new Ranger at Locksley, one Adam of Kirklees, a worthy man and a generous. I thank you for your gold: now take my load and may fortune befriend you."

"God rest you, butcher," answered Robin, laughing, as the other turned on his heel and began his song once more. "Stay—stay—I have a thought," he called out after the butcher. "How can I sell meat in this garb?"

The other paused and scratched his head doubtfully.

"I'll give you another piece for your clothes, friend," said Robin, persuasively. "Is it a bargain?"

"I'll do it for another piece," said the butcher. "Ay, and think myself fortunate. This is a very happy day, for sure. Strip yourself, beggar; and you can hand your purse over to me with the rags if you care to!"

Robin laughed again and shook his head. The change was soon effected, and within ten minutes he was leading his spavined horse toward the gates of Nottingham. In the distance he could hear the butcher's loud song losing itself in the forest sounds.

He smeared his face with grease and earth and rubbed his hair awry ere daring to enter the city. Boldly he led his shuffling horse to the market and there took up his place. He had no notion of the price to ask, and the folk, finding him so foolish and easy a man, soon began to crowd about the cart.

Robin gave as much for a penny as the other butchers did for five or six when his customer was poor. If he seemed to be a prosperous citizen who would buy, Robin had quite another price for him.

The butchers about him could not quite understand these novel methods; but they saw with envy that the harebrained fellow was selling all his meat. His loud voice and foolish gestures made them think him some crazy loon who had slipped off with his good man's cart. They entered into conversation with him, and found his witless speech most entertaining.

They had all been bidden to a supper in the Sheriff's buttery that night, this being holiday time; and they begged Robin to join with them, hoping to have no little amusement from him. With a vacant stare he agreed to eat the Sheriff's mutton.

All the time he had sharp eyes and long ears; but could find out nothing of the Sheriff's plans, nor happen on sight of Mistress Fitzwalter. When they were sitting down to the supper in Monceux's buttery he perceived towering high amongst the Sheriff's servants the figure of Master Little John.

"So, friend, my visit here has not been vain," thought Robin, grimly. "Now we shall see and hear things, no doubt." He settled himself to an attack upon the viands, and played his part with the Sheriff's ale, not forgetting to keep up the attitude of foolishness he had adopted in the market.

The laughter grew long and loud, and presently the Sheriff himself came down. He made them a speech and gave a toast. My lord of Hereford, looking very pale and limp, also came into the buttery for a space and made them a Latin grace.

Then Monceux told them, with bristling eyebrows, how he had been instructed by the Bishop of Hereford that the pestilent evil bands whose power had once been broken had re-formed in Sherwood. The Sheriff restated the reward to be given for the head of any malefactor and disturber of their laws, as ordered by Prince John; and said further that in a few days he was going to despatch his men into and about the forest to satisfy the Bishop. "Whilst I am preparing my fellows, there is a chance for all honest citizens and burgesses to earn a fair sum. My lord of Hereford will add his reward to the man who shall recover his money to him, or part of it; and I will give such man freedom from all taxes and levies," added the Sheriff, importantly.

Robin wondered whether Little John had spoken of the company. While he was eyeing darkly the burly figure of Master Nailor, the latter came over to him under a pretence of filling Robin's glass.

"By my skin, Locksley," whispered the giant into his startled ear, "this is a foolish adventure! Your head is as good as off your shoulders in this place. Hasten to leave it soon as you can, for fear the Bishop may know you as I have done."

Robin only stared in his new half-vacant manner. Little John moved away to another part of the room. Hard questions formed themselves in Robin's mind—how had Little John known him? Stranger still, why did not my lord of Hereford recognize Master John Little Nailor? He had been foremost in the business with the Bishop. Robin recollected, all at once, that when the Bishop had briefly come in to bless the supper, Little John had gone out hurriedly with some dishes.

That was it, no doubt; but a mystery still remained. Robin decided to pierce it ere the night was done. Some of the guests were far gone in their cups already; and Monceux had given over the buttery to the butchers for the night. "I'll stay here then," decided Robin; and, pretending to be suddenly overcome by the strong ale, he tumbled himself down upon the rush-strewn floor.

He set up a great snoring, until Little John, taking him by the heels, dragged him through the kitchen into a little larder, and there shut the door on him. "Lie there, nasty pig," cried Little John from outside with disgusted air, for his fellow servants to note. "Lie there in a clean sty for once; and if you grunt again I will surely souse you under the pump!" At this threat Robin's snores abated somewhat in their violence.

"*I* would drop him into the river forthwith," spoke a harsh voice, startling Robin into fierce astonishment. There was no mistaking those tones: so cruel, so false, so malicious. "Roger and Micah—Micah and Roger." One of these two villains it was of a surety! But Robin had seen them both slain on the day of that battle wherein poor Will of Cloudesley had perished.

Trembling with amazement, he cautiously got upon his knees and peeped through the keyhole. In the flagged kitchen, amidst the reek of hot foods and disordered dishes, were two men—one of them Little John. The other was dressed as a cook, and as he turned his face towards the light of the fire Robin knew him for one of the two traitor outlaws. He had changed little.

Little John answered his remark over his shoulder: "You would do many a rash thing, Roger, if you could," was all he said; but he spoke in sneering tone.

"Ay, marry; and one thing I would do, right instantly, dear gossip," said Roger, busying himself with the dishes. Robin saw that they shone like gold in the ruddy light of the fire. "I would not have *you* as helpmate in this kitchen had I the ordering of matters. Big hands and heavy hands and thieving hands. Ah, I need not be wizard to know them when I see them!"

"You shall feel them, little Roger," said Little John, very angry. And he soundly cuffed the cook about the head. Roger snarlingly drew back and snatched up a dish. Full viciously he flung it at Little John, and after it another and another.

The first struck the giant's shoulder and fell clattering upon the red tiles. The second dish struck Little John as he recoiled and cut his forehead and head. Blood ran down instantly over his cheek. The third smashed itself against the wall harmlessly. Drawing in his breath, Little John commenced a long chase of his foe, who had raced off to the other side of the table.

Neither man spoke, but each eyed the other warily. Anger shone on one face, jealous hate upon the other. They moved round and round the table carefully.

There were knives in plenty upon it; and every now and again Roger would seize one and fling it hurriedly at his enemy. Little John ruthlessly followed him, without flinching or abating his set purpose by one jot.

At last he made a dart upon Roger and the chase grew furious. Dishes, plates, covers, pots and pans—all that came in the way of them went flying. The noise was awful; then suddenly ceased—for Little

John had grasped his prey by the short skirt of his tunic. In another second of time Roger was secured, fluttering, cursing, and green with a sick terror.

Little John lifted him up bodily and flung him with all his strength against the wall of the kitchen. He rebounded from the wall to the dresser; and in convulsive agony gripped hold of those utensils near him. All fell, with reverberations of sound, downward with him to the ground. There Roger lay still—save for a slight and hideous twitching of his mouth.

Little John opened the door to Robin. "Hasten—hasten away from here, soon as you can. There is danger and death."

"And you?"

"I shall escape. I have a story for them." Little John suddenly pushed Robin back into the larder. " 'Tis too late: be silent on your life."

Some servants, alarmed by the din, entered. They found Little John, the new kitchen drawer, bending in consternation over the lifeless form of the cook. "Run, run," cried he, scarce glancing at them. "Here is Roger the cook suddenly dying. His brain has given way. See how the foam flecks upon his lips. Get me water for him. Or stay, help me carry him to his bed."

Little John picked him up tenderly and with a face full of seeming concern. The others, aghast at the mere thought of touching a madman, shrank back. The giant carried the unconscious Roger out of the kitchen.

The servants came and busied themselves in restoring the kitchen to order. One of them opened the larder; but Robin had laid himself full length upon the top shelf. So he was not discovered.

The night wore on and most of the servants went yawningly to bed. Little John returned, telling the few who remained that the cook was recovered from his fit; but was still delirious and unsafe. "I will bank the fire and sleep here, so that I may be able to go to him," continued Little John, with a kind air. "By my wits, but he did mightily scare me when first the distemper showed in him. He sliced me with the spit. See how my head is cut, and my cheek shows you how his horrid teeth did meet in my flesh."

"Did he indeed bite you, Master Nailor?"

At last he made a dart upon Roger and the chase grew furious. Dishes, plates, covers, pots and pans— all went flying.

"By my bones, he bit and tore me like a wild beast. But since I am so big and not fearful of him I will e'en watch him through the night, unless you choose to do service, Mickleham?"

Mickleham swore roundly that he would not.

"Then get you gone, gossip," said the giant, busying himself with the fire. " 'Tis late; and my lord of Hereford has business abroad at an early hour."

He bade Robin go back into the buttery and stay there until dawn, there being no chance of escape out of the castle at this hour. "Play your part, Locksley, and avoid the Bishop's eyes—even as have I. We may meet on the morrow."

"You have not betrayed us, Little John?"

"Roger the cook was to have sold you. Therefore have I quietened him for the nonce. Here's my hand on it, Locksley: that Little John is loyal. But I do not love Stuteley yet."

"It will come in time," answered Robin, sleepily. "You are both sound fellows. Give you good night, honest John. I'll sleep none the worse for my pillow." He stretched himself amid the trampled rushes of the buttery, and laid his head upon the prone body of one of the sleeping butchers. Full a dozen of them had fallen into slumber to the Sheriff's rush-bottomed buttery floor.

Little John went back to the kitchen and there carefully and silently collected Master Monceux's gold plate. He put it all into a stout sack, tied it up, and waited patiently for dawn.

CHAPTER 19

ROBIN WOKE from a heavy slumber at daybreak. A faint noise from without the buttery disturbed him. He very quietly rose up, and, picking his way across the room, came to the entrance to the kitchens. He opened one of the doors and found a passage, grey-lit by the first gleam of dawn.

At the end of it was the figure of a man. His height revealed him for Little John. Over his shoulders was a short sack.

Seeing Robin, he beckoned to him; then whispered his plans. But Robin did not intend to leave Nottingham so soon.

"Go, Little John, and take that which is in your sack——"

"I shall bring it to you, gossip," spoke Little John, in a muffled voice: "to your haunts in Barnesdale. You shall see who is the better servant—Stuteley or myself. Here have I the Sheriff's plate——"

An audacious notion flashed upon Robin.

"Take it to our cave in Barnesdale, honest John," said he, swiftly, indicating the sack, "and, harkee; I will follow later with such a guest as never our greenwood has carried. Lay out a royal feast and kill one of the fattest bucks. Take my dagger in token to them that I have sent you."

"Who will you bring with you, gossip? Not my lord of Hereford?"

"I will bring Monceux himself," said Robin, boldly. "Leave the business in my hands. Go now, if you know a safe road from out of this place."

"I have a friend at the gate who will ask me no questions," answered Little John, softly. "But you?"

"My wit shall lead me out from Nottingham," Robin told him.

Little John let himself out by one of the postern doors, and found means to convey the Sheriff's plate through the streets. Afterwards when he reached the gate, he continued to win his passage by pure statesmanship, pretending that he had been sent out at that strange hour to snare young rabbits for his lord's breakfast!

Meanwhile, Robin returned to the buttery, and waited for events to shape themselves. Ere long the butchers began yawning and quarrelling betwixt themselves; and Robin artfully persuaded them, by setting one against the other, to a free fight.

The servants separated them, and in anger bade them all begone. Robin besought them to let him stay, saying that he wished an audience with my lord the Sheriff.

"Out upon you, pestilent fellow!" cried one of the servants. "You scum of the earth! This comes of hobnobbing with such rascals. Go hence quickly, with your fellows, or we will break all your bones."

So were they all bustled out into the cold streets, and Robin, in his butcher's smock, went back, as if very crestfallen, to his empty cart and lean horse.

In due season the servants found that the Sheriff's new kitchen hand was gone, and with him the gold plate. Then they remembered how he had been found with the cook.

Roger was plucked out of his bed, with all his bruises and wounds upon him, to give evidence before Monceux, who was in a great fume. All that spite and jealousy might do Roger performed with gusto, and so fixed the blame upon Little John that no one else was even suspected.

Roger would have now spoken as to Barnesdale, and betrayed the secret caves to the Sheriff; but he had once before persuaded them to search the cave near Gamewell, with ill results.

"Enough of these tales," snarled the Sheriff; "keep them for the Bishop's ears. *I* am concerned for my plate; and will recover it ere I put forth on any other enterprise."

He sent out his archers and men-at-arms, with such an incoherent description of Little John that near all the tall men of Nottingham were brought under arrest. The gatekeeper who had been so foolish as to open to Little John became so fearful of the Sheriff's anger that, when they questioned him, he vowed by all the saints that he had clapped eyes on no such fellow in his life.

Monceux, getting more and more enraged, chanced at last upon the butchers. He bade them all to be brought before him.

Small comfort did he gather from any, least of all from Robin, who behaved in so foolish a manner before the great man that all who had not believed him crazy before were now well sure of it.

He would persist in talking to the irate lord of his own affairs: how he had just inherited a farm with many head of cattle—such beasts! how he had sold some of them in the market on the previous day for large moneys; how he intended to always sell at Nottingham, since there the people were so rich and generous.

"I have full five hundred and ten horned beasts upon my land that I will sell for a just figure," said Robin. "Ay, to him who will pay me in right money will I sell them for twenty pieces. Is that too much to ask, lording?"

Monceux, in the midst of his frenzy, suddenly quieted down. This was the idiot butcher of whom people had been chattering. No use to bluster and threaten him.

Five hundred and ten fat beasts for twenty pieces! Was ever such a fool? "I'll buy your beasts of you, butcher," said Monceux, "and will give you twice the money you ask."

At this Robin was quite overcome, and fell to praising him to the skies. For the moment the missing plate was forgotten.

"Drive in your beasts, butcher," said Monceux.

"They are but at Gamewell, Excellence," said Robin; "not more than a mile beyond it at most. Will you not come and choose your own beasts? The day is fine."

The Sheriff dismissed all but Robin, in order that they might settle it quietly. If he did not close upon this bargain straightway it would be lost to him.

After some hesitation, "I will go with you, butcher," spoke Master Monceux. After all, what had he to fear? Surely no man, be he ever so wicked and desperate an outlaw, would *dare* to lay hands upon the Sheriff of Nottingham!

Monceux had all along suspected the Bishop of Hereford's story.

There were no robbers in Sherwood now—the Bishop had invented the tale in order to cover up some disgraceful carousal, and had bribed his men. It had been a plot by which my lord of Hereford had been able to foist himself and his company upon the Sheriff, and so gain both free lodging in Nottingham and save giving in charity to the poor folk of the town.

Thus Master Monceux argued swiftly within himself.

"Get ready, butcher, for," he said, briskly, "I will join you in a few minutes."

He laid a solemn and dreadful charge upon the captain of his men-at-arms and upon those of his household to find him his plate ere he returned. He swore that their own goods should be seized and sold if they failed him in this matter!

Then he affected to be going in secret search himself.

So the two of them, without guard, went off together, Robin driving his shambling horse and rickety cart beside the Sheriff's little fat brown pony.

They passed through the gate, and Monceux left word there that his archers were to follow him to Gamewell so soon as they had returned from their searching for his plate.

Robin was very gay, and kept the Sheriff amused with his foolish chattering. Monceux congratulated himself more and more.

They had drawn nigh to Gamewell, and to that little gravel pit wherein was one of the hidden passages to the Barnesdale caves. Peering irresolute through the tree trunks far off to their right, Robin spied a herd of deer.

They stood and trembled at sight of Robin and the Sheriff, preparing to stampede.

Robin guessed that they had been driven by the greenwood men all that day—that perchance Stuteley and the rest were near the beasts, in ambush. Reining in his lean horse, he turned in his cart to call to the Sheriff.

"See, Excellence, here are my beasts, coming to welcome me! Now choose those which your eyes like and pay me the gold."

Monceux saw then that he had been duped, and flew into a terrible passion. Robin cut his reproaches very short, however; and, taking off his butcher's smock, blew on his horn that short, queer signal.

The Sheriff turned to fly, but had not travelled a hundred yards ere, hearing an uncomfortable hissing sound made by an arrow as it flew just over his head, thought it better to stop. Robin had hidden his bow and quiver in the straw at the bottom of the butcher's cart. He now stood up and sped his shafts all round and about the poor Sheriff.

Then Monceux reined up his fat pony and surrendered himself grudgingly, trying to bargain all the while. "If I give you my horse, and a golden penny, will you let me go, butcher?" said he, whiningly. "Did I not treat you well last night, giving you a fair supper and much ale? This is ill requiting my usage of you, butcher."

Suddenly he saw himself surrounded by the men of the greenwood, headed by Stuteley. Robin nodded, and in a moment the Sheriff was seized and hurried away to the gravel pit, and his pony was set galloping in the direction of Nottingham with empty saddle.

The greenwood men soon brought their captive through the dangerous passage, having first blindfolded him. Within five hours of his departure from Nottingham my lord the Sheriff found himself in a strange, unknown part of Sherwood, seated amongst two score and ten wild fellows, to a wilder meal of venison, brown bread, and wine.

With a shock of surprise he saw that the hot, juicy portion of the King's beast handed to him as his share was smoking fragrantly upon a golden plate. He glanced around from the merry faces of the lawless men to the dishes and plates from which they were eating. All were of gold and very familiar.

His rolling eye encountered that of Little John's, coolly helping himself to a second serve. "You rascal! You rogue!" spluttered Monceux. "You scum of the kitchens! Where is my plate? You shall be shred into little pieces for this trick, and you also, false butcher."

"Nay, Excellence," said a gentle voice near to him, "this is no butcher; but rather Master Robin o' th' Hood, a good yeoman and right Saxon. Some call him Robin of Locksley. Let me fill your goblet, Excellence, for you have spilled all the wine."

Monceux glared at the speaker, a handsome lad dressed gaily in page's costume. The Sheriff's frown would have frightened most people, but the dark-haired boy only laughed and tossed his head in a queerly fascinating way. The Sheriff, relaxing, held out his goblet, and smiled back upon the page.

"Well done, Master Gilbert of Blois!" cried Robin, who sat at the Sheriff's left hand. "Now tell me how you discovered me, and I will love you——"

The lad blushed furiously. "I knew you from the first, Robin o' th' Hood," he answered, defiantly.

"In truth?" questioned Robin, slily, and with his own suspicions growing. No wonder he had seen nothing of Marian in Nottingham town.

"In truth—well, no," submitted the page. "Let me fill your tankard, friend. But very soon I did discover you. Is this the stag that you killed, Robin o' th' Hood?" he added, innocently.

Robin nodded; and the Sheriff flashed another look of anger upon him. "Sit you beside me, Gilbert," Robin ordered; "I am very fain to have speech with you."

Marian, with her woman's intuition, knew from his tone that she also was discovered. Yet she braved it out. "I will fill all the cups, Robin o' th' Hood," she said, firmly, with an adorable little shake of her black curls; "then will hear your adventures as a Nottingham butcher, which I see you are dying to tell to us."

The page skipped lightly from under Robin's threatening hand, and the merry men laughed loud and long. "He calls you Robin o' th' Hood, Master!" cried John Berry, roaring like a bull. For some reason this nickname tickled him mightily. He kept repeating it in all kinds of tones, and those about him began to laugh also.

" 'Tis a very excellent name," said Robin, a little vexed. "A merry name, a man's name, and a name to my heart! I do adopt it from this day; for is not Robin Fitzooth of Locksley dead? My lord the Sheriff can tell you that he is, for he has burned him. Laugh at it, or like it, friends, which you will. But pledge me in it, for I have paid the reckoning."

Little John, Stuteley, and Much rose to their feet together in their hurry to be first. The others were not slow in following them.

"Long life to you and happiness, Robin o' th' Hood! Here's fortune's best and confusion to all your enemies! Huzza, Robin o' th' Hood!"

The darkening woods echoed it back to them. "Robin o' th' Hood! Robin—Hood!"

"You will have to be christened, gossip," said Little John, with an air of importance; "and surely I know the man who will be sponsor. But you spoke just now of a reckoning; and I do see that our guest is become fidgety. Shall I tot up the bill for him?"

"Do so, friend."

The Sheriff appeared uneasy at this. "I have not my purse with me," he began, apologetically.

"How did you purpose paying me for my beasts?" asked Robin.

"Why—that is—I have, of course, a small sum about me."

"What is that sum, gossip?" questioned Little John, very kindly.

" 'Tis no more than forty pieces of gold," said Monceux, recollecting that he had named this amount to Robin.

"Is that all?"

"I have not another penny-piece, good Master Hood," replied the Sheriff.

"If that is true, then you shall pay no more than ten pieces of gold for your entertainment, Excellence," decreed Robin. "Speak I soothly, men of the greenwood?"

"The Sheriff should swear by his patron saint that he will never more molest us," said one of the company, wisely; and this addition was carried unanimously.

"So be it, then," cried Little John, approaching Monceux. "Now, swear by your life and your patron saint——"

"I will swear it by St. George, who is patron of us all," cried the fat Sheriff, vigorously; and he swore that never again would he disturb or distress them in Sherwood.

"Let me catch anyone of you *out* of it!" thought he to himself.

Then he paid them ten pieces of gold; and having done this, rose up to go.

It was already full dusk. "Gossip," observed Little John, reprovingly, "you did not hand me your wallet, but took out instead the ten golden pieces. Let me see for myself that thirty remain. Mayhap some evil person has robbed you unbeknown."

"Nay—I do not think that," said the Sheriff, quickly; "I take great care of my belongings——"

"Yet you may have been despoiled," persisted Little John; "permit me to satisfy myself and this company that you have had honorable treatment in these happy woods."

With a groan Monceux yielded his wallet, and Stuteley counted out the money in it with a loud voice; otherwise the company was silent. "There is another wallet, gossip," said the inexorable Little John, pointing towards the Sheriff's belt.

In all they counted out one hundred gold pieces. "We must add another 'nought' to the foot of our bill, Excellence," said Robin, gravely. "Be of good heart; what is 'nought' but nothing? Ten pounds and a 'nought' added to it is a most reasonable account for such royal fare. Take then this money which you first gave me; we will keep the wallets."

" 'Tis monstrous! 'Tis an enormity," bellowed Monceux, flying out. "Already you have stolen my plates, and now would strip me utterly! 'Tis rank villainy, and I promise you all——"

"You have promised enough tonight, Sheriff," retorted Robin: "away with him, Stuteley, and go you, too, Little John. Take our guest through the secret path so far as the roadway by Nottingham gate. There he may find his archers waiting for him. Be speedy."

They nodded and grasped the struggling Sheriff by either arm. His eyes were speedily bandaged by little Gilbert, and he made an undignified exit. Whilst the rest busied themselves removing the remains of the feast, Robin spoke quietly with the page.

"Since Little John has happily returned to us, Master Gilbert," said Robin, " 'tis clear that he will want his quarters again. So I must move you."

"It matters not, Robin."

"You are over young to consort with such wild company, Gilbert," Robin continued; "and so I will take you to a safe asylum, unless, of course, you would sooner return into Nottingham."

"I have now no real home in Nottingham," said Marian, frankly. "My father has gone to London to find us a home there. He has been offered a post in the King's household. So soon as he had departed they sent for me to attend at the Sheriff's castle, saying I was to become maid to the demoiselle Marie. This I would not; and so escaped in the early dawn of the day——"

"I have a friend at Gamewell," said Robin, diffidently. "In sooth, it is mine own uncle, and he surely would not refuse me in this. Will you go with me, Gilbert, at once? Soon it will be night indeed."

"I'll go anywhere with you, Robin," answered the little page.

Yet Robin would not affect to recognize Marian, though his heart was thumping in his body. He led her silently, hastily, through the strange passages towards Gamewell, thinking how he should bring a welcome for the maid.

"You are not talkative, friend Robin," murmured his companion once.

"My heart is too full for speech, Gilbert," said Robin, softly then; and this answer seemed to satisfy Master Gilbert of Blois. Under the night he smiled happily to himself.

"Is this your bad hand, Robin?" he asked, presently, "the one that I did wound? Poor fingers! I am sorry now. Can you forgive me, Robin?"

CHAPTER 20

WHEN THEY HAD reached the little hut nearby the pleasance, Robin bade her stay. "I now must play Yellow Lady," said he, lightly. "She is the spirit of this grove, and under her guise I can venture near to the house. Lend me your cloak— the color will not matter on so dark a night."

"I will not be left alone here," said Marian at this, with great decision. "Not for all the Montfichets in Christendom. I'll go with you."

They crossed the pleasance side by side. Lights burned within Gamewell to guide them.

"I am not afraid, Robin," announced Master Gilbert of Blois, courageously. "You know I am no coward."

"Take my hand then," said Robin; "I like to feel that you are with me."

"Yet you have but known me a day," said Marian, trying to peep at him. Her tone was questioning and full of pretty malice.

He had a mind then to take her in his arms, but again forbore. "Be silent now," whispered he; "I must proclaim myself. I have scarce knowledge of the servants here, my chief friend being old Warrenton, and he is in the greenwood."

"Let us go back there," suggested his companion; "I am willing to risk the wild beasts and the Sheriff's wrath."

" 'Tis no place for you," said Robin. "Here you will be both safe and comfortable."

"I do not like the shape of this house," argued Marian. "I do not feel that I will be happy in it."

"It is a home worthy to be your sister's, let alone yours, Master Gilbert. Now be done with your grumbling, for here you shall stay until your father's return."

At this she made a grimace, but obeyed him meekly, notwithstanding. As they drew near to the courtyard, Robin bade her follow him cautiously until they had made a full circle of it, and crept round to the front of the hall.

By good fortune the bridge was down. Old Gamewell had no fear of the world, it would seem. They might pretend now that they had crossed to the hall from the road. Robin wound his horn suddenly and confidently.

The dogs within Gamewell began to bark and growl, and presently they heard sounds of approach. In a moment more the doors were opened and they saw a servant armed with a lanthorn and a stick.

"I would have audience with Master Montfichet," said Robin, in a bold voice. "Pray take me to him at once."

"Do you come from Nottingham?" asked the man, civilly.

"I left there this day," replied Robin.

"Follow me," said the servant, briefly. He waited until they were safely inside; then closed the doors carefully. He led them across the court to the inner doors.

Here another fellow was in waiting, also carrying a light. "These are travellers from Nottingham, desiring audience of Master Gamewell," observed the first servant.

"Your names, gentles?" asked the second.

"I am Robin o' th' Hood, and this is Master Gilbert of Blois," said Robin, at once.

They were escorted into the great hall, and there, sat beside the open hearth, was old Squire George. He made a pathetic figure. Robin felt his heart go out to him.

Yet even when he had satisfied himself in a single glance as to the identity of one of the late-coming guests, Montfichet gave no sign. His was a strange nature, and he could not forgive Robin his innocent deceit.

"Sir," said Robin, respectfully, "I do feel shame in coming before you without waiting for your word of welcome. My errand must be my excuse."

" 'Tis Robin Fitzooth!" said old Montfichet, then. "I was told that you had been killed long since."

"Robin Fitzooth is truly dead, sir. Behold in his place Robin o' th' Hood. I come to ask a service at your hands for the memory of this dead man, and in redemption of your promise given to him once in Nottingham."

"Ask it, friend."

The Squire's tones were kinder. Looking at him, Robin saw that he had aged. There were no longer signs of that fastidious attention to his apparel which had characterized Montfichet of Gamewell.

"There is, sir, a maid who, losing her father on a journey to London, hath had great trouble put upon her by the Sheriff. Monceux would persecute her, in short, and she has flown from the city. Now, I would ask an asylum for her here."

"She shall be made welcome and given full freedom of Gamewell," answered Montfichet, rising. "I shall rejoice to see her here, in sooth, for my days lack company. When will you bring her to me, Master Robin o' th' Hood, and pray what makes you wear so strange a name?"

He spoke quite in his old manner, and half-smiled at them. He glanced toward Master Gilbert of Blois. "Is this your little esquire, young Stuteley?" asked he, lifting his brows. "Truly he has grown out of all memory."

Robin felt himself to be in an awkward fix. His eyes glanced from one to the other. Marian, at last, took pity on his distress. "Good my lord," said she, with that pretty shake of her dark curls, "I am the maid for whom Master Robin pleads so earnestly. I am Marian Fitzwalter out of her petticoats and into a boy's clothes. I had no other way of flying from Nottingham, so behold me for the nonce as Gilbert of Blois."

The Squire listened, and slowly his face relaxed. Anything spirited or daring always appealed to him strongly. "You are a pretty page, I swear, Master Gilbert! Sure it will be hard for you to make fairer maid than man. Welcome either way to Gamewell. I'll keep you safe from

Monceux; I have no love for him in any case. You have fasted today, no doubt; I'll have supper brought us here."

"We have already supped, sir," said Robin, relieved to find this easy way out of a difficult business. He had the hope that Marian would in some way bring about a reconciliation between him and the Squire.

"We will sup a second time," said Montfichet. "Ho there! Bring us a pasty and a flagon! Hurry, knaves, bring us the best of our larder. Come, Robin, sit here at my right hand, and you, Gilbert, by his side. And so already it has come to this, Robin? Will not the greenwoods seem dull tomorrow?"

"Mayhap I might change them for a seat at your table on occasion, sir?" asked Robin.

"To see how badly I treat my guest? Is that it? Come when you will, Robin o' th' Hood. Tell me now, why did you choose this name? Another was offered you."

"Ask Master Gilbert here, sir—he is responsible for't. And, honestly, I do like the name—'tis uncommon. May I pledge you, sir? Here's to our friendship! May we grow old in it and ripe in it!"

"I have no wish, Robin, to grow either old or ripe," said Marian, settling herself. "Let us eat first, and make our speeches afterward. Help me to the pasty before you, and do not chatter so much."

Squire George nodded in approval. "Spoken like a man," cried he. "Robin is too full of words tonight. Ay, but I am right glad to see him here, for all that! Fill your glass, kinsman, and the lady's. Nay, look not so distressed at her; up to the top, man, up to the top! This is no time for half-measures."

★   ★   ★

In the morning when Robin came blithely from his bed—the first bed that he had known for many months—he found the Squire waiting for him in the hall. His face was grave. "I must speed you, Robin," said he; "I have news that Monceux is abroad, and will attack your company at Barnesdale."

Robin had told him all, and the Squire had neither approved nor disapproved. Working in his mind was jealous wonderment that Robin should prefer such a life to that which might have been his at Gamewell. The Squire made no show of this, however.

"I will guard Mistress Fitzwalter from all harm, rely upon me. And go, since you must. Here is our Master Gilbert—Gilbert no more. I should scarcely have known her."

Marian entered from the other end of the hall. The maids had found her a dress, grey-blue as her eyes. She bloomed like an early rose on this sweet spring morning.

"And you are going to leave me, Robin?" she said, mournfully.

The Squire had disappeared. Robin, approaching, took her hand. He looked up from it, and saw the golden arrow gleaming in her hair—that arrow which had so strangely marked the beginning of his troubles. Marian smiled, and her eyes invited him.

And so these two kissed each other frankly, mouth to mouth.

★   ★   ★

A little later Robin was speeding through the forest. His feet were light, and he sang softly to himself as he trod the springy grass.

Suddenly a sad song broke upon his ear. 'Twas a doleful song, full of tears; and Robin, in consternation, stopped short.

Along the woodland path there came towards him a minstrel carrying a harp and trailing a rope. "Marry, friend, but your harp is out of all harmony!" began Robin.

"I do not play upon it," retorted the minstrel.

"You sing a sad song," said Robin; "and I, who am happy, am put out of countenance by it. Therefore sing it not until I am far from you."

"My heart overflows with sorrow," said the minstrel, "and so I must sing of sadness and of death."

"Tell me your sorrow, friend," Robin begged, "and walk with me back upon the road. Like as not I can help you."

"I should not speak my grief to you," the minstrel told him, "for you are happy."

"One who lives in the greenwood cannot be otherwise," observed Robin. "Come, walk with me, and coil the rope."

"I had brought it," said the minstrel, "so that I might hang myself to some old oak, and thus fittingly end the wretched, misfortunate life of Allan-a-Dale."

Robin perceived that there was a story to follow. "Walk with me, gossip, and ease your heart in confidence," he said, cheerfully. "I can likely help you. Today is my lucky day."

"Know then, happy stranger, that I have lost my dear, and through no fault of mine own," said Allan-a-Dale, as they walked together. "A wealthy baron has taken my love from me, and will marry her this very day; so I have come into these quiet woods that I may kill myself, for never can I live without my Fennel."

"Is that her name? 'Tis very quaint."

" 'Tis a fitting name, gossip. Fennel means 'Worthy of all praise,' and she is the most worthy of all maids."

"Perchance you do not know many maids, friend," said Robin. "Tell me, is she dark-haired, and are her eyes sweet as violets?"

"In sooth, her eyes are blue enough, gossip," said Allan; "but her hair is like finespun gold. And she has a little straight nose, and such a tender smile. Marry, when I think upon her many perfections my heart doth leap, to sink again when I mind me that I have lost her."

"And why have you lost her, Allan-a-Dale?"

"Look you, 'tis this way. The Normans overrun us, and are in such favor that none may say them nay. This baron coveted the land wherein my love dwells; so her brother, who was lord of it, was one day found still and stark—killed whilst hunting, folks say. Thus the maid became heir-at-law, and the baron wooed her, thrusting me aside."

"Nay, but surely——" began Robin.

"Hear me out, gossip," Allan said. "You think I am light overborne, no doubt; but never should this Norman dog have triumphed had it been man to man. But who can deal with a snake in th' grass? The wretch has poisoned my Fennel against me, and 'tis she who has cast me into despair, while she is to be wedded with mine enemy."

"Does she love you, Allan?"

"Once she loved me right well. Here is the little ring which she gave me when we were betrothed."

"Enough," said Robin, "this wedding shall not be. Can you keep your own counsel? Follow me then; and on your love for Fennel, see nothing of the way in which I lead you. Hasten."

He brought the minstrel into Barnesdale woods and to their most secret haunt. Then he summoned the greenwood men and told them first of the Sheriff's plans and then gave out the grievous story of Allan-a-Dale.

"Where is this marriage to be held?" asked Little John.

"In Plympton church," sighed the minstrel.

"Then to Plympton we will go, by my beard!" cried the giant, "and Monceux may meanwhile scour Barnesdale for us in vain! Thus virtue is plainly its own reward."

"Well planned, indeed, Little John. Fill quivers, friends, and let us go. This shall be a strange marriage day for your baron, Allan—if the lady be not stubborn. You must move her, if she be cross with you. We will do all other duties."

They travelled through one of their many secret ways towards Plympton. The sun shone high in the heavens ere they had come within sight of the small square church.

Without the building they espied a guard of ten archers liveried in scarlet and gold. Robin bade the rest to approach under cover of the hedgerows. He then borrowed Allan's cloak and harp, and stepped out boldly towards the church.

A few villagers were gathered about the archers; and Robin mingled with these, asking many quaint questions, and giving odd answers to any who asked in turn of him. Hearing the laughter and chattering, the Bishop who was to perform the marriage came to the church door all in his fine robes and looked severely forth.

"What is the meaning of this unseemliness?" asked he, in well-known tones.

Robin saw that here was my lord of Hereford again! He answered, modestly: "I am a harper, good my lord. Shall I not make a song to fit this happy day?"

"Welcome, minstrel, if such you are," said the Bishop. "Music pleases me right well, and you shall sing to us."

"I must not tune my harp nor pluck the strings in melody until the bride and bridegroom have come," Robin answered, wisely; "such a thing would bring ill fortune on us, and on them."

"You will not have long to wait," cried the Bishop, "for here they come. Stand on one side, worthy people."

He busied himself in welcome of the bridegroom—a grave old man, dressed up very fine. The bride was clothed in white samite, and her hair shone like the sun. Her pretty eyes were dark with weeping; but she walked with a proud air, as women will who feel that they are martyring themselves for their love's sake. She had but two maids with her, roguish girls both. One held up her mistress's gown from the ground; the other carried flowers in plenty.

"Now by all the songs I have ever sung, surely never have marriage bells rung for so strange a pair!" cried Robin, boldly. He had stopped them as they were passing into the church. "Lady," he asked, "do you love this man? For if you do not then you are on your way to commit sacrilege."

"Stand aside, fool," cried the bridegroom, wrathfully.

"Do you love this man?" persisted Robin. "Speak now or never. I am a minstrel, and I know maids' hearts. Many songs have I made in their honor, and never have I found worse things in them than pride or vanity."

"I give my hand to him, minstrel, and that is enough," the girl answered at last. She made a movement towards the aisle.

"And Allan?" whispered Robin, looking straight into her eyes.

At this she gave a little gasp of fear and love, then glanced irresolutely towards the shrivelled baron. "I will *not* marry you!" she cried, suddenly.

Robin laughed and, dropping the harp, clapped his horn to his lips. Even as the archers sprang upon him, the greenwood men appeared.

"Mercy me!" cried out the Bishop, seeking to escape, "here are those rascal fellows who did maltreat me so in Sherwood."

The archers were prisoners everyone, and the baron too, ere my lord of Hereford had done exclaiming. Stutely and Much pushed Allan-a-Dale forward. "This is the man, good my lord, to whom you shall marry the maid," cried Robin, flourishing his bow, "if she is willing."

"Will you marry *me*, dear heart?" pleaded Allan-a-Dale. "I am your true love, and the stories they told to you were all false."

"Own to it, baron!" roared Little John, shaking up the unfortunate old man. "Tell her that you did lie in your straggling beard when you said that Allan was untrue."

"Ay, ay, I spoke falsely; ay, I own to it. Have done with me, villain."

"Spare him, Little John, for the nonce. Now, my lord, marry them for us, for I am ready to sing you my song."

"They must be called in church three times by their names; such is the law," the Bishop protested.

Robin impatiently plucked the Bishop's loose gown from off his back and threw it over Little John's shoulders. The big fellow thrust himself firmly into it and stood with arms akimbo. "By the faith o' my body," cried Robin, "this cloth makes you a man!"

Little John went to the church door, and all began to laugh consumedly at him. Even the maid Fennel forgot her vexations. Seeing that she smiled, Allan opened his arms to her, and she found her way into them.

Little John called their names seven times, in case three should not be enough. Then Robin turned to the Bishop and swore that he should marry these two forthwith. The gown was given back to him, and my lord of Hereford commenced the service. He thought it more polite to obey, remembering his last experience with this madcap outlaw.

"Who gives this maid in marriage?" asked the Bishop, in due season.

"I do," said Robin, "I give her heartily to my good friend, Allan-a-Dale, and he who takes her from him shall buy her dearly."

CHAPTER 21

THEY BETOOK THEMSELVES to Barnesdale after the wedding, leaving my lord of Hereford gownless and fuming in the organ loft of the little church at Plympton. His guard was variously disposed about the sacred edifice: two of the bowmen being locked up in the tiny crypt, three in the belfry, "to ring us a wedding peal," as Robin said, and the others in the vestry or under the choir seats in the chancel. The old baron had been forced to climb a high tree, and had been left in the branches of it feebly railing at them.

Then they all came back into Barnesdale, there to make a proper wedding feast, after which Allan carried off his bride and her maids to his own home in the north, promising stoutly to return to them in due season.

The days came and went, and Monceux began to hope fondly that the outlaws had gone out of Sherwood. On the third morning after Allan's marriage the Bishop of Hereford came bursting into Nottingham with the old baron and the humiliated guard. The Sheriff's hopes were shattered under the furious indignation of the baron and my lord of Hereford.

It appeared that they had been released from their various positions of confinement during the evening of the marriage day, and had forthwith hurried to the baron's castle. Thence they had set out for Allan's home in the east of the county, near to Southwell, a pretty place.

Arrived there, they had demanded reparation and the maid Fennel, and in order to be able to declare the marriage false, the Bishop had sent in a petition to the Pope whereto Mistress Fennel was led to place her hand in writing. Allan's answer was to tear the petition into little pieces and fling it at the feet of the messenger who had brought it.

Whereupon the Bishop had withdrawn and the baron had commenced an attack upon the place. After an hour or so of vain storming, Allan, at the head of a small band of retainers, had issued forth and mightily discomfited the baron and his men, beating them heartily out of the neighborhood of Southwell.

These matters, instigated and brought about by one Master Robin o' th' Hood, cried aloud for summary vengeance.

The Sheriff doubled and trebled the reward offered for his head, mentioning him above all others who were known to aid and abet him. Little John ranked next in point of infamous merit in the Sheriff's reckoning, for Monceux remembered his golden plate.

The people of Nottingham, hearing continually of this pother, fell a-chattering between themselves, and ere a week was out Monceux's reward of a hundred golden pieces for the head of Robin Hood was the one theme of conversation in the city.

No one identified him with Robin of Locksley—that brave misguided youth being so entirely dead to their minds—and he was variously named as Hood, Robin Hood, Captain Hood, and Master Robin.

A travelling tinker came at length upon the talk of the town. He had been sitting on the bench without the "Sign of the Sixteen Does," dozing and drinking, and at last seeking to do both at once.

Mine host stood nearby, discussing the eternal Robin.

"Folk do say that Master Monceux has sent into Lincoln for more men-at-arms and horses, and that when he has these to hand he will soon scourge Captain Hood from our forest."

"Of whom speak you?" asked the tinker, suddenly waking up.

"Of this Robin of the Greenwood," said the innkeeper, "but you will never earn the Sheriff's hundred pieces!"

Then the tinker arose upon his dignity, and eyed the innkeeper reproachfully.

"And why will I not earn the hundred pieces, gossip?" said he, with a deadly calm in his manner.

"Where our Sheriff has failed, and a Bishop also, it is not likely that a mere tinker will succeed," mine host answered. "Pay me for your ale, gossip, and go on your way."

The tinker approached and laid a heavy hand upon the innkeeper's fat shoulder. "Friend," he said, impressively, "I am one not noted either for dullness or lack of courage. I do perpend that to earn these pieces of which you speak one must perform some worthy business. Tell it to me, and you and Nottingham shall see then what Middle the Tinker thinks on it."

At this a great clacking began, so that Master Middle only came to the gist of it in an hour. He valiantly proclaimed his intention, so soon as he *did* understand, of taking Robin Hood single-handed. "Why send into Lincoln and the shires when Middle the Tinker will do this business for you, gossips? I will go into your Sherwood this very day. Give me the warrant, and I'll read it to Robin to purpose, I promise you!"

They pushed him, laughing and jesting between themselves, towards Nottingham Castle, and there thrust him into the hall.

"Here is a champion come to take your pieces, Master Monceux," someone called out. "Here is Middle, the potvaliant," cried another.

Master Middle asked for the warrant, and obtained it. Then he sallied forth, accompanied by the customers from the "Sign of the Sixteen Does" as far as the gates of the city. There he made them a long speech and left them.

They watched him making determinedly along the white road towards Barnesdale; then returned to their tankards and their talk.

Master Middle reached Gamewell without mishap; and the brisk air having revived him much, he gradually came into a placid frame of mind.

In this happy condition he encountered presently a comely youth, with a little beard and a friendly tongue.

"Give you good-den, gossip," cried the youth. "I hear there is sad news abroad. I fear all is not well with the world."

"Since I live in Banbury, good friend," the tinker replied, "I cannot speak for the world. But Banbury is always willing to listen, and learn."

"Harkee, then—this is the news I have heard: that in Nottingham town they have put two tinkers in the stocks for drinking too much ale and beer!"

"If that is all," said Middle, contemptuously, "your news is not worth a groat; while as for drinking good ale, 'tis not you who would willingly lose your part of it."

"By my faith, gossip, you are right!" laughed the youth. "But now give me your news, since mine is worth so little. You who go from town to town must come by many strange items."

"All that I have heard," the tinker said, thinking of the Sheriff's pieces, "is very good. I am in search of an outlaw whom men call Robin Hood. In my wallet I have a warrant to take him wherever I can; and if you can tell me where he is I will make a man of you, friend."

"Let me see the warrant," said Robin, for 'twas he, "and if I find it to be right I will take you to him this very day."

"That I will not do," cried Middle, readily, "I will trust no man with my warrant; and if you will not help me, gossip, why, pass on and good riddance to you."

He began to stride along the road again, and until Robin had called him thrice would not turn about. "If you will come with me to a certain inn on Watling Street, good friend," called Robin, encouragingly, "I'll e'en show you Robin o' th' Hood!"

At this, Middle turned his head, and then came back to Robin. "Lead the way, gossip," said he, at length. "I'll walk behind you. I have my stick."

Robin made no reply, but started at a good pace. He led the tinker through the forest by many devious ways until they had arrived at a little inn on Watling Street. It was styled the "Falcon," and mine host came willingly to serve these guests.

The tinker asked for ale, Robin for wine. They sat at talk for near an hour, Robin explaining much about this Robin o' th' Hood. The tinker drank his ale and listened; then pronounced his plan for taking the outlaw. This made a lengthy history, and was so dry withal that Master Middle must needs fill and empty his tankard many times.

In the end he fell asleep. Robin deftly opened his pouch then, took out the warrant, read it, and put it into his own wallet. He called mine host, and, telling him that the tinker would pay the reckoning so soon as he awoke, Robin left the "Falcon" and Master Middle together.

Having leisure for the whimsey, Robin bethought him to stay awhile and see what Middle might do, for in a way he had taken Robin's fancy.

So Robin hid and waited events.

Presently the tinker awoke and called for the landlord. "Gossip," said he to mine host, "I have a grave charge to lay upon you. In this house, whilst I did rest in the thought that you were an honest man and one loving the King, my pouch has been opened and many matters of importance taken from it. I had in it, item, a warrant, granted under the hand and seal of my lord the Sheriff of Nottingham, authorizing the arrest of a notorious rascal, one Robin Hood of Barnesdale. Item, a crust of bread. Item, six single keys, useful withal. Item, twelve silver pennies, the which I have earned this week in fair labor——"

"I wonder to hear you speak so of Robin Hood, friend," answered the landlord. "Was he not with you just now? And did he not clink glasses with you in all amity?"

"Was Robin o' th' Hood *that* little bag of bones?" cried Middle, in great vexation. "God-a-mercy, but now I see it all. He has taken my warrant and my pennies! Let me go after him, gossip; be sure that I will bring him back right soon."

"There is first the reckoning to be paid, good friend," said the landlord.

"Why, I would pay you with all pleasure, had I the means," the tinker replied. "At this moment I have but my stick and my bag of tools. I will leave them with you as hostages."

"Give me your leathern coat as well," said mine host, sharply; "the hammer and tools are naught to me."

"It would seem that I am fallen from one thief to another," snapped Middle. "If you will walk with me to the green I'll give you such a crack as shall drive some honesty into your thick skull."

"You are wasting your breath and my leisure," the other retorted, contemptuously. "Get you gone after your quarry."

Middle thought this to be good advice, and he strode forth from the "Falcon" in a black mood.

Ere he had gone half a mile upon the road he perceived Robin demurely walking under the trees a little in front of him. "Ho there!

You villain!" shouted Middle. "Stay your steps. I am most desperately in need of you this day!"

Robin turned about with a surprised face. "Well met again, tinker," cried he. "Have you found Robin Hood?"

"Marry, that have I!" roared Middle, plunging at him.

Robin had his sword at his side and tried to draw it; but the tinker was too speedy for him. Middle laid on his blows with so much vigor that for a while he had Robin at his mercy.

The greenwood rang with the noise of the fight, for now Robin had plucked out his sword. 'Twas steel against oak; brute force matched against skill. Indignation gave Middle the advantage, and he fought with such fury that Robin's sides began to ache.

"Hold your hand, tinker," called Robin, at last. "I cry a boon of you."

"I would rather hang you upon this tree ere granting it to you," said Middle, commencing afresh.

But Robin had had time to blow his horn in urgent summons of Stuteley and Little John.

In a brief space they appeared, with most of the greenwood men at their heels, and Master Middle was seized and disarmed rudely enough.

"This rascal tinker had made my bones quite sore," said Robin, ruefully.

"Is that your trouble?" said Little John. "Let me discover now if I may do the like for him."

"Not so, Little John," Robin said then. "This was my own quarrel, and I deserved all that this rogue has bestowed on me. He had a warrant for my arrest, which I have stolen from him."

"With twelve silver pennies, a crust of bread, and six little keys," remarked Middle, with emphasis.

"Here are the keys and the crust, gossip," answered Robin, smiling-ly. "And here the pennies, turned by me into gold. Here also, if you will, is my hand."

"I take it heartily, with the pence!" cried Middle, seizing the slim, frank hand of the outlaw. "By my leathern coat, by my pots and pans, I swear I like you, friend Hood, and will serve you and your men honestly. Do you want a tinker? Nay; but I'll swear you do—who else can mend and grind your swords and patch your pannikins? Will you take me, little man, who can fight so well, and who knows how to play a bold game?"

"Marry, I will take you, tinker—if the rest be willing, and you will swear the oath. But it rests not with me, for this is a band of freemen, without a leader."

"Not so, Robin," cried Little John, glancing up from close perusal of the Sheriff's warrant. "We have a leader, and you are the man! Master Monceux of Nottingham has ordained it. Herein you are described as Robin o' th' Hood, leader and captain of that band of evil robbers infesting Barnesdale and our forest of Sherwood! The Bishop of Hereford has put his blessing on the Sheriff's choice by excommunicating you. Shall we not accept Monceux's word for it, comrades all?" he added, turning around. "He has named a leader for us whom we can trust."

It was carried with acclamation, and Robin found himself leader of the greenwood men willy-nilly, for good and all. Warrenton was hugely delighted; and the tinker seemed pleased that he had helped in bringing about so excellent an arrangement. Master Middle swore the oath of allegiance in good set terms, and they all repaired to Barnesdale to call a full council and ratify their choice of captain.

CHAPTER 22

ITHIN THE NEXT few days came Allan-a-Dale into Barnesdale with his lady and her two maids. Allan had the story to tell of the Bishop's encounter with him and the baron's onslaught upon his house in Southwell. Allan explained that, although he had triumphed over his enemies for the present, tidings had been brought to him that the Bishop was plotting fresh mischief against them at Southwell, and had already excommunicated both Allan-a-Dale and his pretty wife.

"In that case you must take up your life with us," said Robin. "The greenwood is the abode of liberty and justice; 'tis *our* commonwealth, in truth, and a happy enough place to live in even in wintertime. We will find you a cave."

"There's Fennel," explained Allan, dubiously; "I do not think that she will like to live in a cave."

This presented a difficulty. So Allan went over to where Fennel stood waiting with her maids, and explained things to her. "So long as I am with you, dear heart," answered Fennel, laughing, "I do not care if I live under a tree or in a house. Do that which you think best for us."

Therefore, they came into the greenwood, and were found a cave opening from one of the larger passages—a dry and excellent home in these long summer months.

In the meantime little Midge had fallen sick, and Much the Miller wept loudly over him as he lay, pale and languid, on a rude couch of dry leaves. All the company sorrowed over this small Lincoln fellow, for he had been a merry companion, and Robin himself sought to bring him back to health with such simple remedies as he knew.

"Captain," said Much, with a woebegone countenance, " 'tis all useless, our doctoring—I am about to lose the best friend that ever I have known. Can you get a priest to pray beside Midge's bed?"

"I did know of a right worthy priest," Robin answered, sorrowfully, "but he has gone from these parts. He would have been just the one to cheer us all."

"I have heard tell of a jovial fellow who has but lately come to our parish," said Middle the Tinker. "You must know, comrades, that I was born near to Fountain's Abbey, in York, and that once a year at least I visit my old mother there. Now, I promise you, that never such a frolicsome priest did you know as this one who has come to our priory. He can bend a bow with any man, and sing you a good song."

"I would dearly love such a man to minister to me," pleaded poor Midge. "I believe on my soul that he could cast out the fever from my bones. Bring him to me, Much, as you love me."

This settled matters forthwith. "I will go to the world's end for you, if there be need," sobbed the honest miller. "Give me leave, Captain, to go in search of this worthy friar."

"I will go with you, Much, and Little John shall come also," began Robin; but now a fresh difficulty arose. All of them wished to go wherever Robin went; he was their captain, they said, and so must be protected.

In the end it was arranged that Stuteley should remain with two score of men in Barnesdale, to guard their caves and keep the Sheriff at bay if occasion arose. (In truth, however, Master Monceux had full hands just now with affairs of state, although the greenwood men did not know of this. The King was grievously ill; and Monceux had gone to London, with the Bishop of Hereford and many of the neighboring barons, under Royal command.)

Robin asked Mistress Fennel to give the sick man such nursing as she would to Allan himself; and she sweetly promised that Midge should suffer in no way by his captain's absence. Then Robin, with the rest of the band—fifteen in all—set off for York.

It so happened that Master Simeon Carfax was departing from the old town at nigh the same moment, with *his* face set nodding homewards.

Warrenton, Little John, Much the Miller, and Master Middle were of Robin's company. Also there was John Berry, the forester, and that one called Hal, who had been so much at the right hand of poor Will o' th' Green in other days.

This little company travelled speedily, and within three days they had brought themselves over the borders into the county of York.

Another two days brought them within a league of Fountain's Abbey or Dale, as some folk call it.

As they neared the Abbey Robin walked on in front of the rest and held his bow free in his hand.

Presently he came to a stream, and heard sounds of a jovial song floating towards him. He hid under a bush and watched alertly. At length, approaching the far bank, Robin espied a knight, clad in chain armor and very merry.

He sang, in a lusty voice, a hearty woodland song. "Now by my bones!" thought Robin, puzzled, "but I have heard this song before."

He peeped forth again, and saw that the knight filled up the spaces of his song with bites from a great pasty which he held in his hand. His face was turned from Robin.

Robin called out suddenly upon him, fitting an arrow to his bow as he did so. "I pray you, Sir Knight, to carry me across this stream," said Robin, covering the stranger with his weapon.

"Put down your bow, forester," shouted the knight, "and I will safely carry you across the brook. 'Tis our duty in life to help each other, and I do see that you are a man worthy of some attention."

His voice troubled Robin as his song had done; but whilst he was searching his memory to fit a name to this courteous knight, the latter had waded across to him. "Jump upon my back, forester, and I'll bring you to shore." He spoke through the bars of his closed visor.

Robin had cast down his bow; and now, without thinking, jumped upon the knight's shoulders. The knight carried him safely over the brook.

"Now, gossip, you shall carry me over this stream," said the knight, serenely; "one good turn deserves another, as you know."

"Nay, but I shall wet my feet," Robin commenced.

"No more than I have wetted mine," retorted the other. "Besides, yonder is your bow, and small use are your arrows without it."

Robin perceived then that he had been too hasty. He considered for a moment. "Leave your sword behind as I do my bow, Sir Knight," he said, presently, "and I will carry you across the river."

The knight laughed and agreed, and Robin took him upon his back. It was all that Robin could do to bring himself and his load to the bank; but at last he managed it. He set the knight down, then seized his bow. "Now, friend, yonder is your sword. I'll e'en crave that you shall carry me on your shoulders once more!"

The knight eyed Robin solemnly. " 'Tis written in the Scriptures, forester, that we should not be weary in well-doing," he observed, "so for this reason I will do your behest. Get upon my back once more."

This time Robin carried his bow and smiled within himself. He found, however, that the knight was holding him very lightly. Just as he had opened his mouth in expostulation, the knight suddenly released his hold of Robin's legs, and shook him into the running water. Then, laughing heartily, he regained the other bank and his broadsword.

Robin, with wet skin and spoiled bow, struggled back to the bank wherefrom he had first started out. He began to revile the knight in set terms, and challenged him to fight.

" 'Tis only fair, forester, that we should go halfway to each other," answered the knight, unconcernedly, "if so be we are able to fight. I will come to the middle of the stream, and if I do not find you there, I shall know you to be afraid."

Robin waded out to him with drawn sword; and there in the centre of the stream they fought together valiantly for near a quarter of an hour. "I crave a boon of you, Sir Knight," cried Robin, then feeling himself in danger of being drowned.

" 'Tis yours, forester," spluttered the knight, still holding fast to his manner of courtesy.

Forthwith Robin found his horn, and blew it somehow, all wet as it was.

"I too claim a boon," cried the knight.

" 'Tis yours," answered Robin, hearing joyfully the approach of his men.

The knight produced a whistle and caused a shrill note to issue forth from it. Even as Warrenton and the rest came leaping to Robin's rescue on one hand, twenty and five great dogs sprang out of the bushes on the opposite bank.

Warrenton and his fellows immediately sped a volley of arrows at the yelping beasts; but, jumping and leaping, they caught the arrows in their mouths, even as they flew!

"I never have seen the like of this in my days!" cried Little John, amazed. " 'Tis rank sorcery and witchcraft."

"Take off your dogs, Friar," cried Middle, who was the least surprised of them all, "else ill will befall both them and you."

"He calls you friar," said Robin, astounded; "are you not a knight, in sooth?"

"I am but a poor anchorite, a curtal friar," replied the other, pushing out for his side of the river. "By name Friar Tuck of Fountain's Dale. Are these your men, forester?"

"This is Robin Hood, come in all amity and peace from Nottingham to bring you to a sickbedside," the tinker told him. " 'Tis a sorry welcome that you accord to him!"

"I am Robin Fitzooth," said Robin, having in his turn regained the riverbank. "And surely your name is *not* Tuck, as you say."

The knight then lifted his visor, and Robin gave a cry of joy. It was the merry face of the Clerk of Copmanhurst that beamed upon him from under the mailed cap. "God save you, dear friend, why did you not say 'twas you?"

"To tell truth, Robin," answered the clerk, comically, "you scarce gave me pause to eat my pie, let alone announce myself. Do I see Master Hal, and my good friend Warrenton? Wait until I have chained my dogs, and I will give you all such welcome as this place does know."

⋆　　⋆　　⋆

They stayed with the worthy friar of Fountain's Dale long enough for them to be all refreshed and rested; then started upon the return journey into Barnesdale with good speed. Friar Tuck—for so we must know him now—said he would go with them gladly, and bring his dogs also, for a year had been sufficient for his liking of Fountain's Abbey. The place was too quiet and deadly; and although he had succeeded to these dumb and faithful friends, he had employed much time in the training of them.

Robin bethought him of poor Midge waiting patiently their return, and so allowed no pause.

They came back to Barnesdale within three days, having encountered and levied toll upon some rich merchants—penitents bound with presents for the Priory of York.

Midge was found to be vastly recovered from his sickness, thanks to the nursing of Mistress Fennel and her maids. He welcomed the friar in his own droll way, begging to be forgiven by Master Tuck for not giving him reason to perform prayers for an outlaw's soul, and offering to be shrived, notwithstanding, if the priest felt aggrieved.

Little John, remembering his own words of many days afore, said: " 'Tis a pity indeed that the good friar should have made this grievous long journey—all for naught! By my faith, but here is a notion for the use of him and for yourself, Robin. Your name is not your own until Mother Church has put it properly upon you. So therefore let us have a christening, since by good fortune we may not have a burying."

"I am the man to fix your new name upon you right bravely," cried Tuck, whistling to his dogs. "Come, we will have such a christening as these woods have ne'er dreamed of. Get me a basin of water and a book."

"Nay," said Robin, laughing, "I think that you baptized me heartily enough in the river by Fountain's Dale! 'Twill be fitting, to my mind, if now we have the feast which follows upon all christenings. Bring out of our best, comrades, and let good cheer and the right wine fill our bodies. Afterward we can hold carnival, and the friar shall show how he can use the bow."

"Ay, marry, friend," laughed the fat clerk, "and I have learned other things in this year beside that. You are wondering to see me so changed, doubtless, but I must tell you that the life at Fountain's Dale has not been an easy one. I have had to hold mine own against the earls and squires of the borders, who have sought to rob me often enough, thinking that every son of Mother Church must needs be wealthy. So I have learned to use the broadsword and quarterstaff as well as the bow."

"Father," exclaimed Hal, "you knew how to play all these very prettily when you were Clerk of Copmanhurst, though then you chose to have folks believe that naught but holiness was in you."

"A man should not boast of all there is in him," answered the friar. "But now, since I am found out, you know me for what I am."

"I am well content with you, anyway," Robin told him.

The worthy friar would not stay altogether with them in Barnesdale. He left his dogs there—save three—and returned to Copmanhurst, when the little hermitage knew him again as master. Each day he would come into Barnesdale, howbeit, to give news to Robin and hear the items that the greenwood men had for him. 'Twas from Friar Tuck that the outlaws learned much as to travellers through Sherwood ere inquiring of them whether they were rich, whether worthy, or whether they were poor and deserving of help rather than taxing.

CHAPTER 23

ASTER CARFAX had by this time arrived in Nottingham, all eager to marry his cold bride. He found, however, that this was a happiness not yet to be, for matters were in a grievous state in the Sheriff's household.

My lord of Hereford was very wroth with them all, and had sent Monceux back to his native city with much to think upon. The Bishop had taken the opportunity of laying formal complaint at Court before the King; and his Majesty had told Master Monceux that when he went back to Nottingham it must be to keep the Royal forest free of all evildoers. Otherwise a new Sheriff would be found for Nottingham, and that right soon.

Henry, the King, was near to his own end, and had become very irritable in consequence of his illness. His sons tried his scanty patience sorely with their waywardness and their ingratitude. So Monceux had none too pleasant a reception at Court, and returned therefrom with a heavy heart.

Simeon Carfax was therefore despatched into Sherwood to find the tinker, so that Middle might be whipped and put into the stocks for having failed; also Carfax was to secure Robin and the ringleaders at all hazard. To this end Master Simeon was given command of the Sheriff's own men-at-arms, and a great body of citizens from the town wards, each man having the promise of a large reward and freedom thenceforth from all taxes.

The news soon came to Robin, and he and his men retired at once into the innermost parts of Barnesdale, and secured their caves by covering the mouths of them with barricades artfully concealed behind green boughs and the like.

So Carfax and his fellows searched without avail for near three weeks, only occasionally having evidence of the greenwood men by finding the feet and antlers of the King's deer lying here and there in the forest. The Sheriff's men laid many traps for Robin, but all in vain.

Stuteley, being of venturesome mind, must needs attempt all manner of tricks upon this motley company of soldiers. He would dig a pit with Little John and Much, and hide it up with branches and earth, so that Master Carfax might stray into it and haply break his neck.

At last Carfax bethought him of a good plot. He had nigh fallen into one of Will Stuteley's pits, but suddenly stayed his men from demolishing it. He planned instead to pretend to be trapped in the pit that very night; and, having hidden his fellows all round about, he walked out boldly at dusk with but three of them, and fell a-talking loudly of his schemes for capturing Robin Hood.

He walked carelessly up to the hidden pit and with great outcry fell into it, the others with him running off then as if in deadly alarm. Then Master Carfax began a loud lament, and made such a noise that Stuteley must hear it.

Young Will came bounding joyfully to the pit's edge, and, spying Carfax therein, fell into an ecstasy of delight. He railed at Simeon very pleasantly, and made merry at the other's supposed mishap. But presently Carfax blew his horn, and shortly Stuteley found the position reversed. After a desperate struggle he was overpowered and carried off, although not without being seen by another of Robin's men. This man brought Robin the bad news within an hour of Will Stuteley's capture.

The greenwood men flung prudence to the winds and sallied forth. They pursued and came up with the rear guard of the enemy, and a terrible battle was fought. Thirteen of Robin's brave fellows were wounded, five of them so grievously as to die soon afterward of their wounds, and as many of the Nottingham soldiery also were slain.

Carfax returned to Nottingham, however—this time in some triumph. His men had beaten back the outlaws, and he had secured the lieutenant of the band, a "desperate villain, next to Robin Hood himself in deeds of violence and disorder."

So all agreed; and by dint and hard swearing soon wove a noose to fit Will Stuteley's thin neck. Monceux, in grave satisfaction, ordered that their prisoner should be hanged and quartered, within a week, in the streets of Nottingham, as a warning and example to all wrongdoers.

The Sheriff gave a feast to all the soldiery and doubled the reward upon Robin's head. Until *he* was caught Monceux could but remain uneasy, for Henry of England was a man of his word.

Robin was sorely grieved at the loss of Stuteley, and swore that he would save his little squire or die. He went, therefore, to Gamewell to discover from Marian precisely how they had arranged for the hanging of Stuteley, for she was able to go into Nottingham in her page's dress.

Marian had learned it all. "First, he will be tortured to tell the secret of your hiding place, dear heart," she told Robin, in bated breath. "Then he will suffer the full penalty, and will be hanged from a gallows with three other poor wretches. Last of all he is to be quartered, and his body flung to the people."

She burst into weeping, and sobbed so grievously that Robin was hard put to it to keep back his own tears. "Did you learn who these others might be?" he asked her, to change her thoughts and to satisfy himself that no other friend was with little Will.

"They are the three sons of a poor widow, who lives in the forest. They found the body of one of the deer, and, being very hungry, were carrying it from the forest to their little home. Someone, passing by, accused them of having first killed it, and this quarrel came to the Sheriff's ears. Master Carfax then affected to recognize them as being three greenwood men; and they have been tried summarily and found guilty, and will be hanged together with Will."

"I swear that this shall not be," cried Robin, in heat, "since no doubt I am to blame for leaving the slain deer in their way."

"It was, I believe, the very stag that I did kill," said Marian, in a troubled voice. "They have been in prison for near a month; and the beast was found outside part of the woods. Shall I not go and give myself up in their place? Since I have had this dreadful guilty thought in my mind I have known no moment's peace; but, coward-like, I do not dare to be honest with myself."

"Be of good courage, dear maid," said Robin. "We have killed many of the King's deer since the day I first did meet with Master Gilbert of Blois. For we are hungry every day, prithee, and the beasts are many. Also in this season they are very wild and ferocious—'tis like this one was killed in a battle royal between itself and another stag. But to make all sure, we will rescue the widow's three sons with my Stuteley from the Sheriff's foul clutches."

"Go not into danger, dear heart, for my sake," Marian pleaded, and she held him close to her as though she never would let him depart again.

* * *

Robin went back to his men, and they made their plans. Little John was given the second place of command, and it was agreed that upon the morning on which Stuteley and the others were to be hanged the greenwood men should risk all by marching into Nottingham to the rescue.

The dawn of this eventful morning broke bright and sunny. Robin was clothed in a gay scarlet dress and his men wore their mantles of Lincoln-green cloth. They were armed with broadswords, and each carried a full quiver of new arrows, fashioned for them during the past winter by the cunning hands of Warrenton.

They marched boldly towards Nottingham, leaving Allan-a-Dale with his little dame and six of the outlaws to keep house for them, as it were. When they were within a mile of Nottingham gates, Robin called a halt, and said: "I hold it good, comrades, that we stay here in hiding, and send forth someone to hear the news. There comes upon the road a palmer—see you him nearby the gates? Who will go forth and engage him in talk?"

"I will," said Midge, at once; "for I am used to deal with holy men."

So Midge went out from them, whilst they all hid themselves and waited. When he was close to the palmer, Midge said, amiably: "I pray you, old palmer, tell me if you know where and when these robbers are to die? Doubtless you have passed the very spot?"

"That have I, indeed," answered the palmer, sadly, "and 'tis a sorry sight to see. By the Sheriff's castle, out upon the roadway, they have built an angled gallows tree to bear the four of them at once. They are to die at noon, after the torturing is done. I cannot bear the sight; and so have turned my back upon it."

The palmer spoke in a muffled voice; and as his hood had been pulled well over his head, Midge could not see what manner of man he might exactly be. He carried his long stick with its little cross at the top; and had sandalled feet, like any monk. Midge noticed idly how small his feet were for a man of his size, but gave no second thought to the matter.

"Who will shrive these poor fellows, then, if you have turned your back upon them?" asked Midge, reproachfully. This seemed to present itself as a new idea to the palmer.

"Do you think, friend," he inquired, in a troubled way, "that I should undertake the office?"

"By Saint Peter and Saint Mary, I do indeed," cried Midge, roundly. "Would you leave them to the empty prayers which the Sheriff's chaplain will pour coldly over them? Nay, in sooth, if your heart be turned to sympathy, surely you are the man to administer this last consolation to these poor fellows."

"If it might be permitted I would dearly love to shrive them," said the palmer, still hesitating. "But I am only a poor palmer."

"Keep close to me," Midge told him, valiantly, "and you shall shrive these good fellows an it become necessary. That I promise you."

He returned to Robin and told him that the execution had been fixed to take place outside Nottingham Castle at noon. "We must hasten then," said Robin. "Go you first, Little John; and we will tread close upon your heels."

Little John swam the moat, and sprang upon the warder of the city gates suddenly, whilst he was craning his neck to get a view of the Sheriff's procession of death. The big outlaw seized his victim from behind, and clapped his great hand over his mouth. Very soon the warder was prisoner in the round tower by the gate; and Little John had slipped himself into his uniform.

Little John then lowered the bridge quietly, and passed the rest of them into Nottingham. Midge and the palmer came last of all. "Now spread yourselves about into groups of twos and threes," said Robin, "and have your swords ready when you hear my horn. Little John, prithee draw the bridge again, so that none may suspect us; but leave the winch loose, for we may have to use it hastily. Go you first, and Heaven speed thee."

Will Stuteley at length came out of the castle surrounded by the Sheriff's guards; and behind him walked dejectedly the widow's three sons. Poor Will looked ghastly pale, and marks of the torturings showed upon his skin. His face was drawn and lined with anguish.

Monceux was there, dressed out in his best; and was blowing out his fat cheeks in vast self-importance. Beside the Sheriff was Master Carfax, lean-faced as ever. They were mounted on white horses; and behind them were two score of archers and pikemen.

Stuteley, seeing that no help appeared at hand, asked, in a weak voice, that he might have words with the Sheriff.

Monceux went up to him and bade him speak out.

Stuteley said, in a sad tone: "Sheriff, seeing that I must die today, grant me this one boon, that I may not be hanged upon a gallows tree, but rather that I die with my sword in my hand, fighting you and all your men to the last."

The Sheriff laughed coarsely: "Not so, my man; you shall die instead a shameful death, and after you your master, Robin Hood, that false butcher, so soon as I have him fast."

"That you will never do," answered Stuteley, with prophecy, in his weak voice. "But unbind my hands, Sheriff, for your soul's sake, and let me meet my end valiantly."

"To the gallows with him!" roared Monceux, giving the sign to the executioner; and Stuteley was hustled into the rude cart which was to bear him under the gallows until his neck had been leashed. Then it would be drawn roughly away and the unhappy man would swing out over the tail of it into another world.

Two fellows had great knives with them ready to cut him down, and quarter his body whilst life was in it, as the cruel sentence had ordained.

"Let me, at the least, shrive this man's soul ere it be hurled into eternity," said the palmer, stepping toward.

Monceux's face grew black with rage; and yet he scarcely liked to refuse, for fear it should injure him too much in the eyes of the people. "Perform the duty quickly then, Sir Priest," he snarled; and then rode back to Carfax. "Watch the palmer narrowly," he told him, "and do you secure him afterwards. Methinks he is some ally of these rascal outlaws; and, in any case, we shall do no harm in questioning him."

The palmer had hardly begun to string his beads when Little John commenced to elbow a path for himself through the crowd. He roughly thrust the soldiers aside as if they had been so many children, and came up to the edge of the cart. "I pray you, Will, take leave of your true friend here before you die," cried Little John.

The palmer had fallen back at his approach; and stood in some hesitancy. In a moment Monceux saw what happened. "Seize that man!" he shouted to his pikemen. "He is that villain who did rob us of our gold plate, who nearly slew Roger, our cook. He is of the band—seize him; and he too shall hang!"

"Not so fast, gossip," Little John answered, with an ugly look; "I must needs borrow my friend of you for a while."

He had cut Stuteley's bands with two quick strokes of his dagger, and having wrenched a pike from out of one of the soldiers' hands, flung it to little Will. "Now, by my freedom, here's your prayer answered, comrade," cried Little John. "I have found you a weapon—do your best with it!"

The soldiers had recovered from their temporary surprise and flung themselves upon the prisoner and his would-be rescuer. Robin, from the back of the Sheriff's bowmen, sounded his horn, and instantly all became confusion and riot. In the mêlée the palmer sought to slip away unnoticed, but was detected by the keen eyes of Carfax. Master Simeon rode round with six of his fellows and caused them to seize the holy man, and bind him fast with leathern thongs.

But this small success was more than outweighed by the reverse suffered by Monceux and his men. Taken in assault at the rear, they had no chance with the greenwood men. Robin himself had released the widow's three sons, and they had not been slow in arming themselves. Some of those in the crowd, having secret sympathy with the outlaws and hating the Sheriff heartily for many small injustices, also flung themselves into the fray.

The greenwood men cleared the green square before the Sheriff's home by repeated rushes and desperate chargings. Broken heads and cut knees there were in plenty; and lucky the man who escaped with so little as these. Carfax won a place of safety for Master Monceux, and fell back slowly, with him the unwilling palmer, until shelter of the castle gates had been attained. Then the soldiers and pikemen grew very valiant, and shot out clouds of arrows, through the loopholes in the castle towers, upon townsmen and rioters alike.

Half a score of men were killed ere this day was ended, amongst them being that very apprentice who had wrestled on the day of Nottingham Fair with little Stuteley, the tumbler, for Squire o' th' Hall's purse. Robin had an arrow through his hand, and nigh broke the shaft in pulling it out.

The greenwood men, well satisfied with the day's work, commenced an orderly retreat. Little John lowered the bridge for them, when they reached the city gates, and all fell back into Sherwood in good style. Stuteley had been rescued, and walked joyfully by the side of his master. Next to him was Little John, and near him the widow's three sons. They had already asked for and obtained permission to take up a free life in the woods of Sherwood.

Two of the band had been killed by the murderous arrows of the Sheriff's fellows, and most of the outlaws bore wounds of some sort. Yet they were not cast down. Sorrow sat upon them for the loss of those two brave hearts, but for their own hurts they cared naught. The bodies of their comrades were being carried with them into the free and happy woods, and there should find rest.

"Tell me, Midge," said Robin, presently, and looking round for him, "what did become of the palmer who was so wishing to be of service to our Stuteley? He seemed a likeable old man, and I would not that we should seem ungrateful."

"I much fear me that Monceux's fellows did capture him, the same who bore off thee, Will," said Midge. "But they will scarcely do him hurt, being a holy man."

"I have no trust in either of them," Robin answered, vexed, "and I am grievously angry with you, Midge, for keeping this news to yourself. The palmer must be recovered from Monceux, and at once. I will bethink me upon some plan to this end."

They walked on in silence. After a while, "I ne'er thought, Master," said Stuteley, brokenly, "that I should see these woods again—nor meet Little John, either in quarrel or in friendship, nor see any of your dear faces again."

"By my crown, which is the hardest part of me," Little John cried, "I swear that in future you shall meet me how you will, gossip. Here's my hand on it."

Thus began the great friendship between these two, which was to last them all their days. Robin was glad enough of it; but the doubtful fate of the palmer still troubled him sorely. If he had known then that bitter truth which he was to learn very shortly he would have ridden back forthwith into Nottingham town, there to end this story at once. Life had, however, many years and queer twists in it yet for Robin Hood of Barnesdale.

CHAPTER 24

HE TIME OF Nottingham Fair
had come round once more, and again the Sheriff would give a prize.
Monceux determined to make the prize a good one, such as might tempt
any archer. He hoped thus that Robin might be lured into Nottingham.

He smiled to himself in grim satisfaction, and rubbed his hands
softly together. To tell truth, he had been expecting Robin any moment during these last ten days, and had wondered why he had not
come. The palmer should have proved a bait in himself, so the Sheriff
imagined.

But Robin only learned on the eve of the Fair the whole truth about
that holy man.

It was in this way. For ten nights had Robin waited at the trysting
place for sight of Marian; and had waited in vain.

At last doubt grew into suspicion, and suspicion into fierce terror.
Had Marian been abducted by Monceux, and did the Squire fear to
tell him?

On the night before the Fair he took courage and marched up to the
castle entrance, then wound his horn for the bridge to be lowered. Now,
if Monceux could but have known, Robin would have been easy prey.

He rushed across the bridge soon as it had fallen, clangingly, upon
the buttresses. The same old servant met him at the gates, holding it
open just a little way so that he might peer forth. Robin pulled his cloak
about himself.

"I would see Master Montfichet, and at once," he began.

"My master is in London," replied the man, eyeing him.

"Did he journey alone? Did not Mistress Fitzwalter go with him? When did they go?"

Robin's questions came all of a rush. "My master hath been gone near two weeks. He went alone from here. But tell me who you are, clamoring so noisily with your questioning?"

"I am Robin Hood," said Robin, in desperation, "and now, for the love of Heaven, give me news of Mistress Fitzwalter."

"She left here on the day after my lord's departure."

"Hath left Gamewell?" Robin gasped. "How? In what way?"

The man sniggered. "To tell truth, Excellence, she did leave us in strange guise. I have pondered more than ever upon the ways of women since the day. Mistress would have our maids make her a monk's gown, and I was bid to fashion her a staff such as these palmers carry in their hands. Then with sandalled feet——"

"Did she go forth from here upon the day of the rioting in Nottingham, when Stuteley and the others escaped?"

"It was upon the morning of that day," the man replied; "and I promise you, we have not seen her since."

Robin turned abruptly from him. Next minute he was running blindly under the night towards the city gates.

*   *   *

The Sheriff's prize had been announced far and wide. For the best archer there was an Arab horse, coal-black and worth a bag of gold, and with the horse there would be a saddle of silver and fine leather. Also a silk purse, worked by the demoiselle Marie, containing a hundred pieces.

There were other rewards for the quarterstaff and singlestick, but this year there would be no tourney.

It was a fête day, and folk crowded into Nottingham by all gates. These had been lowered hospitably and were to remain down all day. The stages had been erected for quarterstaff.

There was a fellow, one Nat of Nottingham, who was believed to be the finest player at the game for many miles around. Several had tried their skill with Nat, but he had soon knocked every man of them off the stage rudely to the ground. He began boasting then of his prowess, and called them all cowardly and the like.

A lame beggar who had pushed himself well to the front of the ring about the stage came in for a share of Nat's abuse. This was a strange-looking fellow, with very dirty ragged clothes upon him, and a black patch over one eye. He wore a beard, pointed and untrimmed, and he listened very calmly to the other's noisy chattering.

"Come up here, you dirty villain; and I'll dust your rags for you," cried Nat, flourishing his staff.

"If you will use a shorter staff than this, Master Windbag," said the beggar, quietly, and showing his stick, "I'll take all the beating *you* can give me."

With scornful laughter Nat accepted this challenge.

The beggar took off his ragged coat and limped painfully onto the stage.

They fenced for an opening, both playing well. The beggar, for all his limp and one eye, had a pretty notion of the sport, but he had the queerest gait upon him; and as he hobbled round and round the stage under Nat's blows the people laughed continuously.

Nat caught him smartly upon the right arm a sounding thwack. The beggar made as if to drop his staff forthright, and Nat lifted himself for another and crushing blow.

But the one-eyed man recovered his guard, sprang suddenly on one side, and, as Nat's staff was descending vainly, the beggar dealt his foe a back thrust so neatly, so heartily, and so swiftly that Nat was swept off the stage into the crowd as a fly off a table.

The beggar waited the full time for him to return; and then claimed the prize.

The victory of this queer unknown was popular. Nat was a great bully and braggart, and many of them had suffered insult at his hands. Therefore, when the beggar went to fetch his prize from the Sheriff's own hand, there was great cheering and applause. He found Monceux seated in a handsome booth, with his daughter and her maids, nearby the archery rings. Here the shooting was in progress.

The Sheriff narrowly watched each competitor, and glanced often towards Mistress Monceux. The demoiselle Marie had one of her women sitting near her feet, so that every movement she made might be observed. The Sheriff's daughter signalled "No," and "No" again to her father as the various bowmen took their places.

The beggar paused to watch the contest. It seemed to amuse him exceedingly.

Master Patch was thus for some minutes close to the Sheriff's tent. His patched eye was turned towards it, and he seemed to be blissfully unaware of the great man's near presence. But he had taken due note, nevertheless, of Master Monceux and his cold daughter, and the maid sitting so forlornly upon the hard ground at the latter's feet.

One of the Nottingham men, a tanner by trade, had so far been most successful, and like Nat, he began to be disdainful of the rest, and to swagger it somewhat each time his turn to shoot came round. "The prize will surely be thine, Arthur-à-Bland," cried Monceux, loudly clapping his hands together after this fellow had made a fair shot.

"Indeed, I do not think that Master Hood himself would beat me today," admitted Arthur-à-Bland, conceitedly.

The beggar heard both remark and answer. "Thou speakest well, gossip," he said, "here in Nottingham town; yet I would venture to advise thee, were this pretty place in Sherwood and the bold Robin within earshot."

The archer turned towards him. "What do *you* know, old Patch-and-Rags, of Robin Hood?" he sneered, angrily.

"I know too much of him," answered the beggar. "Once, like you, gossip, I boasted of my skill with the bow—'twas in Sherwood, whilst I was walking with a stranger who had met me very civilly upon the road. Says he: 'If you can hit yon mark I'll know you a better archer than Robin Hood.' So I flew my shaft arrogantly, and 'twas a tidy shot, near two hundred paces. My arrow struck the mark fairly. 'What say you, stranger?' says I. He made for reply such a bowshot as never I have seen before; for, having stepped back a score of yards, he yet was able to speed his arrow so cleverly as to split mine own from end to end. 'Thou art Robin Hood,' I said then, and I had fear upon me."

"What then?" asked Arthur-à-Bland, composedly.

"For my boasting he gave me a drubbing," the beggar went on, "and for my archery five silver crowns."

"Then thou canst bend the bow?" said Arthur. "Will you not attempt my lord Sheriff's prize, old Patch-and-Rags?"

The beggar dealt his foe
a back thrust so neatly and
so swiftly that Nat was
swept off the stage into the crowd
as a fly off a table.

"Marry, I would most willingly," cried the beggar, "but for my lame leg and blind eye."

"One does not need a leg to shoot arrows, nor yet two eyes. Take aim, gossip, and show us how you played the sport in Sherwood on that day."

The archer's tone was mocking; but the beggar only replied that he had already won a prize and was content.

Just then one of the Sheriff's guards approached him.

"My master would have speech with you, friend," said he.

"And so you have met bold Robin Hood?" asked Monceux, so soon as the beggar stood before him.

"Well do I know it," the beggar answered, writhing his eye in fiery glance about the Sheriff's tent. "My body is full sore yet from the beating he gave me."

"Are you sure 'twas Robin Hood?"

"That am I. He is a slim, slight man with long hair, and small, fair beard."

"If you could lead me to him, friend, I would reward you well," said the Sheriff, in malicious tones.

"I will show the place where we met soon as you will, Excellence," replied the beggar.

Monceux nodded, and made a sign of dismissal. "I will speak further with you later, friend," he said.

The beggar went back to the archer and said that now he would take a shot with him. "I may as well win two prizes as one," he continued, affably, "for the horse will help me carry my pieces."

Arthur-à-Bland was greatly incensed at this speech, and took aim with hands that trembled with anger. However, he made a pretty shot, and a round of cheering met his effort.

The beggar took the bow which one of the archers held out to him, and fitted his arrow to it with a great show of care. When at last he released the arrow all got ready to laugh and jeer at him.

He contrived, however, to surprise them once again, for his arrow was found to be a full inch nearer the middle of the mark than all the others.

They shot again and again, and at length Arthur-à-Bland lodged his shaft in the center of the target. "Now mend that shot, Master Patch, an you can," cried he.

"Nay, I fear that I must now yield the prize to you, gossip," declared the beggar. "Yet I will even do my best."

He aimed with every circumstance of effort, and flew his shaft with a loud sigh. It rose up high in the air as though it must fly altogether wide of the target, and folk had already opened their mouths to laugh, when suddenly it dropped in a graceful curve towards the mark, the steel point struck exactly on the point of the other's arrow, just where it had lodged loosely in the bull, and Master Bland's arrow came tumbling to the ground, leaving the beggar's shaft shaking in the very hole its opponent's arrow had made.

This wondrous feat of archery evoked the loudest applause, and had not the Sheriff been so foolish a man, must have awakened suspicion in his breast. But, no—Master Monceux pompously gave over the Arab horse with its saddle, and the purse of gold to the victorious beggar; and then turned to leave the sports.

He bade Master Carfax to see that the beggar did not go far away. The Sheriff did not mean to lose his gifts so easily. But the beggar was very willing to keep near to the Sheriff, and asked very humbly that he might be given a place in Monceux's household, instead of taking his horse, which was of small use to one of his trade.

"I will accept your offer," said Monceux, "on the understanding that you will take the captaincy of my archers."

With such a fellow as this in his household Monceux felt that he would soon lay Robin Hood by the heels. So he strutted to his horse, and was lifted thereon in fine self-satisfaction. His daughter mounted her palfrey, and Carfax led the beast gently, whilst the maids had to hurry over the rough stones as best they might.

The beggar gripped his staff and limped along beside the women. His roving eye implored a glance from the grey-blue eyes of the maid who had sat so uncomfortably at her mistress's knee. She moved, with downcast looks, after the rest, and only dared once peep at this strange ragged fellow.

His lips moved, making her a signal, then were shut resolutely.

*   *   *

That night Monceux kept open house and grew noisy in his cups. He swore that Robin Hood was both coward and villain not to have come into Nottingham to take his chance of winning the horse and purse.

Even as he spoke an arrow came flying in through one of the narrow windows of the Sheriff's hall, and, curving, fell with a rattle upon the table in front of the startled Monceux. Attached to it was an empty purse, Monceux's own—that one indeed which had that morn held the hundred pieces so comfortably! "Where is that rascal beggar?" cried the Sheriff, suddenly having his doubts.

"Where is my maid?" shrilled the demoiselle Marie, rushing in upon her father.

"I did not send for her," shouted Monceux, seeing it all. "Haste thee, Simeon, pursue them. They cannot be far away."

"Excellence, the Arab steed hath been stolen, and by thy beggar guest," cried one of the servants, running in at the other door. "Even now he has gained the bridge, carrying your new maid a-pillion, Mistress. None may hope to catch them on that fleet horse."

"They cannot win through the gates. After them, Simeon, as you love me. I never will look on you again if you do not capture Robin Hood and this girl."

Mistress Monceux was quite beside herself with fury.

"Alas, Mistress," said the servant, "the gates of Nottingham stand wide; did not my master order it so but this very morn?"

"Silence!" roared Monceux; and, unable to control his rage, he struck the fellow to the ground. "After them, Simeon, and take what men you will."

Master Carfax had other duty before him, however, for his gentle lady had relapsed into a screaming hysteria. They slapped her hands and poured wine between her lips, and finally her maids had to cut her laces and put her to bed.

CHAPTER 25

DAYS PASSED INTO weeks and weeks into months, and Robin Hood was still to seek. The Sheriff waged an intermittent warfare with him, scoring a few minor successes; then Robin moved himself and his men farther afield. Many of the Nottingham apprentices and other roving spirits joined when they might with Robin and his band.

Arthur-à-Bland, the tanner, who had so nearly won the Sheriff's prize, had often in these days envious thoughts for the outlaws in their free life. Anything was better, to his mind, than oak bark and ditch water and the smell of half-tanned hides. Also he was ambitious to beat Robin at his own game. By dint of perseverance Arthur had once come very nigh to emulating that masterly feat of archery by which Robin had wrested the purse of gold and the Arab horse from him. Vastly elated at this promise of success, the tanner had flung down his trade and had marched off towards Barnesdale, armed with his bow and a long pike-staff. He strode across the close turf, browning now under an August sun, and was soon far away from the highroad and the small protection it afforded. He espied a herd of deer, and prepared himself to shoot one of them. Just as his bow was bent Robin came out of the bushes on his left hand; and, not noticing the tanner, the young outlaw began to move stealthily round to the windward side of the beasts in order that they might make a fairer mark for his arrows.

"What makes you here so like a thief, gossip?" enquired Arthur-à-Bland, arrogantly. "I am a keeper in this forest, and it is my duty to stay you."

"Have you any assistants, friend?" Robin asked, scarcely glancing towards him. "For it is not one man alone who will stop me."

"Truly, gossip," cried Arthur, "I have no better assistant than this good oak-graff; but he will do all that I want. For your sword and your arrows I care not one straw—if I can get but a knock at your poll you will ask me no further question."

Robin unbuckled his belt at this; and, flinging his bow upon the ground, tore down a young sapling that was growing nearby. With his dagger he quickly lopped it into shape; and then strode up to the tanner.

"Eight foot and a half, and 'twill knock down a calf," sang Arthur, flourishing his staff still more, "and I hope it will knock down you."

Robin sparred with him for a little, and then, making a sudden feint, bestowed such a blow on Master Bland that the blood ran down his cheek from his broken pate.

But the tanner did not accept this favor without making some return, and soon was giving Robin as good as he gave. The wood rang with the noise of their blows, and the tanner laid on his strokes as if he were beating hides.

"Hold your hand," cried Robin, at last. "You have done enough, and I will make you free of these woods."

"Why, God-a-mercy," said Arthur, "I may thank my staff for that, good fellow; not you."

"Well, well, gossip, let that be as it may. But ere we continue, tell me your name and trade, at the least. I fain would know who 'tis who hath beaten me so well."

"I am a tanner, gossip," replied Arthur, jovially now, "and by my soul, if you will come to my pits I will tan your hide for naught."

"In sooth you have already done me that service," said Robin, ruefully. "But, harkee, if you will leave your tan-pots and come with me, as sure as my name is Robin Hood, you shall not want gold or fee."

"If you be Robin Hood," said Arthur, "then I am Arthur-à-Bland; and I have come to live with you and my cousin Little John, in the free woods of Barnesdale. That is, if you will have me."

"I have already given you freedom of the woods, and you shall see what welcome Little John can offer," answered Robin. "But tell me, friend, are you not that archer who so nearly won the Sheriff's horse from me in Nottingham town?"

The tanner acknowledged himself to be the man, and since Robin put it so handsomely to him he forgot all his hard thoughts about the defeat. They joined hands in friendship and went together to find Little John, who seemed right glad to find his cousin ready to join the band.

The day was spent in the usual free and happy manner. And when time for supper came round with the dusk Robin asked Little John for the name and style of their guest at supper this night. "For," said Robin, "you must have got me at least a bishop, a baron, or a knight, or some squire from the north country, to meet our new comrade tonight."

"We have no guest, Master," answered Little John, regretfully.

"Then have I no stomach for my supper," Robin cried. "Go you at once, Little John, and you, Stuteley, and you also, Much, and find us such a guest, worthy of our company, and well able to pay for the pleasure of it."

"Where may they find so desirable a man?" asked the little ferret Midge, eagerly.

"Go into Watling Street," Robin told them. "At this time o' th' year there are many people passing that way."

"May Heaven send us a guest speedily," said Arthur-à-Bland, "for I am growing wondrous hungry."

The three outlaws started off at once and in high spirits, the adventure being one much to their liking. They had scarcely watched the great highroad known to all as Watling Street (and which runs from Dover in Kent to Chester town) for many minutes, when they espied a knight riding by in a very forlorn and careless manner. One foot was in the stirrups, the other out; his visor was raised above his eyes, and his face was pinched and woebegone.

Little John approached the stranger and bade him stay; for who can judge of a man's wealth by his looks? The outlaw saluted the knight courteously and informed him that his master was fasting, having waited supper for him a full three hours.

The knight reined in his sorry steed, and glanced toward his questioner with lacklustre eye. Little John repeated his speech.

"And who is your master?" asked the knight then.

"None other than Robin Hood, of Barnesdale," Little John returned, laying his great hand on the knight's bridle. "He bids us speed you to the feast."

Seeing the other two, the knight shrugged his shoulders.

" 'Tis clear that this is an invitation which will brook no refusal," he said. "So I will go with you, friends."

When they were returned to Barnesdale, Robin saluted the knight very magnificently; and his horse having been cared for, all sat down to a plentiful supper of venison, pheasants, and various small birds.

After partaking liberally of the good cheer, the knight brightened up considerably and declared that he had not enjoyed so good a meal for nigh three weeks; and he vowed that if ever Robin and his comrades should come to his country he would entertain them with an equally worthy and honorable repast.

This was not, however, the exact payment which Robin had intended. He thanked the knight, therefore, and reminded him that a yeoman like himself might hardly offer such a supper to a knight as a gift of charity.

"I have no money, Master Hood, nevertheless," answered the knight, frankly. "I have so little of this world's goods in sooth that I should be ashamed to offer that which I have."

"Money, however little, always finds a welcome from us," said Robin, smiling. "Will you deem me too impertinent, Sir Knight, if I ask what moneys you have?"

"I have, of my own, ten silver pennies," said the knight. "Here they are, and I wish they were a hundred times as many." He handed Little John his pouch; and the big fellow soon had knowledge of its contents. It was as the knight said, no more nor less.

Robin filled his guest a bumper of wine, and made a sign for Little John to hand back the pouch.

"Pledge me, Sir Knight," cried the merry outlaw, "and pledge me heartily, for these be sorry times. I see that your armor is bent and that your clothes are worn. Tell me now, were you a yeoman and made a knight by force? Or have you been bad steward to yourself and wasted your property in lawsuits and the like? Be not bashful with me, we shall not betray your secrets."

"I am a Norman knight in my own right; and I have always lived a sober and quiet life," the sorrowful knight replied. "My father, and his father, and his father's father were all knights of the King; but, as is often the case, friend Robin, rich men sometimes find their riches fly away from them. Until within this last year I have contrived, by dint of care and labor, to live on the few hundreds of rent and the like which fall to me year by year; but now I have only these ten pennies of silver and my wife and children three."

Robin asked how his moneys had gone from him.

"I lost them through misfortune and naught else," the knight declared, sighing. "I have a son—a good youth—who, when he was but twenty years of age, could play prettily in jousts and tournaments and other knightly games. He had the ill luck to push his sports too far; and did kill a knight of Lancashire in a battle *à outrance*. To save my boy I had to sell my lands and mortgage my estates; and this not being enough, in the end I have had to borrow money from my lord of Hereford."

"A most worthy Bishop," said Robin, ironically; "I know him well."

"He seemeth to be a hard man in law," said the knight; "and since I cannot pay him the four hundred pieces he has promised to foreclose his mortgage on our home."

"Have you not any friends who would become a surety for you, Sir Knight?" queried Robin, thoughtfully.

"None. My friends have fallen away from me in mine adversity as leaves from an autumn tree."

"Fill your goblet again, Sir Knight," Robin commanded; and he turned to whisper a word in Marian's ear. She nodded, and beckoned Little John and Much the Miller to her side.

"Here is health and prosperity to you, gallant Robin," the knight said, tilting his goblet, "and my best thanks for your cheer. Would that I might make better recompense."

The two outlaws, with Mistress Marian, had now consulted the others, and all seemed to be agreed. Warrenton, as treasurer to the band, was sent into one of the inner caves, and presently returned, bearing a bag of gold. He counted it out before the knight; and there were four times one hundred golden pieces.

"Take this loan from us, Sir Knight, and pay your debt to the Bishop," Robin told him. "Nay, no thanks; you are but exchanging creditors. Mayhap we shall not be so hard on you as was the Christian Bishop; yet again, we may be harder. Who can say, where human nature is concerned?"

Much now appeared, dragging a bale of cloth. "The knight should have a suit worthy of his rank, Master, do you not think?"

"Measure him twenty ells of it," Robin ordered.

"Give him your Arab horse also," whispered Marian; "it is a gift which will come back to you fourfold, for this is a worthy man. My father doth know him well."

So the horse was given also, and Robin bade Arthur-à-Bland ride as esquire to the knight; to be good use and to fulfil his first duty as one of the band.

The knight was sorrowful no longer. He could scarcely voice his thanks to them; and was nigh overcome when time for his departure came round on the following morning.

"God save you, comrades," said he, with deep feeling in his tones, "and give me a grateful heart."

"We shall wait for you twelve months from today, here in this place," said Robin, smiling cheerfully. "And then you will repay us for the loan of the gold."

"I shall return it to you within a year," replied the knight, firmly. "So sure as I am Sir Richard of the Lee, the money shall be returned, with interest beside. Look for me in the early days of March, friends, for then I expect to have good news of my son."

"Then, or later, Sir Knight, as you will," said Robin.

CHAPTER 26

HE SHERIFF having failed to en-
snare Robin Hood, and Master Simeon having done so little better, it
became clear that a more wise person than either must attempt the
business. The demoiselle Marie had recovered from her fit of anger, and
announced her intention of showing them both how such an affair
should be approached. To this end she employed herself in archery and
won some accomplishment in the sport; then she caused Master
Fitzwalter's house to be searched thoroughly and any writings of his to
be brought to her.

Mistress Monceux engaged her fingers next in a pretty schooling,
teaching them to hold a pen as awkwardly as might Master Fitzwalter
himself. So she produced at last a writing purporting to come from him
to Maid Marian, his daughter. She wrote it simply and in few words:—

*"This to my dear child Marian, from her affectionate father, Henry
Fitzwalter, now in the Court of St. James, in London town. I send you
all greetings, and am well both in mind and spirit. I pray God that He
has kept you as jealously in my long absence from home. This is to tell
you, dear heart, that, after all, I shall return to Nottingham, mayhap
very soon, and that you are to provide accordingly. I have had tidings
of you given to me by my lord Bishop of Hereford, and now send you
this by the hand of his man, who returns to Nottingham on other
business of my lord's. I pray you to remain closely in Nottingham during
my absence.*

"(Signed) FITZWALTER, Warden of the City Gates.
"The twenty-fifth day of August, 1188."

The demoiselle Marie had made several attempts before she had succeeded in producing a letter so entirely to her satisfaction; and when she had sealed the above with the Fitzwalter arms and had addressed it, she felt such a glow of pride in it that she could scarce bring herself to part with the missive.

At length she bade one of her maids fetch Master Simeon to her. When, all delighted, he stood before her, his love handed him the note.

"Take this, dear fool," said she, kindly, "and bring it to the hand of the maid Fitzwalter. She is with the outlaws in Barnesdale, hidden in one of their deeps, no doubt. I care not how you give it to her so long as you are speedy."

"I will send it by the hand of Roger, your father's cook. He is well acquainted with their hiding places."

"That would be to spoil my plot at its outset," Marie answered, cuttingly. "Gather your wandering wits, and bethink you of some more likely messenger. Have you not someone in this town who can be trusted?"

"I have the very man for it," suddenly cried Carfax. "There is a young knight, one who hath been exiled by the King for plotting with Prince John. He is the only son of our fiery neighbor Montfichet. He hath done secret work for the Prince, and will do it again if he believes that he hath need for it."

"You are forever employed in doubtful business," said Marie, crossly. "I do not like your fiddling with Prince John. You may be sure that Richard will succeed to the throne; and then we shall see where your plottings have brought you."

"Richard hath already succeeded," said Carfax, whisperingly. "I had the news but an hour since. Old Henry of Angevin is King no more— he is dead. And Richard, *Cœur de Lion*, as the commoners do call him, hath gone to Palestine, all unknowing that he is King!"

"So you think that John may seize the throne?" sneered Marie Monceux, unconvinced. "Let it be, I tell you, Simeon. In any case we must destroy these outlaws of Sherwood or they will destroy us. If they be not exterminated by the end of this year my father will cease to be Sheriff."

"May the Lord forbid!" cried Carfax, startled.

"Ay, and we shall be poor folk, Simeon, unworthy of you, no doubt. But that is not yet. Take this note, and send it how you will so long as it comes to this girl's hands within two days."

Carfax accepted the charge; and went into the lodgings of one who had entered the town within the last few hours—none other, indeed, than Geoffrey de Montfichet, who had brought Master Simeon the startling news of the King's sudden death.

Geoffrey perceived that he might openly show himself now if the Sheriff would but ignore the dead King's decree of exile passed upon him. He was sounding Carfax in the matter, and the wily go-between was temporizing in his usual way—trying to make some gain to himself out of one or the other of them.

"If you will but carry this letter to Mistress Fitzwalter, who is with thy cousin Robin Fitzooth in Barnesdale, Sir Knight," said Simeon, plausibly, "you will win the gratitude of the Sheriff's daughter, at the least; and she doth rule the roost here, as I can tell you. 'Tis but a letter from Master Fitzwalter to his child."

"I know the woods and will take the note," Geoffrey said. "See to it that Monceux does not move against me."

"His girl will tie his hands, if need be," grinned Carfax. "Ay, she can drive us all. God speed you, Sir Knight."

*   *   *

It fell out that whilst Robin was walking alone near the highroad to York, close to that very bridge whereon he had fought with Little John, he perceived a smart stranger dressed in scarlet and silk. Just as Robin espied this gay gentleman and was marvelling at his daring in walking these woods so coolly, unattended by squire or guard, the knight deftly fitted an arrow to his bow, and with a clever shot brought down a fine stag.

"Well hit," cried Robin, who could never abstain from admiration of a good bowman. "You have used your bow full well, Sir Knight."

The scarlet knight turned towards Robin, and, taking him for some husbandman or hind, called out in high tones, asking how he dared to speak to his betters in that insolent way.

"How is one to know one's betters, Sir Knight?" queried Robin, cheerfully. "A noble is not always known by his dress, but rather by his manners and his deeds."

"Your insolence shall be well paid for," returned the other, putting by his bow and drawing his sword. Without further argument he approached Robin angrily, and struck at him with meaning.

Robin was too quick for him, however, and caught the blow upon the edge of his own trusty blade. After a few passes Robin feinted, and, catching the other unawares, dealt him a thwack with the flat of his blade. The scarlet stranger reeled under the blow.

"I find you are not so mean a person as I had thought," observed he, in a series of gasps. "Yet, even now, 'tis not amiss that you should have a lesson."

With that the two engaged heartily, and fought for nigh an hour, without either side gaining an advantage.

At length he succeeded in pricking Robin on the cheek.

"Hast enough, fellow?"

"A rest would be welcome," admitted Robin, with a laugh.

They called a truce and sat down side by side beneath a tree. The stranger eyed Robin thoughtfully; and Robin glanced back at him, with his suspicions slowly growing to certainty. Presently:

"You are he whom they call Robin Hood, I take it," said the stranger, "although I do not know you by such a strange name."

"It is my own name," replied the outlaw, "and I am proud of it. Are you not Geoffrey of Gamewell?"

"That *was* my name, Cousin, even as yours was once Robin Fitzooth, but now I call myself Will Scarlett. 'Tis a whimsey; but since Geoffrey Montfichet has a bigger price on his head than I can afford to pay, why, I have buried him under a prettier name! But tell me why you are dressed so plainly. On my life, I did not know you when first we met."

"A man should have clothes to suit his work, Cousin," argued Robin. "And 'tis a wonder to me that you should have been able to kill yon stag with such a wild color upon you. Howbeit, thy arrow was shrewd enough, and I'll say no more than to tell how well pleased I am to have fallen in with you again. Here's my hand in all true affection, Cousin Scarlett."

"And mine, Cousin Hood."

They carried the stag between them to Barnesdale; and Robin learned that his cousin had a letter with him for Marian. When Robin heard who had given it to Will Scarlett his suspicions were immediately awakened.

"However, let us give Marian the letter, and see what she may think upon it," he observed. "There cannot be much harm in that."

Thus did Mistress Monceux succeed admirably in the first part of her scheme.

★   ★   ★

Soon as Marian had had her letter she was all agog to go back into Nottingham. She showed the scroll to Robin, and though his heart misgave him he could hardly say her nay. No doubt as to the genuineness of the letter occurred to Marian: she knew her father's peculiarly awkward handwriting too well. Certainly the phrasing of it seemed a little too easy for so plain a man, yet since he had been so long in London he had, of course, acquired Court ways.

On the third week in September Marian determined to return to her old home, and take the risk of any treachery.

"Allan-a-Dale and Fennel shall go with you, dear heart," said Robin. "Why not? They can appear as your father's guests, and the two maids will help you keep house. Also Warrenton shall go as Allan's man. I can be sure that these faithful ones will guard my pretty love from all harm."

"Am I indeed your pretty love?" asked Marian, in foolish happiness; "are you sure that you would not have some other maid—to wit, the demoiselle Marie? She hath an eye for you, as I know—for all she seemeth so much our enemy. Trust a woman for finding out another woman's secret!"

Mistress Fennel was not loth to leave the greenwood. In the summer months the life was none too bad a one, but now that September mists and rains were upon Barnesdale, the young wife shivered and complained. "Hereford is the only one we need fear, after all," Allan admitted; "your old baron would never look for us in Nottingham."

"And the Bishop is in London," said Marian, showing her letter. "See what my father saith."

Therefore Robin and his men were left to their own devices in the matter of cooking and kitchen work soon as September's third week had come and gone. Allan-a-Dale, Warrenton, the two girls and their two maids, all travelled into Nottingham on the best horses that the outlaws could provide, under escort so far as Gamewell. They were secretly watched into the town, that Robin might be sure no one attempted any treachery.

It was arranged that Allan should come himself to Gamewell, and seek the Squire's friendship on some near occasion. Then he might tell the old man about Marian and how she had left his roof.

Montfichet would not be vexed with her, Marian felt. If he were, she would come herself, and coax him. Also either Allan or Warrenton would find means to send Robin news of the household, and tell him whether Fitzwalter returned as the latter promised.

So all safeguards that wit could devise were taken, and Robin, having kissed her little fingers very tenderly, left Marian with her cortège upon the road by Gamewell, and having satisfied himself that all had gained safe entrance to Nottingham, journeyed back to the caves at Barnesdale with quiet mien. His heart told him to suspect some evil plot—yet where could he find one? Scarlett, his own cousin, had brought the letter, and Marian had recognized the writing.

Oh, how dull the caves and the woods seemed without her! Tuck and the miller had employed themselves in cooking them all a royal dinner; and Stuteley tried his best to lighten the gloom. Robin laughed with them, and sought to hide his grief, feeling it to be unmanly.

But never had he enjoyed a feast so little in the free woods as this one. Good food and good company he had, but not that salt with which to savor them—a merry heart.

CHAPTER 27

THE AUTUMN RIPENED into winter. Allan found means to send Robin news of them often: Master Fitzwalter had not returned; but had sent another letter saying that he would do so ere long. They all were happy and unmolested in the city. Of the Sheriff and his daughter they had seen nothing. That Warrenton was well, and that they had gotten them a man cook and other servants.

Marian wrote little crabbed messages to him. Brief and ill-spelt as they were, they became Robin's chiefest treasures. Marian forbore making any attempt to see her love, for fear that she might be watched and followed, and so bring about Robin's capture. She fretted sorely at this restraint placed upon her by Allan's more prudent hands.

The demoiselle Marie had made a miscalculation. She knew that presently Robin would seek Marian, even in the lion's mouth. *Then* would come the day of the Sheriff's triumph.

The little house of the Fitzwalters was spied upon from within. No one bethought them of this new cook. Had Little John once espied him there would have been a different tale to tell, however.

He had offered his services to Warrenton at a small premium, saying that he had lost his last place with being too fond of his bed.

He said his name was Roger de Burgh, and that he came of good family. The wages he asked were so small, and he seemed so willing, and had been so frank as to his failing, that Marian bade him take up his quarters forthwith in her father's house.

Life passed uneventfully for them in the Fitzwalter household. It was neither happy nor unhappy. Mistress Fennel found it vastly more amusing than the draughty caves of Barnesdale; but then Mistress Fennel had her dear—and Marian had not. She was vaguely disturbed at her father's lengthened absence. Surely he should by now have determined where he would live—Nottingham or London.

The months crawled on and Christmas came and went.

Marian was still tied to Nottingham streets and Robin to Barnesdale woods. This state of inactivity had told much upon the greenwood men—upon Little John most of all.

At last the big fellow fell out with Friar Tuck, and began to grumble at everyone in turn. Robin, in despair, bade him go into Nottingham, to see how the land lay there. "If you must be breaking someone's head, Little John, let it be one of our enemies who shall suffer. But have a care, for your tongue is as long as your body. Choose a cunning disguise therefor."

"I will go as a beggar," said Little John, brightening up at the prospect of adventure. "For a beggar may chatter as much as he will—'tis part of his trade."

So clad all in rags, and bent double as though with age, Little John went forth from their caves upon a February morning. He supported himself with a stout oak staff, and carried two great bags upon his shoulders. One held his food, and the other was to be refuge for anything of note that he might find left about—such as Sheriff's plate, to wit, or a Bishop's valuables.

He encountered four fellows of the like profession nearby Nottingham north gate. One was dumb, another blind, the other two halt and lame. "Give you good morrow, brothers," said he, in a gruff voice. "It's my fortune that brings me to you, for I am in sore need of company. What is there a-doing in Nottingham since the bells be ringing a-merrily? Are they hanging a man, or skinning a beggar?"

"Neither one nor the other, you crooked churl," replied one of the crippled beggars. "The Sheriff is returned from London with his daughter, and the folk are giving him a welcome such as you will never have from the city! Stand back, for there is no room for you there. Four of us as it is are too many, and we have come here to settle who shall go on and who turn back."

"And how will you settle such a knotty point, gossip?"

"Marry, with our sticks," retorted the beggar, threateningly. "But first we will dispose of you"; and he made a fierce blow at Little John.

"If it be a fight that your stomachs are yearning for—why, I am the man for you all," Little John said at once, "and I will beat the four of you heartily, whether you be friends or enemies." Then he began to twirl his staff right merrily, and gave the dumb fellow such a crack upon his crown that he began to roar lustily.

"Why, I am a doctor, then, since I can cure dumbness," cried the outlaw. "Now let me see whether I can mend your broken leg, gossip," and he cut the first cripple so suddenly across the shins that he dropped his staff and commenced to dance with pain. "Now for your eyes, friend."

But the blind one did not wait for the cure. He took to his heels forthwith, running surprisingly straight. The other lame one ran after him full as fast.

Little John caught them after a short chase, and dusted their rags thoroughly.

"Give you good day, brothers," said he, then, well satisfied. "Now I am going to welcome the Sheriff, and, as you say Nottingham is too small a place for us all, therefore speed you towards Lincoln; 'tis a pretty town and none too far for such strong legs."

His flourishing stick spoke even more eloquently. The four of them shuffled away speedily, sore in their minds and bodies.

Nottingham was gay indeed. The Sheriff had returned from London, where he had been in order to gain more time for the capture of Robin Hood and his men. His daughter had complete faith in her scheme—it was bound in the end to be successful.

"Be patient, and all will be well," she told her father. But Christmas was the end of the time which Prince John had allowed Monceux for Robin's capture. Therefore, both the Sheriff and his daughter had journeyed to Court to see what instructions had been left, and whether they might not get the time extended.

They contrived by spending much money in bribes, and in giving grand entertainments, to achieve their ends. King Richard was away in the Holy Land. Prince John was well employed in stirring up the barons to espouse him as King while there was such an opening. There was thus no actual monarch, and none in the Court to care much about the Sheriff or Robin. Those high in authority accepted the Sheriff's bribes, and bade him take till Doomsday.

Squire Montfichet, who was, as we know, a staunch supporter of the old order of things, would recognize no other King than Richard. As a matter of fact, the old man had no great love for him, but he was, after all, the true King, and Montfichet threw all his weight into the scale against John. The Saxon nobles were also active, feeling that now was their chance to recover power.

So Monceux and the demoiselle saw for themselves that they had nothing to fear from the Court, at any rate. They had stayed and enjoyed themselves in the city, and the Sheriff was able to make himself presently very useful.

The Princess of Aragon, one of the Court beauties, had need of an escort to York. She was going there to be married (much against her royal will) to one of the great Saxon notables. This was an arrangement made by the Richard party, in the hopes of winning the Saxons to themselves, as against John, who had already Salisbury, De Bray, and the cunning Fitzurse upon his side.

The Sheriff had arrived with his train in great state, just as Little John entered Nottingham. The outlaw came in by the north gate, as Monceux, proud of escorting the pretty Princess, entered by the south. Nottingham was gay with bunting and flags, and the bells were ringing noisily.

It was a royal procession, and soon as Little John was able to join with it his bag began to swell rapidly. Many a pocket did his sharp knife slice away from the side of unsuspecting wealthy citizens.

Sports were held in the fields, and the beggar had a merry time of it. Towards nightfall his bags were both filled, and he began to think it about time to attend to the commissions which Robin had laid upon him. This was to convey a letter to Marian, and to discover how Allan-a-Dale and his little wife were faring.

Little John shuffled with his bags along the narrow streets until he came to the house. He began to cry his wares, calling out that he was ready to change new goods for old ones, that he would buy old clothes and give good money for them.

Marian and the rest had, however, gone to see the sights, for there were to be illuminations. Only Roger the cook had been left in charge, and he, having glanced once at the noisy beggar, angrily bade him begone.

Little John only shouted the louder, and the cook furiously flung to the casement windows. The beggar passed by the house slowly, still calling "old clothes," as if he had not even noticed the angry cook.

Yet Roger's few angry words had awoke sharp recognition in Little John. "By my rags and bags," muttered he, amazed, "this rascal needeth much killing!" The scene in the Sheriff's kitchen arose before him. "This time I will fling you into the river, Master Roger—be sure of it. I wonder what evil hath brought you to this house of all others! If by chance you have harmed any one of them, vengeance shall fall upon you swift and deadly."

A thin rain had commenced to fall, and so the beggar turned back.

The house was dark and silent. The beggar stopped in front of it uncertainly, grumbling under his breath at the driving rain. Just as he was about to move towards the door, the click of its latch warned him to jump back into the shadows of the next house.

A white face looked out of the Fitzwalter home, stealthily peering right and left. Little John crept farther into the shadows.

The cook came out into the wet road. He seemed to be scared and troubled. After a moment's pause he returned to the house, entered it silently, and Little John heard the latch click once more.

"Now, what mischief is in the air?" thought Little John. "Some knavish business doubtless, or my friend Roger would not be in it. By my faith, I do mistrust that man."

He went back into the middle of the road with his sacks, and commenced crying his wares afresh. Almost at once Roger opened the door again. "A murrain upon you, noisy rascal," he called; "can you not be still?"

"Ay, truly, an it pay me," answered Little John, lurching towards him, as though he were tipsy. "Can I strike a bargain with you, gossip?"

"What have you in the sacks, beggar?"

"Everything in the world, brother. I have gifts for the rich, presents for the poor."

"Have you anything fit for a cook?" asked Roger.

"I have a basting spoon and a spit."

"I will give you meat and bread—much as you can carry—if you have such a spoon as my kitchen lacks," whispered Roger.

Little John dived his hand into a sack, and brought out a silver ladle, which he had stolen from a shop that day. Roger took it eagerly, and his fingers were icy cold.

"Put your sacks down by the door, dear gossip," said Roger, after a moment's pause. "*Here* they will be out of the rain. I must go within to examine this ladle."

"Have you not a tankard of ale to give me?" begged Little John. "I am worn with the day."

"Enter, friend," Roger said then. "Tread lightly, for fear we disturb my folk." He took Little John into the dark passage. "I'll bring your sacks in for you, whilst you are here," continued Roger, very obligingly; and before the other could say him yea or nay, he had pulled the sacks into the house and had closed the door tightly.

It was very dark, and Little John thought it only prudent to keep his fingers on his knife. He heard the cook rustling about near to him, and presently came a faint sound as if one of the sacks had bulged forward and shifted its contents. "Hasten with the ale, good friend," whispered Little John, hoarsely. "I feel mighty drowsy in this close place; soon I shall be asleep."

Roger's voice answered him then softly from the end of the narrow hall, and almost at once the cook appeared with a lantern. He came creakingly over the boards, and handed Little John a mug of beer. "Your ladle is of the right sort, dear gossip," he announced, "and I will give you a penny for it."

"Twenty silver pennies is my price for the spoon," answered Little John, tossing off the ale at a draught. "Give it to me, brother, or return me my spoon. I do not find your ale to my taste," he added, wiping his mouth.

Roger opened the door roughly. "Then begone, ungrateful churl," he cried, forgetting his caution. He tried to push Little John roughly out into the night. "What! Would you try to steal my bags?" roared Little

John, suddenly snatching hold of Roger by the scruff of his neck. "You villain—you rascally wretch—you withered apple!"

He tossed and shook Roger like a rat, and finally flung him into the centre of the muddy road. "Help! help!" screamed the cook, at the full pitch of his voice. "Help! A thief, a thief! Help! Murder! Help!"

His cries at once attracted notice. The dull, dead street became instantly alive. With an angry exclamation Little John dashed into the passage, seized up his bags, and fled, stepping upon the writhing body of the cook as he ran.

Little John turned the first corner at top speed. Three men rushed at him with drawn swords. He swung his bags right and left and felled two of them. The third he butted with his head, and the man asked no more.

Under the wet driving night Little John ran. The bags sadly impeded him, but he would not let them go. He darted down a little court to avoid a dozen clutching hands, and fancied he had now safety.

He paused, drawing in his breath with a sob. The race had tried him terribly. The court was all dark, and his pursuers had overshot it; next instant, however, they recovered the scent and were upon him full cry.

Little John, snatching his bags, dashed up to the end of the alley. There was a door, which yielded to him.

Next instant he had plunged into the open lighted space before Nottingham Castle, into the midst of a shouting throng. The illuminations had not been a success, owing to the rain, but they gave enough light to achieve Little John's undoing. The beggar was seized and his bags were torn from him, just as those other pursuers sprang out through the alley.

"He hath robbed a house, and killed a man," shouted the foremost. "Hold him fast and sure."

"Nay—I have killed no one," cried the giant, struggling hopelessly and desperately. "Take my bags an you will; I was but bearing them to my master."

"Pretty goods to be carrying, indeed," said a voice, as someone turned one bag upside down. Onto the hard wet stones rolled a number of things collected by this industrious outlaw—pockets, daggers, purses, knives, pieces of gold, and pennies of silver, a motley company of valuables.

"They are my master's," panted Little John, furiously. "Let them be."

"See what he hath in the other sack," cried another. "He seemeth to have robbed our butchers also." The sack was opened, and the contents laid bare.

A sudden silence fell upon the crowd, a silence of horror and hate. Then a thousand tongues spoke at once, and Little John, frozen cold with loathing, saw under the flickering lamps a dreadful thing.

Out of the second sack had fallen the limbless trunk of a dead man, cold and appalling even in this uncertain light. A head, severed through the jugular arteries, rolled at his feet, grinning and ghastly.

" 'Tis Master Fitzwalter," whispered one, in a lull. "Dead and dishonored——"

The clamor became deafening, and Little John felt his senses failing fast. He was beaten and struck at by them all; they tore at him, and cursed him.

Their blows and their rage were as nothing beside the thought of that awful thing upon the ground. The crowd and the lamps reeled and swam before the outlaw's eyes and became blurred.

But the grim vision of that dreadful body became plainer and plainer to him. It assumed terrible proportions, shutting out all else.

CHAPTER 28

S THE DAYS sped on and nothing was heard of Little John, Robin began to grow more and more anxious. He made up his mind to go himself into Nottingham and there see Marian, and discover and (if need be) rescue his faithful herdsman.

All the greenwood men were against him in this, however, and for once had their own way. "Let me go, Master," begged Stuteley; "for my life is of little account compared with yours."

"I will go," said Scarlett. "There is no such animus in the Sheriff's mind against me as he hath against the rest of you. I can ask for Master Carfax and he will perforce treat me fairly."

"I am not so sure of it," said Robin, significantly; "I would not trust Master Simeon further than a rope would hold him. Still, what you say is fair enough, Cousin, and if you will go into the city for us we shall all be grateful. For my part, I would dearly like to accompany you."

"Your duty is here," answered Scarlett. "Rely on me. I will find out what hath chanced to Little John, and will also attend Mistress Fitzwalter."

Will Scarlett started at once, and bore himself so well that he made sight of Gamewell within two hours. He paused for a moment without his father's house, regarding the old place with half-scornful eyes. Then, "What is to be, must be," said Will, to hearten himself.

He walked on toward Nottingham meditatively. If he could have met old Gamewell then and there he would have stopped him and asked his forgiveness. 'Twas in the morning, the sweet fresh morn, in the happy woods, wherein birds fluttered and sang tenderly, and the peaceful deer fed placidly on the close grass of the glades.

This sylvan picture was disturbed rudely for him. A stag, wild and furious, dashed out suddenly from amongst the trees, scattering the does in terrified alarm. The vicious beast eyed Will in his bright dress, and, lowering its head, charged at him furiously. Will nimbly sprang aside, and having gained shelter of an oak, scrambled hurriedly into its branches.

The stag turned about and dashed itself at the tree.

"Now am I right glad not to be in your path, gentle friend," murmured Scarlett, trying to fix himself on the branches so that he might be able to draw an arrow. "Sorry indeed would be anyone's plight who should encounter you in this black humor."

Scarcely had he spoken when he saw the stag suddenly startle and fix its glances rigidly on the bushes to the left of it. These were parted by a delicate hand, and through the opening appeared the figure of a young girl. She advanced, unconscious alike of Will's horrified gaze and the evil fury of the stag.

She saw the beast, standing as if irresolute, there, and held out her hand to it with a pretty gesture, making a little sound with her lips as if to call it to her side. "For the love of God, dear lady——" cried Will.

And then the words died on his throat. With a savage snort of rage the beast had rushed at this easy victim, and with a side blow of its antlers had stretched her upon the ground. It now lowered its head, preparing to gore her to death.

Already its cruel horns had brushed across her once. A piteous cry rang through the woods. Will set his teeth, and swung himself to the ground noiselessly.

Then he quickly dropped to his knee, and was aiming his shaft whilst the stag was making ready for a more deadly effort. Will's arrow struck it with terrific force full in the center of its forehead. The stag fell dead across the body of the fainting maid.

Will Scarlett had soon dragged the beast from off the girl, and had picked her up in his strong arms. He bore her swiftly to the side of one of the many brooks in the vale.

He dashed cool water upon her face, roughly almost, in his agony of fear that she was already dead, and he could have shed tears of joy to see those poor closed eyelids tremble. He redoubled his efforts; and presently she gave a little gasp: "Where am I, what is't?"

"You are here, dear maid, in the forest of Sherwood, and are safe."

She opened her eyes then, and sat up. "Methinks that there was danger about me, and death," she said, wonderingly. Then recognition shone in her face, and she incontinently began to bind her fallen hair and tidy her disordered dress. "Is it you, indeed, Master Scarlett?" she asked.

"Ay, 'tis I. And, thank Heaven, in time to do you a service." Will's tones were deep and full of feeling.

"I am always in your debt, Master Will," she said, pouting, "and now you have me at grievous disadvantage. Tell me where you have been, and why you did leave Cousin Richard and France?"

"Once I had no safety there," replied Will, with meaning, "neither for myself nor for my heart. As for my leaving Richard's Court, why, foolishly, I would be always where you are."

"So you have followed me, then; is that what I am to believe?" The maid smiled. "I will confess, I did know that you were come to London, and I was glad, Will, for I had not too many friends in England, nor have them now, it would seem. But why was there no safety for you in London? And where have you hidden yourself of late?"

"There is a price upon my head. I am in exile. You know me as Will Scarlett, but in sooth my name is not so Saxon."

"I hate the Saxons," said the maid, pettishly. She had risen to her feet, but still was troubled about her tumbled hair. "I am to be married to one, and so have run away. That is why I am wandering in this stupid wood."

"Call it not stupid, it hath brought you to me once more," whispered Will, taking her hands; "and so you do not love this man after all? Is it so? Had I but known!"

"Didst leave London because of *that*?" asked she, lightly. "Ay, but men know how to cozen us! I'll not believe a foolish thing, not if you were to tell it me a thousand times."

"I'll tell it to you once, sweetheart. I did leave London because I learned that you were to be married to another. Life had no more to teach me than that one thing, and it was enough. For what was left for me to learn? I had loved you and loved you so well, and had loved you in vain."

"Had loved, Will? Is thy love so small, then, that it burns out like a candle, within an hour? I had believed——"

But Master Scarlett suddenly took this wilful maid to his heart. "I do love you, oh, my dear, with all my body and my life—till the end of ends, in waking and sleeping. And so I pledge my troth."

She struggled out of his arms. "I am encumbered with wild beasts at each step," cried she, all rosy and breathless. "One would kill me for blind rage, the other for love. Oh, I do not know which to fear the most. There, you may kiss my hand, Will, and I will take you for my man, since it seems that I am to be married whether I will or no. But *you* must carry the tidings to my Saxon in York, and, beshrew me, I hope he will not take it too hardly, for your sake."

"And yours also." Scarlett was holding her again.

"I like you well enough to be sorry if he should hurt you," said this teasing little Princess. She looked up at him, and then dropped her lashes. "Do you *truly* love me, Will? For truly do I love you."

And so the Princess of Aragon elected to marry Geoffrey of Montfichet, notwithstanding the politic choice of husband made for her by the wise old men in London town.

They walked on together towards Nottingham, quietly, and in deep content with the world.

They encountered a stately little cavalcade nearby the gates of the city, and knew themselves observed ere they could hope to avoid them. Putting a bold face on it, the lovers stood on one side, to permit this company to pass them.

An old man, richly dressed, came first, followed at a respectful distance by six horsemen.

The Princess watched them in happy indifference. Her frank glance roved from one to the other of the would-be steadfast faces before her. She turned her head to gaze again at the absorbed old man who led the company.

Then she checked herself in a little exclamation; and hastily averted her face. It was too late; the old fellow had been roused from his apathy. He reined in his grey horse, and asked over his shoulder: "Who are these, Jacquelaine?"

The esquire so addressed at once rode forward, but before he could speak his master had discovered an answer for himself. He had fixed fierce eyes upon Master Scarlett, and made a scornful gesture. "So 'tis you, Geoffrey, daring death now for the sake of some country wench? Ay, but you will end upon the gallows, for sure."

"I shall not ask you to pray at my bedside," retorted Scarlett, bitterly.

The Princess suddenly whipped round. "Who are you, Sir Churl, to talk of gallows and the like to us? Hast come from a hanging thyself? There is one afoot in Nottingham, I mind me."

It was now the turn of the old knight to exclaim. "Princess, *you?*" gasped he, in sheer amaze. He tumbled from his horse to the ground, and with old-fashioned courtesy knelt before her. She put out her hand for him to kiss.

"Rise, Master Montfichet, I pray you, 'tis not your place to kneel to me," she said, with her little Court smile.

The other horsemen had dismounted and now stood apart from the trio. The Princess was the first to speak, so soon as the old Squire had risen. "Master Montfichet and Will Scarlett, pray let me make you known to each other," she said, prettily. "This is Squire George of Gamewell, a good friend and honest adviser to me, although I do not always listen to him as I should," she laughed, easily. "*This* is Master Will Scarlett, whom I have known both in France and now again in England. He hath but now saved me from a dreadful death."

She paused; then added quickly and a little nervously: "My life is his, in short, Master Montfichet, and so—and so I have given it to him. We are to be married, and live in the greenwood. Therefore, you are not to speak slightingly of Master Scarlett in my presence."

Consternation, astonishment and gratification struggled together mightily in the Squire's breast. "Geoffrey, you!" he said again. "But this is beyond belief."

"Therefore believe it," spoke the Princess, lightly; "for *that* will show you to be no common man."

"Sir," said Geoffrey, kneeling before his father, "I pray you forgive both my rash words just now and all my seeming ingratitude. I am very fain to be friends again with you, and I do swear to be more dutiful in the years to come. Will you take my hand?"

"Ay, freely as it is offered. God save us; but who am I to be stubborn of will, in the face of these miracles?"

"Do the miracles work happiness for you, Master Montfichet?" enquired the maid, archly.

"Ay, marry. But the King will never consent to this business, be sure of it. *You* marrying my son—a commoner!"

"Your son?" It was now the Princess's turn to be amazed. But soon the matter was explained to her. "So, Will, you have begun by deceiving me; a bad beginning."

"I was trying to tell you, dear heart, when we made this encounter. Was I not saying that my father lived nearby here? Did I not tell you that he was a Norman——"

"There, there, do not fret your dear self. I will marry you, whether you be Will Scarlett or Geoffrey of Montfichet. It is yourself I need, after all."

"Take my steed and ride with us to Gamewell. There, at least, I must keep thee, Princess, until the King hath given his sanction to this marriage. *You* to rule over Gamewell? In sooth I will be a joyful man upon that day."

"And I," murmured Master Scarlett.

So they turned back towards Gamewell, and only when they were in sight of it did Scarlett remember poor Little John. Then he stopped short, reining in the horse which one of the knights had lent to him. The Princess had accepted loan of the esquire Jacquelaine's palfrey.

Will soon had told them this errand which he had come so near to forgetting altogether. "If this be the man they call John Little Nailor," said the Princess, sorrowfully, "why, he is in perilous plight. You have but just ridden through Nottingham, I take it, Master Montfichet, and have some of its news?"

"They do not seem yet to know of your adventurings, Princess."

"No, surely; for what is a woman, missing or to hand, when there is

red murder abroad? This poor fellow, whom I do believe to be innocent, was accused of theft by a rascally cook, and was pursued. 'Twas
the night of our return. They chased him from pillar to post, and
presently caught him close to the castle. He had two bags with him."

" 'Tis Little John, then," cried Scarlett; "I saw him go out with the
sacks across his back."

"In one of them they found many things that other folk had strangely
lost," said the Princess, with a little grimace. "In the other there was the
dead, dishonored body of a good citizen foully done to death."

Her listeners stared in their amazement. "It is a Master Fitzwalter
who hath been so cruelly murdered," continued the Princess, her color
coming and going. "This Little John swears that the cook did kill his
master; and whilst he, Little John, was resting in Fitzwalter's house this
rascal fellow must have changed the sacks."

"Fitzwalter, the warden of the gates? I knew him well. Why, he left
us but three weeks since to travel to Nottingham. It seems that he had
sent a messenger to his girl there that she was to follow him, but either
his letter miscarried or the maid would not. So poor Fitzwalter, busy as
he was, must needs return to meet his death."

"Who is this cook?" asked Scarlett.

"An evil character he hath altogether. Once he was of an outlaw
robber band, headed here in these very woods under one Will of
Cloudesley."

"Tell me, is he called Roger de Burgh?" asked Will.

"That is his name," answered the Princess, surprised; "do you know
aught of him?"

"I know much evil of him," replied her lover; and then he told them
how this very Roger had planned to take his (Will's) life, and how
Robin had saved him.

The Squire nodded. "I remember," said he, slowly.

"Ay, Robin was always a good lad. This news of yours will stagger
him, for he is betrothed to Mistress Fitzwalter, daughter of him who
hath so dreadfully met his end."

"The two of them were arraigned, I must tell you," went on the
Princess, "and both were to be racked. But they did not put it too

hardly upon Master Roger, as I have reason to know, wherefore he was able to maintain his innocence; whilst the other, in his bitter anguish, made confession of a crime which he did never commit."

"And they are hanging him whilst I stand idly here," cried Scarlett, turning to horse. "I must leave you, sweet; forgive me. Here is a man's life in the balance."

"What would you, Will?" she asked, fearfully. "The hanging is fixed for the Thursday in next week."

"Before then he shall be free," said Will Scarlett, firmly. "Farewell, dear heart. Wait for me here at Gamewell; my father will be good host to you, I know."

"The maid Fitzwalter was lodging with us when I was called to London," the Squire began.

"She is now in Nottingham, sir. It is a story which I will tell you later. Now give me farewell, and your blessing."

"God's blessing be in you, Geoffrey, my son," said the Squire. It was the first time for many years that he had called Geoffrey by that name.

"And take all my heart with you, Will." The voice of this little Princess was husky; and a sob sounded in her throat. "Be cautious, and return soon to me."

She watched his swift retreating figure as he sped towards Nottingham, there to argue it with Master Carfax.

CHAPTER 29

THE DAY AFTER Scarlett's depar-
ture found Robin in frantic mood. Two emissaries had he sent out to
gain news of Marian, and neither had returned. He had had now no
direct tidings of her for nigh on three months. Little John's silence, too,
disturbed him.

Robin determined that he would see Marian, at least, this day, or die
in the attempt. So, notwithstanding all that the rest could urge, their
leader started away on foot towards the city.

He walked quickly, and his mind was so filled with dreadful thoughts
that he exercised little of his usual care. Emerging suddenly upon the
highroad, he plunged almost into the arms of his enemy, the Lord
Bishop of Hereford.

It was too late for Robin to retreat, and he was too far away from him
to wind his horn in the hope of rousing his men. The Bishop rode at the
head of a goodly company and had already espied him.

About a mile away, nearby the roadside, was a little tumbledown
cottage. Robin remembered it and saw his only chance of safety. At
once he doubled back through the underwood, much to the surprise of
the Bishop, who thought he had truly disappeared by magic. In a few
minutes Robin had come to the little cottage. The owner of the place, a
little crabbed old woman, rose up with a cry of alarm.

" 'Tis I, Robin Hood; where are your three sons?"

"They are with you, Robin. Well do you know that. Do they not owe
life to you?"

"Help now repay the debt," said Robin, in a breath. "The Bishop will soon be without, and he has many men."

"I will save you, Robin," cried the old woman, bustlingly. "We will change raiment, and you shall go forth as the poor lone woman of this cot. Go without and strip yourself speedily; and throw me your clothes through the doorway."

Robin was in the garden and had slipped out of his Lincoln green in a moment. He clad himself with equal celerity in the old woman's rags, as she flung them out to him one by one.

The Bishop perceived an old decrepit woman hobbling across the road, as he with this company came hastening down it. He bade one of his fellows to stay her, and ask if she had seen such and such a man. The soldier gave her a full and vivid description of Robin Hood. The old woman, thus rudely prevented from gathering her sticks—already she had a little handful of them—answered that there *was* a man within her cottage; and that she would be right glad if my lord Bishop would cause him to be driven out of it. "In sooth, my good gentlemen, he is none other than that vagabond Robin Hood," piped she.

"Enough!" cried the Bishop, triumphantly. "Enter the cottage, men; beat down the door, if need be. A purse of gold pieces is already offered for the capture of Robin Hood, and I will give a hundred beside!"

The old woman was released, and went on gathering twigs for her fire. Little by little she edged towards the forest, and while the Bishop's men were beating down her cottage door she vanished between the trees.

Then she began to run, with surprising quickness, towards Barnesdale.

Stuteley encountered her presently, and was at first prepared to treat her in rough fashion. "Hold your hand, sweet Will," cried Robin, "it is I, your master. Summon our fellows, and return with me speedily. My lord of Hereford is come again to Sherwood."

When Will had done, laughing he blew his horn. "Why, Mistress," said he, turning his grinning face to Robin as though seized with a notion, "is not this the day when the knight Sir Richard of the Lee—he to whom you gave Arthur-à-Bland—swore he would return to pay us our moneys?"

" 'Tis near the time, in sooth," admitted Robin.

"Then surely he hath sent the Bishop to us, not being able to come himself?" argued Will. "We will see if the Bishop is carrying four hundred gold pennies with him. If it be so, then I am right, indeed."

*   *   *

The Bishop, for all his bold words, had not yet nerved himself to give the necessary command of death against the person of Robin Hood. Since he would not come out of the cottage, the door must be beaten down.

When this had been done, the Bishop's men had peeped in. "He is here, hiding," they cried, exultingly. "Shall we slay him with our pikes?"

"Nay, keep watch upon and guard this cottage against all comers. Go, one of you, to Nottingham, with all speed, and bring the Sheriff to us, with many men. Say that I bid him here to settle matters with Robin Hood."

The good Bishop of Hereford did not intend to give this villain a single chance. Were he brought out into the open, he might, by some magic, contrive an escape. Lying in this hut under the pikes of the Bishop's men he was safe, and if the worst came to the worst might readily be slain.

The messenger detached from his escort had not carried the Bishop's message to the Sheriff very far ere his master would have wished to change it. In a moment, whilst my lord of Hereford was complacently gloating over his capture—whilst indeed he was himself peering into the dark cottage in order to catechise his prisoner—there appeared on the highroad the shabby figure of that very old woman who had innocently helped to set the trap.

She called out in a strident voice to the soldiers about her dwelling. "Stand by, lazy rascals," cried she, "stand away from my gates. What are you doing on my ground?"

"Madam," answered the Bishop, turning round to her, "these are my men, and I have given them the order to guard this cottage."

"God-a-mercy!" swore the beldame, harshly. "Things have come to a pass in sooth when our homes may be treated like common jails. Take away this robber and your fellows from my house on the instant, or I will curse you all in eating and drinking and sleeping."

"Not so fast, mother," argued the Bishop, smiling easily at her simulated rage. "All this has been done by my orders, and is therefore in law."

The old woman clapped her hands impatiently. At the signal the greenwood men sprang out on all sides of the cottage. The Bishop saw himself and his men-at-arms trapped; but he determined to make a fight for it. "If one of you but stir an inch towards me, rascals," he cried, spitefully, "it shall be to sound the death of your master Robin Hood. My men have him here under their pikes, and I will command them to kill him forthwith. Further, he shall be killed an you do not at once disperse."

Then Robin stepped out before his men. He flung off the old crone's cap which he had worn so cleverly. "Come, kill me, then, lord," he called, cheerfully. "Here am I, waiting for your pikes and their pokes. Hasten to make sure business of it, for I am in no gentle humor."

The old woman, who, in the garb of Robin Hood, had been lying silent and still so long within the cottage, jumped up then quite nimbly. In all the bald absurdity of her disguise she came to the door of the cottage and looked forth. "Give you good-den, my lord Bishop," piped she; "and what make *you* at so humble a door as this? Do you come to bless me and give me alms?"

"Ay, marry, that does he!" said Stuteley, coming forward. "To you, mother, and to us also. You must know that my lord bears with him a bag of four hundred pieces from Sir Richard of the Lee, who did borrow this money from us to lend it to my lord."

"Now, by all the saints—" began the Bishop.

"They are watching you, brother," said Stuteley, impudently, "so be wary in your speech. Give into my hand the four hundred pieces which you took from the knight I have named. You cannot deny that you *did* take them from him in the June of last year?"

"The knight owned them to me, villain," said the Bishop, furiously. He saw that his men were outnumbered, and that all the outlaws had drawn bows aimed against them and him. A word not to the liking of these desperate fellows would loosen fifty horrid shafts upon him. "Sir Richard did owe them to me," he repeated, omitting the epithet.

"Hark now to that!" said Robin, still in his disguise. "Listen to it, friends, for ye all were witnesses that Sir Richard swore to me that the Bishop had robbed him, and sought to rob him more. Did not you, in honest truth, lend the knight four hundred pieces, my lord?"

"I did not lend him that precise amount," admitted the Bishop. "Four hundred pieces included also the interest of the sum I gave."

"Ho! you gave?" Robin snapped up the word. "You gave it, my lord?"

"I will not bandy words with you, you false villain," shouted the Bishop, suddenly losing control of himself. "Why do you not charge them, men? Take the word from me, and hew these fellows down as they stand."

"They will be well advised to remain as they are," spoke Robin. "See now how we command you all!" He took a bow and arrow out of Much's hands, and sped a shaft so truly towards the purpling Bishop that his mitred cap was sent spinning from off his bald head.

My lord turned green and yellow. He had thought himself dead almost. "Take my money, rascals," he quavered, feebly; and Stuteley approached him, cap in hand.

"Tied to the saddle of my palfrey you will find my all," murmured the Bishop, sighing deeply.

Stuteley took a well-filled bag from under my lord's empty saddle. He spread his cloak upon the road and counted out four hundred pieces into it. "The interest, Master?" asked Will, twinkling to Robin.

"Pay that to this old woman who hath befriended and saved me; and give her, further, two hundred of the pieces on thy cloak," commanded Robin. "We will share with her, even as she hath already shared with me this day."

The outlaws then withdrew, taking with them the old woman and the Bishop's gold. They left him in no great humor; but forbore to provoke him further.

This adventure had, however, banished all hope of Robin making his projected journey into Nottingham. He had perforce to return to the caves at Barnesdale, to get changed again into a more befitting dress. The day was old when he was ready to go out once more; and at Stuteley's entreaty Robin consented to wait until the morning.

The Bishop lost no time in making Nottingham. He and his men were so ashamed of having been overcome so easily by the greenwood men that they had perforce to magnify Robin's band and its prowess twentyfold.

Amongst the many knights who had followed, hopelessly, in the Princess's train was one whose attentions had ever been very noxious to her. This was a coarse, overfed, overconfident Norman, brutally skilful in the games at tourneys and ruthless in battles *à outrance*. His name was Guy of Gisborne, and he hailed from the borders of Lancashire. To him had fallen the rich fat acres of Broadweald, that place for which poor Hugh Fitzooth had wrestled vainly for so long.

He had persecuted her unavailingly—'twas through a scene with him that Scarlett had come so much into the maid's favor. Sir Guy had followed her to Nottingham, meaning to steal her from the Sheriff at first chance. "No Saxon churl shall hope to carry off this prize from me," thought Sir Guy. "Her beauty pleaseth me, and her fortune will help mine own. Therefore, I will follow her meekly until we come nearer to my own land. Then, perhaps, one night pompous Monceux may find her flown. He will be blamed; and none need know whither the little bird has gone and by whom she hath been trapped."

Sir Guy of Gisborne found another in the field with him; the Princess had not waited for him to steal her. The little bird had flown ere Sir Guy's trap had been set.

So the Bishop of Hereford found both the Sheriff and Sir Guy in evil humor. My lord told his story, raging against Robin; the Sheriff had his complaint—directed against the Princess in general and no man in particular.

"Depend on it, Monceux, this rascal hath stolen away your charge," said the Bishop, in order to stir the Sheriff to greater lengths against Robin. "How can you sit here so idly, first losing your gold plate to him and then your gold? Now, with one blow goeth this Princess who was most solemnly committed to your charge, and with her your good name. For, without doubt, this matter will cost you your office."

Monceux was overcome with terror; his eyes started out from his head. "I did hear them speak of some girl betwixt themselves, now that I think on it," continued the Bishop, artfully, noting the effect he had made. " 'This woman shall share with us'—ay, those were Robin's very words. The Princess hath been stolen by him."

"She last was seen walking towards the woods, 'tis true," murmured the unhappy Sheriff. "But, truly, I am not to blame in this plaguey business."

"I will encounter the villain for you, Sheriff," said Sir Guy, with a cunning glance. "And if I do rid you of him, will you swear to stand by me in another matter?"

"Surely, surely."

"Your word on it, then—here in my lord's holy presence," Sir Guy went on. "This girl hath been told by a council of wiseacres that she must marry some Saxon noble. But her heart is given to another—to myself, in short. Swear that you both will help me to win her, and I will take her from your merry Robin and kill him afterward."

They both promised readily that they would do all that he could ask—if only he would kill Robin Hood outright. The Bishop had great influence at Court, and Sir Guy intended that he should smooth matters for him after the abduction of the Princess. The Sheriff was to hold fast to any story that might be necessary, and to swear to the little Princess that Sir Guy of Gisborne was the very Saxon whom she had been ordered to marry.

"All this is settled between us," observed the knight, comfortably. "Give me a number of men, all of them good archers, and put them at my sole command. I will go forth tomorrow in a disguise such as will deceive even your wonderful Robin."

"We will hold over the hanging and flaying of the other rascal until his master can dance beside him," cried the Sheriff, conceiving Robin to be already caught.

CHAPTER 30

ROBIN STARTED OUT early in
the day towards the city. This time nothing should stay him from enter-
ing it—and finding Marian. The demoiselle Marie's plan would surely
have succeeded on this day, for Robin was careless of all things but the
hope of seeing his dear.

Sir Guy of Gisborne was there, however, as Robin's good angel, as we
are to see, although Sir Guy had, in truth, no very merciful feelings
towards the outlaw.

Robin perceived upon the highroad a very strange figure coming
towards him. It seemed to be a three-legged monster at first sight, but
on coming nearer one might see that 'twas really a poorly clad man, who
for a freak had covered up his rags with a capul hide, nothing more nor
less than the sundried skin of a horse, complete with head and tail and
mane.

The skin of the horse's head made a helmet for the man; and the tail
gave him the three-legged appearance.

"Good morrow, gossip," said Robin, cheerily; "by my bow and by
my arrows, I could believe you to be a good archer—you have the
shape of one."

The man took no offence at this greeting, but told Robin that he had
lost his way and was anxious to find it again.

"By my faith, I could have believed that you had lost your wits,"
thought Robin, laughing quietly to himself. "What is your business,
friend?" he asked, aloud; "you are dressed in strange clothes and yet
seem by your speech to be of gentle blood."

"And who are you, forester, to ask me who I am?"

"I am one of the King's rangers," replied Robin; "and 'tis my part to look after the King's deer and save them from the wicked arrows of Robin Hood."

"Do you know Robin Hood?" asked the man, shrewdly eyeing him.

"That do I; and last night I heard that he would be coming alone in a certain part of this wood to meet a maid."

"Is that so indeed?" cried the man, eagerly.

" 'Tis very truth," answered Robin. "And I, knowing this, am going to take him, and carry off both the girl and the reward upon his head."

"Tell me, friend, is this girl a little creature, royal-looking and very beautiful?"

"Marry, she appeared to me a very Princess," cried Robin, with enthusiasm.

"We are well met," remarked the yeoman, presently, and speaking as if come to a decision. "Now I will tell you, friend, that I am in search of Robin Hood myself, and will help you to take him. I am Sir Guy of Gisborne, and can make your fortune for you."

"And I am Robin Hood, so, prithee, make it quickly for me!" cried Robin, imprudently.

Sir Guy was not taken so much aback as Robin had hoped. Quickly he drew his sword from underneath the capul hide, and he smote at Robin full and foul.

Robin parried the thrust with his own true blade, and soon they were at a fierce contest. They fought by the wayside for a long while in a deadly anger, only the sharp clashing of their blades breaking the silence.

Then Robin stumbled over the projecting root of a tree; and Sir Guy, who was quick and heavy with his weapon, wounded Robin in his side.

The outlaw recovered himself adroitly; and, full of sudden rage, stabbed at the knight under and across his guard. The capul hide hindered Sir Guy in his attempt at a parry—the horse head fell across his eyes.

Next instant Sir Guy of Gisborne went staggering backward with a deep groan, Robin's sword through his throat.

"You did bring this upon yourself," muttered Robin, eyeing the body of the knight in vain regret. "Yet you did fall bravely, and in fair fight. You shall be buried honorably."

He dragged the body into the bushes; and, having taken off the horsehide, slipped it upon himself. He then perceived that, hanging from the dead man's belt, there was a little silver whistle. "What may this be?" thought Robin.

Sir Guy, clothed in old and ragged dress, looked to be a plain yeoman, slain in defence of his life, or mayhap a forester. Pulling the hide well over himself, Robin put the little whistle to his lips and blew it shrilly.

Instantly, far off to the right of him, sounded an answering note, and again from behind him there was reply. In about four or five minutes twenty of the Sheriff's best archers came running through the wood to Robin's side.

"Didst signal for us, lording?" asked the leader of them, approaching Robin.

"Ay, see him! I have encountered and slain one of your robber fellows for ye," answered Robin, simulating Sir Guy's voice and manner. "I would have you take up his body upon your shoulders and bear him along this little path, wherefrom he sprang upon me."

The archers obeyed him immediately. "Do you follow us, lording?" they asked.

"I will lead ye," cried Robin, waving his red sword truculently. "Follow me speedily."

Thus he led them after him through the secret paths into Barnesdale, and there blew his horn so suddenly that Stuteley and his fellows were upon the Sheriff's men ere they might drop Sir Guy's dead body to the earth.

Robin bade his men disarm the archers, and tie such of them as would not prove amenable.

Thus the Sheriff was robbed of his best archers; for these fellows, finding the greenwood men to be of such friendly mind, soon joined in with them.

"This is well done, in sooth," said Robin, gently, to himself. "A good day's work; and Monceux will have cause to regret his share in it. Yet am I no nearer Nottingham after all, tho' I have twice sworn that naught should stay me. Stuteley," added he, aloud, calling his squire to his side, "see you that this dead knight be buried with all respect; he fought me well and fairly."

"It shall be done, Master," answered Will Stuteley; "you may be easy about it. But I would have you listen to the talk of these archers— they have grave news of our comrade Little John. It seems that the Sheriff hath seized him for the killing of thy maid's father, and will presently have him dreadfully hanged and burned."

Robin uttered an exclamation of horror. Soon the terrible story was told him, and his brain reeled under the shock of it. All that night he paced the woods until the dawn, then fell incontinently into a deep and heavy slumber.

"Disturb him not nor let him take action until I do return," said the comfortable Friar Tuck, in business-like manner. "I know how his distemper will play upon him, and how he will bring us all to grief if he attempts the city again. Now I may go in and out as I will, being a curtal friar and not now remembered in these parts. I will visit the Sheriff and ask for leave to confess Master Little John. Then I will come back to you with the best news I may."

*   *   *

Geoffrey of Montfichet had ridden into Nottingham on the day before Sir Guy had left it. Carfax had known where the Princess might be found all the while his master, with the Bishop, was busy persuading the Knight of Gisborne that the maid was with Robin. One might be sure, however, that neither Monceux nor Carfax gave out any hint of this knowledge, for to do that would have stayed Sir Guy in his praise-worthy attempt upon the bold outlaw.

Geoffrey—Master Scarlett—had found difficult work before him, but he intended to save Little John. He was convinced that the cook had slain Fitzwalter, most likely at the command of some other person interested in the death.

Who might this be? Who had profited by the death of so unassuming a man as the late city warden?

Carfax treated Scarlett with scant ceremony. The lean-faced fellow devoured the item that the Princess of Aragon was safe at Gamewell, but gave nothing in return. Scarlett had been left to cool his heels in the great hall of Nottingham Castle for near an hour afterward, whilst Simeon Carfax was closeted with the Sheriff.

They were having a tidying of the rooms in honor of the Bishop's visit. Whilst Scarlett impatiently waited the good pleasure of Master Carfax, the maids were busy carrying many things to and fro: fresh rushes to strew my lord's rooms, candles and tapers, silks and cloths, and brown ewers of water. All the rubbish and sweepings of the floors were borne out in great baskets to the courtyard.

One of the maids, a plump, roguish, lazy wench, would only carry her basket so far as the hearth of the hall. A fire was there, why not use it? Also she could ogle and throw sidelong looks at Master Scarlett, who for his beard and thirty-five grave years, was none so bad a man.

This girl was throwing into the open hearth a lot of ends of silk and combings from her mistress's room. She tossed the rubbish on the fire, at the same time eyeing Master Scarlett. Then, finding that he would not notice her, she poutingly returned with her basket upon a fresh journey.

Scarlett came over to the fire to pick up some of the burning scraps. They were drifting over the hearth into the room dangerously, thanks to the maid's carelessness.

He found in his hand a half-burned piece of parchment, which still fizzled and crackled in quaint malicious fashion.

Upon the parchment was an awkward writing, and some of the words showed up very black under the heat. Half-idly, Scarlett tried to make sense of them:

"This . . . dear child Marian, . . . her affectionate father . . . Court of . . . in London town."

So far did Master Scarlett read before suddenly the beginnings of the truth flashed upon him. This was the very letter which he had borne to Marian.

How had it come into the castle? By what strange magic? Could Marian have carried it here herself?

He remembered that she had given it to Robin, and that he had put it into his bosom.

"Mistress, you seem indeed to be very busy this day," said Master Scarlett, affably, to the girl next time she appeared. "Do you prepare me a chamber, for it seems that I am to wait here for a week at least."

"I am tidying my mistress's room, and have had hard work, I promise you," replied the girl, impudently. "Mayhap you will give me a help whilst you wait, Sir Taciturn? This is the fifth basket of rubbish I have borne from the demoiselle Marie's little cupboard."

"I will readily help you if you will help me," said Scarlett, pleasantly. "Canst tell me who wrote this little paper? The writing seemeth familiar to mine eyes."

" 'Tis a piece of my lady's jesting," said the girl, after a glance at the parchment. " 'Twas written in imitation of Master Fitzwalter's hand after we had searched his house last year. Ah, poor man, who would have then imagined so hard a fate for him?" She sighed prodigiously, and rolled her eyes.

"Tell me the story of this murder, Mistress, I pray you."

She was not loth to fall a-chattering, and she told Scarlett all she knew of it. From the rambling history he discovered another strange fact, that Roger de Burgh had been cook in the Sheriff's household before he had gone to the Fitzwalter house. Slowly he began to see that the letter he had so blithely put into Marian's hand was a forgery, done by the clever fingers of the demoiselle Marie.

"So," thought he, swiftly, "Mistress Fitzwalter was persuaded to return to this place in order that Robin Hood might visit her secretly. The house was watched by a spy from the Sheriff's own kitchen. Soon as Robin came, this spy was to give warning; or, if matters pressed, kill him. But after many months of waiting, *Fitzwalter* came instead."

His quick mind, used to the intrigues and plots of a capricious Court, had unravelled the mystery. Yet how could he act upon this knowledge in the midst of the enemy's camp? If the Sheriff could stoop already to such foul business as this, to what further lengths would he not go? Dismissing himself through the girl, Scarlett strode out of the castle. The air seemed fresher and more wholesome without. He enquired and found his way to the house of grief, and there asked audience with its little heartbroken mistress.

*　　*　　*

Whilst Scarlett was plotting and inventing a hundred schemes to save Little John, a poor wandering priest appeared one evening before the gates of Nottingham Castle. Most humbly he begged a little bread and a drink of water; and, having received these, he blessed the place and all within it.

"You should not bless *all* within this castle, Sir Priest," the Sheriff told him. Monceux had pompously administered to the man's simple wants with his own hands. "There is a villain in our cells who hath done wicked murder."

The ragged friar asked who that might be; and when he had heard, said that at the least he would confess this poor misguided fellow and so deliver his soul from everlasting punishment.

The Sheriff was rather doubtful, but seeing that the priest had no weapon upon him, he gave a sign that he should be admitted to Little John's cell.

There the friar found the big outlaw very dejected. "Give you good cheer, brother," said the friar, gently; "I have come to pray with you."

"What assistance can your prayers be to me?" asked Little John, sharply; "I am to be hanged tomorrow morn, and all your prayers will scarce alter that."

"Anger is a great sin," replied the priest.

"I have no sins against God," said Little John; "I have always endeavored to live easily and justly." Then the friar came up close to him, and whispered something in his ear. The outlaw's expression altered at once. "By the Sheriff's rope," muttered he, quite in his old manner, "but I swear that if thou canst get me a weapon——"

"Here is a little dagger," said Friar Tuck, pulling it out from under his gown. " 'Tis small, but tomorrow it may be of use. I can do no more now; but be ready for us tomorrow, when the last moments are come. Robin Hood will not easily let you die, be sure of it."

The friar, after he had left the prison, ran all the way to Barnesdale, under the stars.

CHAPTER 31

IT WAS HARDLY DAWN when a strong guard of soldiers was drawn up without Nottingham Castle, and the prisoner was dragged forth from his cell. Monceux had wisely come to the conclusion that Sir Guy of Gisborne had also failed, and he saw no reason to delay Little John's execution.

Early as was the hour, yet both the Sheriff and the Bishop of Hereford were present. The space before the castle was thronged with people. Beside the prisoner walked the castle chaplain.

The crowd swayed and roared, and a small disturbance broke out on the right of the Sheriff. At once the soldiers hurried to quell it.

As the prisoner neared the gallows, the crowd so bore upon the cart in which he stood upright that progress for a few minutes was out of all question.

Another disturbance broke out in the rear of the procession. Next instant the prisoner was seen to have free hands. He stooped and sliced the cords about his feet, and, releasing himself, all at once he sprang out of the cart.

Then was an uproar indeed. The soldiers had strict orders that the episode of Stuteley's escape was not to be repeated. But whilst they exerted themselves desperately a sudden hail of arrows fell upon them from the sky, as it were. Robin Hood's horn was heard blowing merrily, and the Sheriff saw the huge mob of people break up into billows of contending portions under his very eyes.

"Lock the gates of the city," screamed Carfax, at this juncture. "We have them trapped at last."

Little John was free and had seized an axe. Much and Middle had brought bags of meal with them, and both repeated the miller's old trick of flinging the white meal into the eyes of the enemy.

Robin had broken up his band into small parties, and all were engaged simultaneously.

In less time than it takes to tell, the space without the castle was turned to pandemonium.

Again and again Robin's horn sounded, calling them together, and slowly but surely his small parties formed up into a whole, beating their way through the crowd with their swords and axes. So soon as they were together, with Little John safely in the middle of them, they fell to their bows and sped a cloud of arrows amongst the Sheriff's men.

Then they turned to retreat, and fell back so suddenly that they had made good start ere Monceux had divined their intent. They sped towards the north gate, that one being nearest to Barnesdale.

Crafty Carfax had forestalled them, however. The north gate was closed hard and fast, and the bridge drawn.

The outlaws doubled on their track and charged at their pursuers with lowered pikes and waving axes. The crowd before them yielded sullenly and allowed them passage.

"To the west gate, Robin, hasten," cried a shrill voice. " 'Tis more easily opened than the rest, and the bridge is down—someone hath smashed the winch."

Robin's heart leaped in his body—'twas the voice of Gilbert of Blois! "Marian," breathed he, overcome with terror for her, "oh, my dearest!"

"Follow, follow!" she cried, with flashing eyes; "there is not a moment to be lost."

Robin saw that it was a matter of life or death now in any case. "To the west gate!" he called, "Locksley! A Locksley!"

It was the old battle cry, and only a few of them remembered it. Yet it served and served well. The greenwood men formed up into close ranks, and all followed the little page, shouting lustily, "Locksley! A Locksley!"

In the rush and hurry Robin saw that Scarlett was there, and Warrenton and Allan-a-Dale. And with the little page ran another, a fair-haired boy, with strangely familiar face.

" 'Tis Fennel," whispered Allan, at Robin's side. "She would not be left."

He spoke as they ran, with the enemy now in full pursuit of them. Every now and again the outlaws turned and sped a hail of arrows into the mob behind them.

The west bridge was gained, and Scarlett had dispossessed the warder of his keys in a moment. He unlocked the gates and flung them wide open.

The two boys—for so they seemed—raced through and over the broken bridge, and Allan followed next. The outlaws were soon free of the town, and once more in their own element, but Little John must needs go back to cover the retreat with Stuteley.

Carfax and the Sheriff were close at hand with their men, furious and determined. Even as the last of Robin's men gained and fell over the bridge, Little John was wounded seriously by a shaft from Simeon Carfax's bow.

His cry brought Robin back to his side. In a moment Robin's arms were about him. "Lean on my shoulder, dear heart," cried Robin, and sure 'twas a ludicrous sight to see this stripling seeking to hold up the great form of Little John.

They ran along in this way, and the outlaws formed a bodyguard about them. Allan and those in front had fired the dry furze and grasses, and the smoke began to roll heavily against the faces of the soldiers.

This gave the greenwood men a small advantage, and they gained the open country; but not for long did the honors of this day rest on one side or the other. The Sheriff and his fellows broke through the fire; and then it was seen that some of them were mounted on fleet horses.

Little John begged to be left behind; and again did Robin try to rally him. Onward they ran; and presently found themselves approaching a hill, thickly wooded about the base.

They gained cover of these trees, and turned at bay. Hidden behind tree trunks they sent forth a death volume of peacock shafts to the Sheriff. Master Carfax was seen to fall, and with him six of the horsemen.

The soldiers halted and prepared their crossbows. A volley of their arrows crashed and splintered the trees, whilst Carfax rose up stiffly to give fresh orders. A duello commenced of longbow against crossbow; and as the freebooters could deliver near a dozen shafts to each bolt, they more than held their own.

When a bolt *did* strike, however, death was instant. A man was shot near to Marian, and fell with his head shattered and ghastly. She gave a little scream, and put her hands over her eyes.

Robin bade her keep near to him—"Behind me, sweetheart," cried he, feverishly, "that naught may hurt you save through me."

So they fought for near an hour; and then the greenwood men saw that reinforcements were coming to their enemies. Robin's horn gave once more the order for retreat.

Slowly they fell back through the woods and up the rising ground. "Alas, alas!" cried poor Mistress Fennel, wringing her hands in utter forgetfulness that now she was dressed as a man. "We are undone! Here come others to meet us, with pikes and many men!"

Robin saw that upon the hilltop there was a grey castle. From its open gate there poured out a motley crowd of men armed rudely with pikes and with staves. They rushed downward to intercept the outlaws as it seemed, and Robin thought that, in truth, he and his merry men were trapped at last.

But—oh, joyful sight!—foremost among those coming from the castle was the once mournful knight Sir Richard of the Lee. He was smiling now and very excited. "A Hood! A Hood!" he cried. "To the rescue. A Hood!"

Never was there more welcome sight and hearing than this. Without a word the outlaws raced up to meet their timely friends, and gained shelter of the castle, whilst Sir Richard kept the Sheriff and his fellows at bay. Then, when all were safely across the little drawbridge, the knight gave the word, and fell back upon his stronghold also. The bridge was drawn and the gates clashed together, almost in the frantic, hideous face of Master Simeon, upon whose features showed streaks of blood from his wound and rage commingled.

*   *   *

The knight stationed his men about the walls. Soon appeared Monceux beneath them alone, and demanding speech. He commanded the knight to deliver up Robin and his men upon pain of assault and burning of the castle with fire.

Sir Richard replied briefly. "Show me your warrant, Sir Malapert, and I will consider it," he said, from within the gates. And Master Monceux had no warrant with him.

"My word is enough for you, Richard of the Lee," roared he, furiously. "Am I not Sheriff of Nottingham?"

"You cannot be the Sheriff of Nottingham, good man," answered the knight, getting ready to close the wicket, "for he is Master Monceux, and is busy escorting the Princess of Aragon towards York. Go to and mend your manners, rascal, and call away these ruffians with you."

Then Sir Richard snapped to the wicket gate, and returned to Robin. "Well met, bold Robin," he cried, taking him by both hands. "Well met, indeed. I had intended to ride forth this very day to your home in the woods, to pay you your moneys with my thanks added thereto; but you have happily saved me and mine the journey. Welcome to my castle, recovered to me by your generosity."

Sir Richard presented his wife to Robin, and his son, who had but just returned from the Holy Land. The knight told him how the last few months had been most prosperous with him, instead of going so badly as he had feared; and explained that now, from one source and another, he was as rich as of yore. "So when we have feasted I will take you to my treasury, and there count you out thy money and its interest faithfully. Yet in ridding myself of this debt I do not free my life of the obligation."

"You need say no more, Sir Richard," interposed Robin. " 'Tis we who owe *all* to you. As for your debt, why, it hath been repaid me already by my lord of Hereford. Is it not so, Stuteley?"

The little esquire protested solemnly that the Bishop had paid it to them as conscience money. "Then I will pay it again," cried the knight, cheerfully, "sooner than be outdone by a Bishop in the matter of honesty; and I have a few presents for you, but these I will show you later."

Robin thanked him gratefully, and, taking him on one side, told how boy's clothes were covering Mistress Marian and Dame Fennel at this instant. Would the knight's wife take charge of them, and find them some apparel as would ease one of them at least from most uneasy feelings?

That evening, whilst Monceux raged and stormed without, they all sat to a great feast. Little John was already so much recovered of his wound as to sing them a song, whilst Robin made sweet accompaniment upon a harp.

The knight showed Robin presently his treasury, and again implored him to take the four hundred pieces of gold, if he would take no interest. But his guest was firm: "Keep the money, for it is your own. I have but made the Bishop return to you that which he had first stolen from your hands."

Sir Richard again expressed his thanks, and now led them to his armory. Therein Robin saw, placed apart, a hundred strong bows with fine waxen silk strings, and a hundred sheaves of arrows. Every shaft was an ell long, and dressed with peacock's feathers and notched with silver. Beside them were a hundred suits of red and white livery, finely made and stitched. "These are the poor presents we have made for you, Robin," said Sir Richard. "Take them from us, with ten thousand times their weight in gratitude."

One of the knight's own men came forward to give a sheaf of the arrows into Robin's hand, and, behold, it was Arthur-à-Bland!

*Little John was already so much
recovered of his wound as
to sing them a song, whilst Robin
made sweet accompaniment
upon a harp.*

CHAPTER 32

A SEARCHING RAIN continued all that night. They well expected to find the Sheriff and his army encamped against them on the morrow.

Strangely enough, the morning showed the countryside quiet and peaceful as of old. Monceux and his fellows, if there, were well hid indeed—nothing might be seen of them.

From the castle battlement, afar off, mysterious under grey opaque morning, lay Nottingham. The old town seemed to be yet asleep; but there was plenty of movement within its gates for all that. A messenger had come out hastily to Monceux, even while he and Carfax had been perfecting details of the siege which they intended to apply to the knight's castle. This man brought the Sheriff news of such moment as to cause him to give up the hope of catching Robin without another effort. My lord of Hereford had had the news from York—he had sped it to Monceux: "The King is abroad; take care of thyself."

That was the item even as it had come in to Prince John from his cousin Philip of France: "The King is abroad."

Richard of England, the Lion Heart, he whom all thought to be safely out of the country—some said in a foreign prison, others that he was fighting the paynims in the Holy Land. In any case, he had returned, and now all such as the Sheriff and the Bishop of Hereford must put their houses in order, and say, once and for all, that they would be loyal and faithful and plot no more with fickle princes behind their true King's back.

Sir Richard of the Lee, whose son had so lately come home to his father's castle, could, an he had liked, have explained much to them. He knew that the King was in England; for had he not, but a few hours since, parted from him with a pardon in his hand and happiness in his heart?

* * *

Friar Tuck, having been forced to run all night in order that he might be able to bring the news as to Little John in to Robin, had compensated himself for the loss of this repose by lying abed the better part of the next day. Stirring things were going forward in the old city of Nottingham, as we know; but only at dusk, when all was over and Robin and them all were safely lodged in Sir Richard's stronghold, did the worthy friar open his little wicket gate and remember him of his fasting dogs.

He fed them and passed the remaining hours of day in putting them through their tricks; then, feeling that he had well earned a good meal, the friar took out some sumptuous fare from his larder and arranged it conveniently upon the small wooden bench in his cell. He then lit a taper, as the night was at hand, bolted and barred his door, and drew his seat close to the promising board.

He uprolled his eyes, and had commenced a Latin grace, when suddenly came interruption unpleasant and alarming. One of his dogs began to bark, deeply and resentfully. The others followed him in the same note, changing the calm stillness of the night into discordant, frenzied clamor. "Now, who, in the name of all the saints, cometh here?" exclaimed Tuck, wrathfully, proceeding to bundle his supper back into the small larder. "May perdition and all the furies grant that he may evermore know the pangs of an empty stomach!"

His pious wishes were rudely interrupted by a loud knocking upon the door of his hermitage. "Open, open!" cried a strident voice.

"I have no means of helping you, poor traveller," roared the friar. "Go your way into Gamewell, 'tis but a few miles hence upon a straight road."

"I will not stir another yard," said the voice, determinedly; "open your door, or I will batter it down with the hilt of my sword."

The priest then, with anger glowing in his eyes, unbarred the door, and flung it open. Before him stood the figure of a knight, clad in black armor and with vizor down.

The Black Knight strode into the friar's cell without waiting for invitation.

"Have you no supper, Brother?" asked the knight, curtly. "I must beg a bed of you this night, and fain would refresh my body ere I sleep."

"I have naught but half of mine own supper to offer you," replied Tuck; "a little dry bread and a pitcher of water."

"Methinks I can smell better fare than that, Brother"; and the Black Knight offered to look into the larder.

This was more than Tuck could bear, so he caught up his staff and flung himself before his guest in a threatening attitude. "Why, then, if you *will*," cried the knight, and he struck the priest smartly with the flat of his sword.

The friar put down his staff. "Now," said he, with meaning, "since you have struck me we will play this game to a fair finish. Wherefore, if you are a true knight, give me your pledge that you will fight me on tomorrow morn with quarterstaff until one of us shall cry 'Enough.' "

"With all my soul," cried the knight, readily. "And will give more knocks than ever you have given your dogs."

"One gives and takes," retorted Tuck, sententiously; "put up your sword and help me to lay supper, for I am passing hungry."

They spread the supper table between them, and once again the friar sat down hopefully. He spoke his grace with unction, and was surprised to hear his guest echo the Latin words after him. The knight unlaced his helm and took it off. He appeared as a bronzed and bearded man, stern-looking and handsome.

They then attacked the venison pasty right valiantly, and pledged each other in a cup of wine. The good food and comfort warmed them both, and soon they were at a gossip, cheerful and astounding. So they passed the time until the hour grew late; and both fell asleep together, almost in their places, by the despoiled supper table.

In the morning they breakfasted on the remains, and then they washed their faces in the jumping brook. The knight told the priest that he had left his companions at Locksley on the previous evening. He asked so many questions as to Robin Hood and his men that the priest had to fence very skilfully.

If the knight had been in a hurry before he seemed now to have changed his mind. He said that he would wait for his companions, if the priest could bear with him, and Friar Tuck, having taken a great liking to this genial traveller, made no complaint.

"I must presently journey forth to visit a poor man who lieth on a sickbed," said the friar, thinking of Robin.

"Mayhap we may travel together?" suggested the knight. "I am going, so soon as friends have found me, into Gamewell."

"I go into Barnesdale," said Tuck, quickly, "which is in quite another direction."

At last the knight said he must go on, with or without his fellows, and he took up his sword. The friar then got out two quarterstaves, full nine feet long. Without a word he handed one to the knight.

He took it, and eyed the friar whimsically; then, seeing no sign of relenting in him, shrugged his shoulders. He put off his helm again, and both going out to the little glade by the ruined shrine of St. Dunstan, they prepared for a bout with the staves.

For all his plumpness Tuck was no mean opponent at the game. He skipped and flourished about and around the knight in a surprising way; and gave him at last such a crack upon his crown as made the tears start.

Then the Black Knight struck in mighty wrath, and soon the blows of their staves were making the welkin ring. So busy they were as to give no heed of the approach of a goodly company of men.

It was Sir Richard of the Lee, with his son and retinue, journeying in a roundabout way in order to throw Monceux off the scent, and so give Robin a chance to reach his stronghold in Barnesdale. Both knights paused in amazement to see this furious combat.

At last the Black Knight brought down his staff with a noise like felling timber upon the shoulder of the priest. Tuck staggered, and dropped his staff. "Enough, enough," he cried; then fell in a heap upon the wet grass.

The knight flung away his staff and ran to help him. He lifted up the priest's head and put it on his knee. Glancing up, he espied them all staring at him. "Run, one of you, and bring me some water."

Sir Richard of the Lee started when he heard that voice. He turned to his son, but already the young man had doffed his helm and was filling it with water from the brook. He brought it quickly to the Black Knight, and, offering it, kneeled before him in deepest respect and affection.

"I thank you, child," spoke the Black Knight, graciously. "See, this good fellow hath but swooned and already doth revive. Are these your men, and this the father who gave his all for you?"

Sir Richard drew nearer and kneeled as his son had done, whilst the servitors looked on in strange fear. "Arise, honest man," said the Black Knight, with feeling, "I know your story, and have pardoned your son. What can I give to you to show you how we esteem a man just and faithful, even in adversity?"

"Sire," faltered Sir Richard, rising and standing with bared head before him. "If I might ask aught of you I would crave amnesty for myself and for my men. You will hear ere long how we have befriended one Robin Hood, an outlaw of these woods. Through his generous help I was able to disencumber my estates, and yesterday, seeing him hard pressed, I opened my hall to him."

"I will hear the story," the Black Knight said, briefly, "and then I will judge." He turned to Tuck, who now was sitting up, and gazing about him in bewildered fashion. "Take my hand, Brother; let me help you to your feet."

"Tell me," said the friar, leaning on the knight, after he had risen, "was that a bolt from the sky which just now did strike me down?"

"I do fear it was this staff, Brother," answered the other, smiling, "with my poor arm to guide it. 'Twas an ill requital for your hospitality, and I ask your forgiveness."

"So small a thing as man's forgiveness of man," spoke Tuck, sententiously, "I freely accord to you." He peeped at Sir Richard, and recognized him at once as the knight of the woeful visage. He made no sign of this knowledge, however. "Are these your companions, Sir Knight, of whom you did tell me last night?" he asked, indicating the others with a wide gesture.

"Why, yes, and no, Brother," replied the knight, whimsically. "They are not my companions in a sense, and yet I do purpose to make them such forthwith. But come, 'tis time for me to be stirring an I would make an end of my quest. I will be frank with you, Brother. I seek Robin Hood, and had hoped that he might be attending you today in this very place."

The friar put up his hands with an exclamation of horror. "I am a lover of peace, Sir Knight, and do not consort with such as these."

"Nay, I think no harm of Master Hood," the knight hastened to say, "but I much yearn to see and speak with him."

"If that be all, and you will come with me," said Tuck, scenting a good prey for Robin, "I will undertake to show you where these villains say their nightly mass. I could not live long in this wood without knowing somewhat of Master Hood, be sure; and matters of religion have perforce my most earnest attention."

"I will go with you, Brother," said the Black Knight.

The friar led the three to his cell. "Bid all the men return to your castle," the Black Knight commanded, loudly, "save four of those most to be trusted." Under his breath he bade Sir Richard tell his fellows to pretend to disperse, and to follow stealthily after their master soon as an hour was gone.

Friar Tuck had produced some old monkish gowns from under a bench. He bade the seven of them put them on, the three knights and the four chosen men. "We will attend the mass as brothers of my order, which is Dominican, as you may see," explained Tuck, easily. "You, Sir Knight of the iron wrist, shall wear this dress, which was an abbot's once. I would we had a horse for you; it would be more seemly, and less like to rouse suspicion."

Sir Richard said that there were horses with his men in plenty; and one was readily obtained for the Black Knight's use. The little cavalcade set out for Barnesdale, the friar joyfully leading the way. The servitors affected to return to Sir Richard's castle, but hid themselves in the bushes instead.

After going deeper and deeper into the forest they came at last to a part of Watling Street, and there was Robin Hood with a score of his men. He was watching the road for Monceux, having a notion that the Sheriff would try now to take them in the rear.

Recognizing Tuck at once, Robin walked boldly up to them. "By your leave, brothers," cried he, taking hold of the bridle of the knight's horse and stopping him, "we are poor yeomen of the forest, and have no means of support, thanks to the tyranny and injustice of the Norman nobles in this land. But you abbots and churchmen have both fine churches and rents, and plenty of gold without. Wherefore, for charity's sake, give us a little of your spending money."

"We are poor monks, good Master Hood," cried Tuck, in a wheedling tone; "I pray you do not stay us. We are journeying with all speed to a monastery in Fountain's Dale, which we hear hath been deserted by its owners."

"I can tell you much concerning this very place," said Robin. "Give me alms, and I will open my lips to purpose."

The pretended abbot spoke now. "I have been journeying, good Master Hood, with the King," said he, in full deep voice, "and I have spent the greater part of my moneys. Fifty golden pieces is all that I have with me."

"It is the very sum I would ask of thee, Sir Abbot," said Robin, cheerily.

He took the gold which the other freely offered, and divided it into two even sums. One half he gave to those with him, bidding them take it to the treasury, the other he returned to the knight. "For thy courtesy, Sir Abbot, keep this gold for thine own spending. 'Tis like that you will journey with the King again, and need it."

"I will tell you now," said the pretended abbot, "for I see that you are truly Robin Hood, although so small a man, that Richard of the Lion Heart is returned to England, and hath bid me seek you out. He hath heard much of you, and bids you, through me, to come into Nottingham and there partake of his hospitality."

Robin laughed heartily. "That is where we may not venture, Sir Abbot, since we value our skins. But where is your authority?"

The knight produced the King's seal from under his abbot's gown. Robin looked at it, and fell at once upon his knees. "I love a true man," cried he, "and by all hearing my King is such an one. Now that he is come to take sovereignty over us we may hope for justice, even in Nottingham town. I thank you for your tidings, Sir Abbot; and for the love I have of valor and all true kingly virtues, I bid you and your fellows to sup freely with us under my trystal tree." He then offered to lead them into Barnesdale; and the pretended monks, after a short discussion, agreed to accept his offer.

They soon were come before the caves of Barnesdale, and were presented to those of the band already there. Presently Robin blew two blasts upon his horn, and the rest of the greenwood men made their appearance. All were dressed in their new livery, and carried new bows in their left hands. Each one knelt for a moment before Robin, as leader of them, ere taking his place.

A handsome, dark-haired page stood at Robin's right hand, to hold his cup for him and pour him wine. The signal was given. Robin graciously placed the abbot in the place of honor; and under the cool fresh evening, bright still with the aftermath of the day, the banquet was begun.

The Black Knight was struck with astonishment. "By all the saints," thought he, "this is a wondrous sight. There is more obedience shown to this outlaw man than my fellows have shown to me."

CHAPTER 33

AFTER SUPPER Robin signal-
led to his men to bend their bows. The knight was startled, for he
thought they intended to choose him for their target.

He was quickly undeceived, however, for two arrows were set up as
butts for these archers. The knight marvelled indeed to see so small a
mark given in this waning light. A garland of leaves was balanced on the
top of each arrow, and Robin laid down the rules. Whoever failed to
speed his shaft through this garland—and it was to be done without
knocking it off the arrow—was to yield up his own shaft to Robin, and
receive also a buffet from the hand of Friar Tuck.

"Master," said Stuteley, "that may not be, for the good friar is not yet
come to confess us this day." He winked his eyes at Robin, well knowing
that the friar sat near to the other monks.

"Doubtless he will be here ere the game be ended," replied Robin, smiling. "I prithee commence soon as I clap my hands."

Little John, limping, Stuteley and old Warrenton each flew their
arrows truly through the garlands, as did many of the rest. Poor Midge
and Arthur-à-Bland were not so fortunate, for though both came near to
doing it, the garlands unkindly fell off an instant after their shafts had
flown through them.

"Where is the friar?" cried Robin, affecting to peer into the distance,
already blue-grey with twilight. "Surely he is late tonight."

Then Tuck could bear it no longer, but stood up in his place. "Come
near to me, thou villainous archers," he roared, "and I will buffet you
right well."

"Ah, Brother, what are you saying?" cried the knight, anxiously. "Surely you forget our vows and our cloth."

"I forget neither the one nor the other," returned Tuck. "But I would be no true man did I submit to watch quietly such bungling as these fellows have done. Come hither, Midge."

"You know them—you are of this company?" continued the knight, as if in alarm.

"I am very proud to be of it, Brother," said the friar.

"I crave a boon," the knight then said, turning to Robin. "This is a little man who will receive the buffets; and though I seem a priest, yet am I willing to take the blow instead."

"If you would care to have a buffet from me," the friar cried, "you are most welcome. For though my arm is sore still from our play of this morn, I warrant me there is still some strength left in it"; and he rolled up his sleeve.

"Take, then, the first blow," said the knight, "and I promise you I will return it you with interest."

A smile lit up the face of the jolly friar. He turned up the sleeve of his cassock still further, and smote the false abbot such a blow as would have felled an ox.

"Thou hittest well, Brother," the knight remarked, coolly.

The friar was amazed to see him withstand such a blow, and so was Robin. "Now, 'tis my turn," the knight said; and, baring his arm, he dealt Tuck such a blow as to send him flat upon his back.

There was a general laugh at this; but the exertion had caused the abbot's cowl to slip away from his head. The strong face and light beard of the Black Knight showed plainly to them all. "Alas, Your Majesty," cried Sir Richard of the Lee, springing up; "you have betrayed yourself."

"It is the King!" cried Scarlett, in sheer surprise; and reverently he knelt before the Black Knight. Robin glanced questioningly towards the greenwood men; then knelt himself beside Scarlett. At once the whole company fell upon their knees also.

"My lord King," said Robin, in hushed voice, "I crave mercy for my men and for myself. We have not chosen this life from any wickedness, but rather have come to it perforce."

The King towered amongst them. "Swear," cried he, in clear, loud voice. "Swear that you will forsake your wild ways, Robin Fitzooth, and will come with your men into my Court, and be good and faithful subjects from this night, and I will give you all the pardon that you crave."

"We will come into your Court and into your service, Sire," answered Robin, gratefully, "nor ask anything better in this world than that."

The King bade them rise and continue their sports. "Night is come and I must ask a lodging of you—even as your chaplain gave me of his hospitality yester e'en," he said, comfortably. "And tell me, Robin, where is your Marian? What laggard in love are you to be here without her?"

"Nay, Sire," said the little page, coming forward, "Robin is no laggard, nor am I far to seek. He is a very valiant, honorable man, and should indeed be a knight of this realm, if all men had their deserts."

Richard smiled then, and bent his haughty head to kiss the little hand she had extended to him. "Thou speakest truth, lady," he answered. "And I had not forgotten how the fair lands of Broadweald once were in Hugh Fitzooth's honest keeping. It may be that they will return to his son one day, for folks tell me that Guy of Gisborne is no more."

He turned to Scarlett. "And you are Master Geoffrey of Montfichet," said he, fixing his keen eyes on the other's face, "son of my father's friend, George Montfichet of Gamewell? And prithee, Master Geoffrey, what have you done with my little cousin, Aimée of Aragon?"

Scarlett confusedly explained that she was safe in his father's hall at Gamewell. "It seemeth, then, that you also have stolen from our Sheriff at Nottingham, Master Scarlett?" Richard observed, quizzing him. "Surely all men's hands are against Monceux!"

"Even as all men's hands are against venomous reptiles and the like," observed the friar, nodding his head. He had recovered from the buffet which Richard's hand had dealt, and had seated himself conveniently to watch the scene. He was truly the one least put about by it.

The King eyed him, and smiled to note his quiet self-possession. "What can I find for you, Brother?" he asked, indulgently. "Some fat living, where there are no wicked to chastise, and where the work is easy and well endowed?"

"I only wish for peace in this life," replied the friar. "Mine is a simple nature, and I care not for the gewgaws and shams of Court. Give me a good meal and a cup of the right brew, health, and enough for the day, and I ask no more either of my God or of my King."

Richard sighed. "You ask the greatest thing in the world, Brother— contentment. It is not mine to give or to deny. Yet if I can help you to find that wondrous jewel, I will do it right heartily." He glanced curiously from one to the other of the greenwood men. "Which of you is called Allan-a-Dale?" he asked; and when Allan had come forward, "So," said Richard, half-sternly, "you are the man who stole a bride from her man at my church doors of Plympton. What have you to say in excuse of this wickedness?"

"Only that I loved her, Sire, and that she loved me," said Allan. "Your Norman baron would have forced her to wed with him, desiring her lands."

"Which since hath been forfeited by my lord of Hereford," said Richard, quickly. "I know your story, Allan. Take back your lands and hers from me this night, and live in peace and loyalty upon them with your dame. Fennel, she is called, is't not so? 'Tis a pretty name."

"I thank you humbly, Sire," said Allan-a-Dale, joyfully. "And Fennel shall thank you for herself. She will do it far better than I, be sure of it."

"Where is your dame?" said the King, looking about and half-expecting to find her clad like Marian in boy's attire.

"She also is at Gamewell," said Sir Richard, hastily. "We left her there this morning when on our way to Copmanhurst. The Princess will take her into her train, and protect both Mistress Fennel and her lord."

"Our Princess will need a protector for her own self, I am thinking," said the King, thoughtfully. "Come hither, Scarlett, and kneel before me!"

Geoffrey wonderingly did so. "Arise, Geoffrey Earl of Nottingham," cried Richard, striking his shoulder with the flat of his sword; "take back your freedom from my hands, and be no more ashamed to attend our Court disguised and in false pretence. From this moment you have the overlordship of this forest for your father's sake and mine, and you are worthy to ask the hand of any woman in this realm."

It was impossible not to perceive the King's gracious meaning, although Geoffrey could scarce believe in his good fortune. He thanked his King in a voice full of gratitude and affection. "You did say that the Princess of Aragon might need a protector, Sire," he added, trembling at his own audacity. "Will you grant me permission to be her champion and defy the world?"

" 'Tis what I had promised for you, my lord of Nottingham," said Richard, quietly, "and best reason for your knighthood! Watch well over her, and guard her from herself—if need be."

For Much the Miller, for Middle the Tinker, for Little John, Stuteley and old Warrenton the King had kindly words. He knew them all, it seemed; and they marvelled more and more amongst themselves to hear how he was aware of all their histories. There was no adventurer, no man of them whom he did not know by name and fame, at least; and this King proved so gracious and royal a man that all of them loved him forthwith and dubbed him in their hearts a right worthy monarch.

They built a great fire, having now no more fear of Monceux or Hereford, or any one of them. The Sheriff would hold his office from Will Scarlett's hands from now!

The archers from Nottingham who had been held as prisoners were at once released, and the King signalled for Sir Richard's followers to appear. This they did with a rush, and Robin saw then how the King had held them all truly in his hand, for these fellows, and even Sir Richard of the Lee, their master, would have had to obey him had he ordered them to engage the greenwood men in sudden combat.

As it was, all were merry and boon companions. Laughter and song floated upward as the jumping flames of the campfire they had built. The friar sang them the song which Robin had heard so often, and Robin himself played upon the harp. Night came and they slept—King of England and his subjects together, in all joy and happiness. The fire burned low, and deep Sherwood watched over them—forest mother of them all.

★   ★   ★

Next morning the King asked if they had any spare liveries of the scarlet and white. "For," said he, " 'tis only fair that I should lead you into the city of Nottingham clad as you are yourselves, since now you are my bodyguard."

So Nottingham awoke to find a great company of men approaching it. Foremost came a number of archers dressed all in bright liveries and carrying their bows unslung in token of peace. Behind them marched a motley host—the servitors of Sir Richard and of old George of Game-well, and last of all the Sheriff's own archers.

Monceux came out to meet them with Master Simeon, whilst my lord of Hereford watched furtively from the city walls. The chief of the approaching host rode forward, and his stern, dark face was plain to see.

" 'Tis the King!" cried Carfax, who knew Richard well. "Now may our tongues be politic and say the right words."

"Go to meet him, Simeon," whispered the Sheriff, all in a flutter of fear and hope. " 'Tis like that he hath encountered Sir Richard of the Lee, and so will know his story of things. Be prudent, be humble."

But Richard waved Carfax haughtily aside. "I will speak with your master, fellow," he said, harshly. Carfax shrank cringingly to one side, and Monceux dismounted from his milk-white horse to meet his King.

"Greetings and welcome, Sire, from this your faithful city," began Monceux, very hurriedly. "The joyful tidings of your return were brought to me two days agone, and at once I did prepare for your coming."

"With a hanging to wit, and murderous attack upon the castle of this faithful knight," said Richard. "A welcome not much to our mind, Sheriff."

"Sire, when the hanging was going forward I did not then know you were so near," explained Monceux, making matters worse. "And, for the matter of that, 'twas for foul murder that I would have hanged the villain, who did escape through your knight's evil practises. Thereby I do accuse Sir Richard of offending against the laws."

"Enough, Master Monceux," interrupted the King, contemptuously. "The murder was not done by the man whose life you did seek so earnestly to end. The killing of Fitzwalter, my warden of these gates, was due to the foul hands of your own cook, Roger de Burgh. As you have stomach for a hanging, see to it that this fellow be brought to book. Know you this writing?"

And Richard showed him the parchment which Will Scarlett had found in the hearth of the hall at Nottingham Castle.

Monceux turned green and white, and gasped for air. "I had no hand in this dreadful business, Sire, I swear it," he gurgled. "We did conspire between us to entice the maid Fitzwalter into Nottingham, I confess, hoping that Robin Hood, the outlaw, would come to visit her, and we might so trap him. He hath been the author of this mischief, I promise you, and is a villainous wretch. If Roger killed Master Fitzwalter, 'twas done in the belief that he was engaged with Hood."

"As I thought," muttered the new Earl of Nottingham, under his breath.

"Therefore," said Richard, slowly, "you, Monceux, knew all along that Little John was not guilty, and yet did seek to hang him."

"Sire, he stole my plate also, and had been excommunicated by my lord of Hereford."

"Take Roger and hang him speedily," cried the King, to end it. "And bring me to the Bishop. Stay!" he called to the quickly retreating Sheriff; "ere you go, Monceux, learn that from henceforward you must look for patronage from this my lord of Nottingham," he added, with a gesture. "He will be your master, and you will hold the feof of Nottingham Castle at his hands."

"Will Scarlett—Master Geoffrey of Montfichet—you?" gasped Monceux.

"Even I, Master Sheriff," replied the man of many names.

"Know also, Monceux," added Richard, indicating Robin and his men, "these are my archers and especial guards. From now the ban of excommunication must be removed."

The Bishop had come down from the walls and had drawn nigh. "Fetch me book and candle, Carfax," said he, "and I will remove the ban."

"You will be wise to do so, my lord," the King said, significantly. The Bishop deemed it prudent to give no particular heed to his sire's tone. At once he proceeded to take off the ban of excommunication he had so hastily pronounced upon Robin Hood and the rest of his merry men.

"Now, Robin, take payment for your entertainment of me in the woods," the King said, in a voice that would brook no denial. Robin drew near and kneeled before him, doubtfully. "Rise, Robin of Huntingdon, first Earl of the shire!" cried Richard, tapping him with the point of his blade. "Take rank amongst my knights, and learn that thy King recognizeth above the other neither Saxon nor Norman of his subjects—all to me are English; and I love the man who is brave and who dealeth fairly as he may with his fellowmen. You have kept the spirit of liberty alive in this my land, and I hold no anger against you because you have been impatient under wrong."

His proud voice was silent; while Robin Earl of Huntingdon seized his King's hand to his lips and kissed it in a wonderment of gratitude.

CHAPTER 34

IT WAS THE wedding day of four happy people. The day was bright, the sky blue, and Sherwood had taken upon itself early summer raiment.

The old church of Nottingham was already crowded to excess.

The newly banded guard of Royal bowmen, gay in their scarlet and white livery, were formed up in two straight lines from the church door to the lych-gate.

So soon as the weddings were over all would go back to a great feast, given at Gamewell Hall, in honor of the day. Then afterward the two couples would go with the king into London, to be followed within seven days by the rest of the Royal guard. Richard meant to employ these fellows shrewdly and test their loyalty. Not for reasons of sentiment only had he forgiven Robin and his men.

The hour was reached, and at once a small company was seen issuing forth from Nottingham Castle. Against his will Master Monceux had given use of the castle to the two bridegrooms—the newly made Earls of Nottingham and Huntingdon.

With Robin and Geoffrey were, firstly, old George of Gamewell, proud above all others in knowing that he had now a son who would ensure honor to the race of Montfichet all their days. The Squire was happy and radiant. He walked between them, and turned his head ever and again in laughing speech with Sir Richard of the Lee and his heir. Stuteley and Little John were next, the long and short of it; and after them the jovial Friar of Copmanhurst. Arthur-à-Bland, with a gold chain about his neck, given him by the knight Sir Richard, walked with

Middle the Tinker on his left and Much the Miller on his right. Close behind trotted the small complaisant Midge, dressed up very fine in a livery of purple doublet and green hose.

They came to the lych-gate, and the crowd jostled itself in its admiration. As they walked, rather consciously, up the narrow path between the smiling ranks of their fellows the crowd cheered them radiantly.

"A Hood! A Montfichet!" was called and called again. Some maids from the opposite windows threw them kisses and waved pretty kerchiefs in their honor.

Within the church, waiting for them soberly at the chancel steps, was my lord of Hereford, dressed out in his finest and richest robes, and beside him Friar Tuck. For Robin Hood and Will Scarlett the Bishop had enmity and contempt, but towards the Earls of Huntingdon and Nottingham this time-serving man could only profess an abundance of respect.

The brides were to be escorted from Gamewell by no other person than the King himself. He was to give them both in marriage, and had promised them jewels and to spare when they were come to Court.

Loud cheering and noise from the mob without the church told of their approach. The people were wild with joy at having their King amongst them like this.

Citizens, burgesses, apprentices were all in their best, their wives and their sweethearts all dressed out in splendid attire. As the King jumped down from his horse before the lych-gate, and held out his strong hand to help the brides from off their milk-white mares, the whole place became alive with excitement and rapture.

Little maids, with baskets of violets and primroses, flung their offerings prettily under the feet of the two beauteous blushing brides, who leaned so timidly upon the King's proud arms.

At last the service was begun and both couples were well-nigh wed. The Bishop had spoken the Latin service impressively and with unction.

In the first row stood Monceux, in all the pomp of his shrievalty, with his councilmen and aldermen. Master Simeon, with face leaner than ever and in-turning eyes, glared impotently at the chief actors in this historic scene.

Alone missing from it was the cold, colorless beauty of the demoiselle Marie. She had taken herself to her room this morn, and had sworn never to leave it again. But now that the double marriage was nearly made she suddenly appeared, thrusting her way rudely through the gathered crowd at the church door. She was wild-eyed, dishevelled, her dress fastened all awry. Folks looked once at her, and then exchanged glances between themselves.

"Stay this mockery of marriage, my lord," she cried, fiercely facing the Bishop. She had elbowed a path for herself to the chancel steps. "I do forbid the marrying of these two." She pointed a trembling finger from Robin to Marian. "This woman is blood-guilty, and Holy Church may not countenance her." She shrilled, desperately, " 'Twas she who foully killed Master Fitzwalter, her own father, and I have proof of it!"

" 'Tis false!" roared Robin, then beside himself. "You viper—you mean-souled spy! Is no crime too great for you?"

"There is no need for defence," spoke the King; "the charge is too wild and foolish an one. Seize this woman, some of you, and take her without. I will deal with her later." He imperiously signed to his guards, and at once the demoiselle was gripped harshly by both arms.

"Be gentle with her," pleaded Marian; "she is distraught, and hath not command upon herself. I beg of you, Sire, to forgive this; I have no quarrel with Mistress Monceux."

The demoiselle had suddenly become quiet under the fierce hands of Much and Little John. She allowed them to thrust her ignominiously forth. At the door of the church she turned once as though to renew her preposterous charges, but contented herself merely with a single glance towards them of malignant hate. Then she was gone; and people stirred themselves uneasily, as folks do when having been within touch of the plague.

The Sheriff had stared with protruding eyes of horror and dismay upon his daughter. When he saw that she was gone, that the dreadful episode was done, he gasped hurriedly and sat down. His mind became confused, his vision obscured as by a cloud. The service was finished. Robin and Marian, Geoffrey and Aimée (no longer of Aragon) were joined together for the rest of their lives. The Bishop pronounced a blessing; and forgetting himself utterly in the emotion of the moment, spoke fervently and with purpose.

The King kissed the brides, and after him their husbands kissed them also. Then all signed their names in the church books, and the trumpeters and heralds made music for them.

They returned through the streets of Nottingham, gay now with flags and merry with a joyful populace. Loud cheerings rent the air, and people showered flowers and blessings upon them. Before the happy couples ran six of the greenwood men, loyal subjects now, flinging largesse upon the people right and left from out of well-filled bags. All the treasure that they had accumulated in their caves at Barnesdale the King's bowmen freely distributed this day. All were happy—the nightmare of unjust dealings, of Norman oppression, of laws for the poor and none for the rich, was ended. The King had said it, and the King had already made good the promise in his words.

Afterward, at Gamewell, Richard conferred upon Montfichet full rank as Baron of the Realm, with power to speak and vote in the Upper Court of Appeal, the highest rank in the land, next to the King himself. Sir Richard of the Lee and his son became members of the Star Chamber, with grants of land in perpetuity.

Turning to Marian, the King wished her every joy that she could wish herself, and gave to her the lands of Broadweald in Lancashire to hold in her own right forever. "Thus you shall have wealth to share with your Robin; and I counsel you both to make good use of your days. My subjects who are loyal to me shall have no cause to regret it. I will give you, Aimée, the Castle of Aquitaine, which I held under my father's grant until his death. You know how fair a spot it is, and how sweet the sky of France! Help her to administer her riches, Geoffrey, wisely and well; and be you all ready when I shall call upon you. Now God save you all. Amen."

IN ALL SINCERITY there should be no more of this tale, seeing that we have found ourselves at last come from beginning to end of Robin's quarrelings with the Sheriff. Most histories end, and end properly, with just such a marriage as we have seen.

Yet, to tell the truth, however strange and distressful, is the business of a good historian; and so it must be written that in the end of it sad days came again for Robin Hood. For five years he lived in peace and prosperity, a faithful, loyal subject, having two sons born to him in his home in Broadweald. Then came the plague, raging and furious, and claimed amongst many victims Marian Countess of Huntingdon.

For a time Robin was as one distraught. He had no joy left to him. He was as one without energy or hope; a miser robbed of his gold, suddenly and cruelly. He gave his two boys into the charge of Geoffrey of Nottingham, and went on a journey to London, there to beg of the King that he might find him active employment, instead of being but one of a guard of honor, as he and his men had so truly become.

Richard had already gone to France, and John was acting as Regent of England in his absence. "Go, shoot some more of my brother's deer," sneered the Prince, having heard Robin impatiently. "Doubtless if you do but slay enough of them he will make you Privy Councillor at the least when he returns."

This great insult fired Robin's blood; he had been in a strange distemper ever since the fatal day of his beloved's death. He answered the disdainful Prince scornfully; and John, growing white with anger, bade his guards to seize upon him.

Faithful Stuteley helped his master to win freedom from the prison into which he had been flung; and, with the majority of his men, Robin returned to the greenwood life. The King's guard was broken up, for the King had no need of it, nor never would again.

Legends are told of Robin's scornful defiance of the laws, but they are intangible and unauthentic. It is a sure thing, howbeit, that he did not revert to Sherwood and Barnesdale, as some aver, but rather took up his quarters near Haddon Hall, in Derbyshire. There is a curious pile of stones and rocks shown to this day as the ruins of Robin's Castle, where the bold outlaw is believed to have lived and defied his enemies for a year at least. Two stones stand higher than the others. These are supposed to be the seats in the hall of this vanished stronghold whereon Robin and Little John sat delivering judgment on matters of forest law.

Another chronicle gives these stones as being the scene of a wondrous leap done by Robin, to show his men that strength and will were his yet. "Robin Hood's stride," folks say.

One thing is sure—that Prince John did not easily forgive or forget him. After many attempts made upon them at Haddon—some desperate enough, in all conscience—Robin and his men were allowed to be at peace. In one of these encounters Robin was sorely wounded; and none but Little John knew of it.

The wound was in Robin's breast, and looked but a small place. It bled little, yet would not heal; and slowly became inflamed in wider circles. Inwardly it burned him as with a consuming fire, his strength was sapped out from him and his eyes began to lose their shrewdness. No longer could he split an arrow at forty paces, as in olden days.

At last he took Little John on one side. "Dear heart," said he, "I do not feel able to shoot another arrow, and soon the rest will know I am stricken sore. I have it in me to return to London and there give myself to the Prince. Mayhap if I did this he would give you all amnesty here."

"Sooner would I see you dead than you should do such a thing," cried Little John; "I swear it by my soul and by my body! Now listen, dear Master, and I will tell you that I have heard of a wondrous cure for thee. An old beggar came this morn through the woods, and, strangely, when he spied me, asked if there was not one amongst us ill and hopeless."

"This beggar—where is he?"

"He waits below," said Little John, hurriedly. "I bethought me to talk with Stuteley on the matter. The beggar told me that the Abbess of Kirklees had stayed him as he was traveling past her Priory: 'Go to Haddon, Brother, and there you will find Robin Hood sick unto death. Say that in the woods nearby there is one who is practising magic upon him, having made a little image of Robin Hood. At each change of the moon this rascal doth stick a needle into the waxen heart of this image, and so doth Robin slowly die. Tell him that the name of the man is Simeon Carfax.' "

"Ay, by my soul, but I thought as much. What villainy! What foul villainy! Get me a horse, John, and one each for thyself and Stuteley."

The begger had gone when they went to the hall. None had offered to stay him. "Let us go quietly, swiftly," said Robin, "for I feel that my hours are short."

They rode all through the day and night, and came upon the Priory in early dawn—a quaint, strange building, surrounded by heavy trees.

The journey and fierce excitement told upon Robin. His wound was beating red-hot irons into his heart; hardly could they get him from his horse to the gate of Kirklees.

Stuteley rang the bell loudly, and anon the door was opened by a woman shrouded in black. She spoke in a cold low voice. "Is this Robin Earl of Huntingdon?" asked she. "I pray God that it may be true, for at this moment the wizard is meditating his very death."

"Tell us where this miscreant doth make his sorcery, good mother," cried Stuteley, and Little John together, "and not all the magic in the world shall save him from our swords!"

"Go out yonder to the left, where ye will find a little stream; nearby it is a tree blasted by Heaven's fires. Under the tree is the man Carfax*—I have watched and known him for many days. Go quickly, and I will tend your master. See, already he swoons—the hour is very nigh!"

*Carfax was then actually in France, acting against Richard.

The two men gave Robin into her keeping, with a fury of impatience; then, with brandished swords, ran swiftly in search of the wizard. Robin had swooned, and lay a dead weight in the arms of the Prioress.

With amazing strength and tenderness she lifted his slight body and bore it to a little room, near to the entrance of the Priory. She laid the unconscious man upon a couch, then hastily bared his right arm.

She paused an instant to throw back her hood; then taking the scissors of her chatelaine, suddenly and resolutely gashed the great artery in his arm. He gave a cry of pain and started up. "Be still, be still," she muttered, soothing him. "The pain is naught, it will cure thee—lie back and sleep—sleep."

"Who are you?" he asked, feebly, and with swimming eyes. Then blackness came upon him again, and he fell back upon the couch. Out of the night of pain the cold face of the demoiselle Marie smiled mockingly at him!

She raised herself and softly withdrew. As she locked the door upon him she smiled thinly, wickedly. "So, Robin—at last, Robin," she murmured, "I am avenged."

Two hours later Little John returned. Behind him was Stuteley, anxious and ashamed. They had found a man in the woods, and had killed him instantly, in their blind rage, only to discover then that he was but a yeoman, and not him whom they sought.

"I did hear my master's horn, mother," cried Little John, when the Prioress had opened the wicket to them. "Three blasts it gave."

" 'Twas the wind in the trees," said she, serenely. "He sleeps." She prepared to close the wicket quietly. "Disturb him not."

But Little John was alarmed and began to fear a trap. With his sword he hewed and hacked at the stout oak door, whilst Stuteley sought to prise it open.

When it yielded they rushed in upon a sorry scene. Robin lay by the window in a pool of blood, his face very white.

"A boon, a boon!" cried Little John, with the tears streaming from his eyes. "Let me slay this wretch and burn her body in the ruins of this place."

His master answered him with a voice from the grave: " 'Twas always my part never to hurt a woman, John. I will not let you do so

Leaning heavily against
Little John's sobbing breast,
Robin Hood flew his last arrow
out through the window,
far away into the trees.

now. Look to my wishes, both of you. Marian's grave—it is to be kept well and honorably. And my two sons—but Geoffrey will care for them. For me, dear hearts, bury me nearby, in some quiet grave. I could not bear another journey."

They sought to lift him up. "Give me my bow," said Robin, suddenly, "and a good true shaft." He took them from Stuteley's shaking hands, and, leaning heavily against Little John's sobbing breast, Robin Hood flew his last arrow out through the window, far away into the deep green of the trees.

A swift remembrance lit up the dying man's face. "Ah, well," he cried, "Will o' th' Green—you knew! Marian, my heart . . . and that day when first we met, beside the fallen deer! And she is gone, and my last arrow is flown. . . . It is the end, Will——" He fell back into Little John's arms. "Bury me, gossips," he murmured, faintly, "where my arrow hath fallen. There lay a green sod under my head and another beneath my feet, and let my bow be at my side."

His voice became presently silent, as though something had snapped within him. His head dropped gently upon Little John's shoulder.

"He sleeps," whispered Stuteley, again and again, trying to make himself believe it was so. "He is asleep, Little John—let us lay him quietly upon his bed."

So died Robin Fitzooth, first Earl of Huntingdon, under treacherous hands. Nearby Kirklees Abbey they laid to his last rest this bravest of all brave men—the most fearless champion of freedom that the land had ever known.

Robin Hood is dead, and no man can say truly where his grave may be. At the least it but holds his bones. His name lives in our ballads, our history, our hearts—so long as the English tongue is known.

NOTTINGHAM

AFTERWORD

AFTERWORD

The following essay has been adapted from the book Robin Hood *by J. C. Holt. One of Great Britain's premier historians, Holt is a professor of medieval history at the University of Cambridge and master of Fitzwilliam College.*

This book is about a legend rather than a man. The legend began more than 600 years ago. The man, if he existed at all, lived even earlier. He has survived as a hero in ballad, book, poem, and play ever since. He cannot be identified, but there is a quiverful of possibilities. Even the likeliest is little better than a shot in the gloaming. To substantiate Robin Hood's identity, the earliest tales of his doings have to be matched with information from other sources, which are scanty. Moreover, even in the earliest stories there is no sure way of sifting fact from fiction. Hence who he might have been is inseparable from what he was thought to have been: any search for a man involves an analysis of the legend.

The identity of the man matters less than the persistence of the legend. That is the most remarkable thing about him. And the perpetuation of the legend involves others: those who told the stories and those who listened to them. But while the legend survived, the performers and the audience changed from one generation to the next. In each generation it acquired new twists from shifts in the composition, outlook, and interests of the audience, or changes in the level of literacy, or developments in the means of communication. New tales were added to the story. New characters were introduced to the plot. Fresh historical contexts were invented. Minor features of the older tales were expanded into major themes; important elements in the earlier ones were jettisoned. The legend snowballed, collecting fragments of other stories as it rolled along. The central character was repeatedly remodeled. At his first appearance Robin was a yeoman. He was then turned into a nobleman unjustly deprived of his inheritance, later into an Englishman protecting his native countrymen from the domination of the Normans, and finally into a social rebel who, in the peasant's struggle against the grasping landlord, retaliates against the person and property of the oppressor. He is usually heroic, often romantic, occasionally, as a participant in rustic buffoonery, ridiculous—and sometimes just a thief.

The legend is now very different from what it was originally. Both in popular imagination and sociological jargon, Robin has come to provide a model for robbing the rich and giving to the poor. Nothing has taken firmer hold in his modern reputation than this unlikely activity. Yet there is very little warrant for it in the earliest stories. In one of them, Robin lends money to a knight and recovers it by robbing an abbot, but that is only one tale among many. The others are simple adventure stories, tales of combat, contest, disguise, and stratagem. They have nothing to do with robbing the rich and giving to the poor. They are not specifically concerned with class grievances, with needy knights or grasping abbots, and still less with discontented, overburdened peasants.

To say this is not to deprive the original legend of all social content. Its heroes are outlaws, placed in the world of the hardened criminal who roamed the countryside; of the defeated rebel, peasant, knight, or noble who took to the woods rather than submit; of the felon who incurred outlawry, rightly or wrongly, through his failure to appear before the courts or his unwillingness or inability to find the money for paying bribes or fines. The outlaws are engaged in a running battle with the sheriff and his men, who are the real villains of the tale. The woods where they live and roam were, both in legend and real life, the haunts of criminal and guerrilla alike. The outlaws live off the king's deer, which were the object of widespread poaching. Their story evokes a variety of local scenes: the archery of the municipal range, the fencing demonstrations of the banquet hall and marketplace, the halls, kitchens, and prison cells of castles. It relies on familiar activities: not plowing or reaping, but feasting and fighting, buying and selling, hunting and worshipping. In short, it would strike many chords in the audience's sensibilities.

Yet it does so with a light touch. It is useful to compare it as an outlaw tale with another, *The Outlaw's Song*, written shortly after 1305, when the legend of Robin may already have been taking shape. The two stories have common features: both praise the delights of the green-wood, and the author of *The Outlaw's Song* knows that the forest is the haunt of companies of archers whom he may be driven to join. But his plaint is quite precise. He names the justices responsible for his outlawry; specifically condemns the royal ordinance which gave them their commission; and makes it perfectly clear that he has been "indicted out of malice" by a body of false jurors. The piece is specific to a particular time and context. There are other literary fragments similar in tone, but none of them initiated or contributed to a legend. Robin's tale, by contrast, is imprecise. He is an outlaw, but no one explains why. He is in conflict with the sheriff, but no reason is ever given; it is simply that the sheriff represents the law and Robin stands outside it. His story is less committed to immediate circumstances. This is one reason why it has proved so durable.

The legend of Robin Hood was varied and adaptable. It would arouse diverse responses in the audience; it could also invade and absorb other entertainments. At a very early date—certainly by the middle of the 15th century—the tales or *gests* were turned into plays; some have argued that the plays came first. At the same time, Robin was adopted into the May Games, from which his legend in turn gained fresh characters. In its greenwood theme it mingled in one direction with Teutonic myth and a world of woodland sprites, while in another direction it contributed to the conventional setting that Shakespeare used in *As You Like It*.

This helps to explain the tale's potential. But to explain why the potential was realized—to understand why stories that seem on the surface so artless and shallow should have proved so compelling to generation after generation—it is necessary to turn from the social issues to the general terms in which those issues were expressed. They may lack depth, but again and again they play on sensitivities and arouse responses that transcend era, age, and social background.

At first sight Robin's legend is about justice. He is at once an embodiment of honor and an agent of retribution. He corrects the evil which flows from the greed of rich clerics and the corruption of royal officials. But he does not seek to overturn social conventions. On the contrary, he sustains those conventions against the machinations of the wicked and the powerful who exploit and undermine them. Robin keeps his word, unlike the treacherous sheriff. He is devout, unlike the worldly clerics. He is generous, unlike the avaricious abbot. He is courteous, unlike the churlish monks whom he entertains at dinner. Robin makes his world conform to the principles that are supposed to underlie it. Inevitably he wins. Honorable men triumph. Villains get tit for tat. Some are compelled to honor the code by which they have failed to live. Others receive their just deserts from a well-directed arrow. It is all very satisfying.

Robin also foreshadows the world of Superman and the comic strip. He has no practical scheme for improving the human condition. There is no sense at any stage of the legend's history that man's lot might be improved by the sweat of his brow. Robin simply intervenes. He succeeds because he is a superlative archer, a consummate swordsman, and a master of disguise and stratagem. Only the king and, in some traditions, the rustics, beggars, or tradesmen whom he attacks and often persuades to join his band, are his equals. He is invulnerable except to treachery. Robin belongs to that world of heroes and villains in which the heroes are so supreme, so magical in their mastery, that they will always win. Many of the stories, far from embodying social protest, turn on this and nothing else. The sheriff hunts the outlaws. Robin turns the tables; the outlaws win. In such simple adventures lies the legend's continuing appeal.

Originally, however, the tale had another meaning. What is now pure adventure to the young, or laudable social protest to the radical, was at first a glorification of violence to young and old alike. Robin was a product of a society where the threshold that separated lawful behavior from self-help by force of arms was indistinct and easily crossed. It was a society where the exercise of local office and the enforcement of the law were often an instrument of political faction; a society where the defeated party might easily pay the penalty with their heads; a society in which men took to robbery and pillage under the pressure of famine and other adverse circumstances; a society in which crime was tolerated, in which local juries protected the criminals, and in which gangs of knightly bandits might gain royal pardon for extortion, kidnapping, or murder.

Robin and his band vindicate such activity by presenting it as honorable and meritorious. They confound it with other behavior likely to inspire sympathy; there would be few who would not approve of their poaching of the king's deer. They deck it out with the conventions of the day: chivalry toward women, devotion to the Virgin, generosity, courtesy, loyalty, and obedience to the king—in all matters except his deer. But Robin's actions cannot be camouflaged totally. He kills—bloodily and with zest. Violent death is accepted with almost casual brutality. This violence takes two directions. One is toward rebellion—not rebellion against authority, for the outlaws are at one in their veneration of the king, but against the local exercise of that authority by the sheriff. All will be well for them if they can gain access to the king and obtain his pardon. He will appreciate their real value and understand, not so much the justice of their cause, for they have none, but the injustice of their exclusion from his peace and favor, which the sheriff and his men deny to them.

The other route is criminal. The most realistic early tradition of Robin is that he extorted money from travelers whom he waylaid on the Great North Road. They are forced to disgorge under duress. True, those who truthfully admit what they are carrying are allowed to retain it; it is only those who deny their wealth who are forced to hand it over. But it just so happens that the poor and impoverished tell the truth while the wealthy always lie. By such ingenious but transparent logic the victim's untruth is used to give moral justification to his captor's crime of highway robbery.

Though a criminal, Robin is portrayed as heroic, and the myth of Robin Hood contributed to those concocted around the names of Jesse James and Billy the Kid. They also were supposed to kill chivalrously and in self-defense. For them, too, it was claimed that they robbed the rich and gave to the poor. It does not matter that neither the James gang nor Billy the Kid lived up to their legend. What matters is that in Missouri and New Mexico in the 19th century, as in England in the 15th century, men were ready to argue, perhaps even to believe, that criminals behaved with such becoming charity. If the love of justice and adventure contributes to the survival of such tales, so also do human failings: gullibility and self-deception.

The tale of Robin Hood injects make-believe into an everyday environment. It makes violence natural. It presents it as unusually successful, for the outlaws' victims always deserve what they get. It has Robin stand for justice against the corruption and venality of the sheriff; he forces the real world to conform to the ideal. The legend even transforms the real discomfort suffered by those who took to the woods into the idyllic life of the greenwood, in which it never rains and where, with the king's deer at hand, every meal is a feast. And this tale took root in communities that submitted petition after petition to the king in Parliament deploring the "lack of governance" from which England suffered. Men voiced their longing for a more orderly life, free from "injustice" through the usual channels of government. They also took flight in their imagination with an outlawed hero who, at one and the same time, symbolized disorder and set it all to rights. The first person known to have asserted that Robin was "a good man" was a sheriff's clerk writing a parliamentary return in 1432.

Who, then, first relished this rough and ready, but unreal, world of Robin Hood? Criminals, outlaws, and rowdies, certainly, for some of them masqueraded under the name of Robin Hood. But the audience was larger than that. The legend is about yeomen—not the yeoman freeholder, but the yeoman servant of the feudal household. It was spread by minstrels who were themselves employed in the households of the aristocracy. Through them it was broadcast from the hall to the marketplace, from the tavern to the inn, wherever a worthwhile audience might gather, crossing class boundaries. It was played before knights and was sung by peasants. To men who could cock a snook at the sheriff as the enforcer of the law and the agent of the crown, to men who lived in or on the fringe of murderous political conflict, to men ever ready to transgress the line between violent politics and violent crime, to men who partook in the almost national pastime of poaching deer, to all those who shared the widespread aversion to usury, it provided a brittle moral fiber. In time it became a harmless tale fit for children. In its origin it served a bloodier purpose.